Innovative Approaches to Literacy Education

Using the Internet to Support New Literacies

Rachel A. Karchmer
University of Delaware
Newark, Delaware, USA

Marla H. Mallette
Southern Illinois University
Carbondale
Carbondale, Illinois, USA

Julia Kara-Soteriou
University of Bridgeport
Bridgeport, Connecticut, USA

Donald J. Leu, Jr.
University of Connecticut
Storrs, Connecticut, USA

Editors

INTERNATIONAL
Reading Association
800 BARKSDALE ROAD, PO BOX 8139
NEWARK, DE 19714-8139, USA
www.reading.org

The International Reading Association attempts, through its publications, to provide a forum for a wide spectrum of opinions on reading. This policy permits divergent viewpoints without implying the endorsement of the Association.

Director of Publications Dan Mangan
Editorial Director, Books and Special Projects Teresa Curto
Managing Editor, Books Shannon T. Fortner
Acquisitions and Developmental Editor Corinne M. Mooney
Associate Editor Charlene M. Nichols
Production Editor Amy Messick
Assistant Editor Elizabeth C. Hunt
Books and Inventory Assistant Rebecca A. Zell
Permissions Editor Janet S. Parrack
Assistant Permissions Editor Tyanna L. Collins
Production Department Manager Iona Muscella
Supervisor, Electronic Publishing Anette Schütz
Senior Electronic Publishing Specialist R. Lynn Harrison
Electronic Publishing Specialist Lisa M. Kochel
Proofreader Stacey Lynn Sharp

Project Editor Amy Messick

Art Cover Design: Linda Steere; Cover Photographs: Dynamic Graphics (center), Photodisc (all others); pp. 11, 83, 181: © IT Stock

Web addresses in this book were correct as of the publication date but may have become inactive or otherwise modified since that time. If you notice a deactivated or changed Web address, please e-mail books@reading.org with the words "Website Update" in the subject line. In your message, specify the Web link, the book title, and the page number on which the link appears.

Library of Congress Cataloging-in-Publication Data
Innovative approaches to literacy education : using the Internet to support new literacies / Rachel A. Karchmer ... [et al], editors.
      p. cm.
  ISBN 0-87207-555-9
  1. Language arts (Elementary)--Computer-assisted instruction. 2. Computers and literacy. 3. Internet in education. I. Karchmer, Rachel A., 1971-
  LB1576.7.I67 2005
  372.6'078'5--dc22

2005003017

CONTENTS

PREFACE

Rachel A. Karchmer, Marla H. Mallette,
Julia Kara-Soteriou, and Donald J. Leu, Jr.

■ Many of us have enjoyed the story of *Miss Rumphius* (Cooney, 1982). In this delightful book, Barbara Cooney describes how the title character travels the world, accumulating many adventures. Eventually, however, she returns to her home by the sea and discovers a way to make the world a better place by planting lupines, beautiful wildflowers, wherever she goes. The story illustrates how a committed individual can envision a better world and then act on that envisionment, transforming all of our lives. It is an important lesson for each of us. (Leu, Karchmer, & Leu, 1999, p. 636)

For the past several years we have used the Miss Rumphius story as a metaphor for the impressive work taking place over the Internet between classroom teachers and students. Just as Miss Rumphius made the world a better place by sharing the beauty of lupines around the world, teachers are doing the same by developing their own classroom websites to share their good work with others over the Internet. In 2000, with Barbara Cooney's permission, members of the RTEACHER listserv created the Miss Rumphius Award to honor these educators (www.reading.org/resources/community/links_rumphius_info.html). RTEACHER is an IRA-sponsored listserv for K–12 educators interested in discussing literacy and technology issues. To receive the award, websites must be nominated by a member of the list and at least two other members must second the nomination. The awards are categorized in four areas: (1) comprehensive, (2) elementary school, (3) middle school, and (4) high school. Currently, a total of 63 awards have been granted.

The overwhelming interest in the Miss Rumphius Award led us to develop a symposium to be presented at the International Reading Association (IRA) Annual Convention. Ten Miss Rumphius Award winners and four literacy scholars participated in the symposium designed to share both the outstanding work done by the teachers, but also to provide a theoretical framework for their work. The positive feedback we received from the audience led us to consider additional ways of sharing this information with the education community. This book is the result of those conversations.

The Purpose of This Book

The emergence of the Internet as an important new information and communication tool demands that educators think in new ways about what it means to become literate and how to provide effective literacy instruction for their students (International Reading Association, 2001; Karchmer, Mallette, & Leu, 2002; Leu, Kinzer, Coiro, & Cammack, 2004). Thus, the purpose of this book is to make more visible the fundamental changes to literacy, literacy learning, and literacy instruction that are brought forth by information and communication technologies (ICTs).

Although the topic of this book is rich and complex, our strategy is a simple one. We seek to share the lessons learned from pioneering, award-winning teachers who use the Internet and other ICTs in their classrooms. After all, what better place is there to look for good instruction than the classrooms of outstanding teachers who are exploring uncharted territory for all of us? As editors, we provided the contributors with guidelines for writing their chapters. Specifically, we asked them to describe the following areas and include many examples to illustrate their stories: (a) the Miss Rumphius Award–winning project, (b) current technology use in the classroom, and (c) technology's influence on literacy learning and instruction. By paying particular attention to these areas, the chapters follow a similar framework that allows readers to consider the different journeys toward technology implementation.

The stories in this book have been written by the following Miss Rumphius Award winners: Gino Sangiuliano, elementary teacher; Mark Ahlness, grade 3 teacher; Cathleen J. Chamberlain, director of curriculum and instruction, K–12; Susan Silverman, instructional technology integration consultant; Dale Hubert; grade 3 teacher, Marci McGowan, grade 1 teacher; Mary Kreul, grade 4 teacher, and Tim C. Lauer, principal. Each participated in the symposium presented at the IRA Annual Convention. In addition, we include the insights of university scholars in this text.

As those involved in the field of education place more emphasis on research-based practice, it is of utmost importance systematically to study the relationship between literacy and technology and disseminate those findings to the education community. The chapters by Charles K. Kinzer, professor of communications, computing, and technology in education, and Linda D. Labbo, professor of language and literacy education, help us make important connections among theory, research, and practice. The chapters by Denise Johnson, assistant professor, and Julie Coiro, literacy and technology integration specialist, emphasize what we know about preservice and inservice education, highlighting the critical need to provide opportunities for teachers to learn the most effective ways of implementing technology in their classrooms. With this powerful combination of perspectives, we hope to move the literacy community forward to ensure that all students are prepared for the literacy futures they deserve.

This book is valuable and relevant to a wide audience. If you are a teacher, you will discover many new instructional ideas and resources for your classroom. If you are a school administrator, you will encounter new visions of what is possible for your school and district. If you are a teacher in preparation, you will learn important lessons from some of the finest classroom teachers. If you are a scholar, you will discover new ways to view your own work in light of the rapid and profound changes taking place in the field. If you are a policymaker, you will learn how critical it is to develop policies that align with new literacies.

The Organization of This Book

Chapter 1 provides the theoretical premise of how ICTs continually redefine literacies in the classroom. Section I offers the stories of three classroom teachers who have used the new literacies of the Internet as a means for social change. They all are involved in projects that could be classified as community service, yet for their students, the nature of community has become global. That is, the outreach extended through their important efforts with Internet technologies is virtually limitless as they make the world a better place in which to live, learn, and teach. A professor concludes the section by commenting on the previous chapters and discussing the importance of linking schools and communities.

Section II offers the stories of six educators who are involved in the development and implementation of collaborative Internet projects. Their projects bring classrooms together in ways that were not possible before the Internet.

Section III focuses on teacher education. We have included this important area because we cannot forget that each of these teachers spent many hours learning how to use technology. It only makes sense for us to consider ways for colleges of education and school professional development programs to best prepare teachers to take on the challenges described in this book. The appendix is a resource for readers that lists the websites of the collaborative Internet projects discussed throughout the book. Each website is listed by chapter and page number of its first mention.

The teachers featured in this book are pioneers, exploring the classroom integration of new technologies and the new literacies these require. Every day, they explore new territory, transforming the nature of literacy instruction in their classrooms as they integrate the Internet and other ICTs into their curricula. Their pioneering work makes possible new instructional worlds for the many homesteading teachers who follow in their footsteps. In this book, we seek to honor the important work of these exceptional educators.

REFERENCES

International Reading Association (IRA). (2002). *Integrating literacy and technology in the curriculum: A position statement*. Newark, DE: Author.

Karchmer, R.A., Mallette, M.H., & Leu, D.J., Jr. (2002). Early literacy in the digital age: Moving from a singular book literacy to the multiple literacies of networked information and communication technologies. In D.M. Barone & L.M. Morrow (Eds.), *Literacy and young children* (pp. 175–194). New York: Guilford.

Leu, D.J., Jr., Karchmer, R.A., & Leu, D.D. (1999). The Miss Rumphius effect: Envisionments for literacy and learning that transform the Internet. *The Reading Teacher, 52*, 636–642.

Leu, D.J., Jr., Kinzer, C.K., Coiro, J., & Cammack, D. (2004). Toward a theory of new literacies emerging from the Internet and other information and communication technologies. In R.B. Ruddell, & N.J. Unrau, *Theoretical models and processes of reading* (5th ed., pp. 1570–1613). Newark, DE: International Reading Association.

CHILDREN'S LITERATURE

Cooney, B. (1982). *Miss Rumphius*. New York: Viking Press.

CONTRIBUTORS

Mark Ahlness
Grade 3 Teacher
Arbor Heights Elementary School
Seattle School District
Seattle, Washington, USA

Cathleen J. Chamberlain
Director of Curriculum and Instruction, K–12
Oswego City School District
Oswego, New York, USA

Julie Coiro
Literacy and Technology Integration Specialist
University of Connecticut
Storrs, Connecticut, USA

Dale Hubert
Grade 3 Teacher
Creator and Moderator of the Flat Stanley Project
London, Ontario, Canada

Denise Johnson
Assistant Professor
The College of William & Mary
Williamsburg, Virginia, USA

Julia Kara-Soteriou
Assistant Professor of Education (Reading/Language Arts)
University of Bridgeport
Bridgeport, Connecticut, USA

Rachel A. Karchmer
Assistant Professor of Literacy Education
University of Delaware
Newark, Delaware, USA

Charles K. Kinzer
Professor of Communications, Computing, and Technology in Education
Teachers College, Columbia University
New York, New York, USA

Mary Kreul
Grade 4 Teacher
School District of Whitefish Bay
Whitefish Bay, Wisconsin, USA

Linda D. Labbo
Professor of Language and Literacy Education
University of Georgia
Athens, Georgia, USA

Tim C. Lauer
Principal
Lewis Elementary School
Portland, Oregon, USA

Donald J. Leu, Jr.
John and Maria Neag Endowed Chair in Literacy and Technology
University of Connecticut
Storrs, Connecticut, USA

Marla H. Mallette
Assistant Professor of Early Literacy
Southern Illinois University Carbondale
Carbondale, Illinois, USA

Marci McGowan
Grade 1 Teacher
H.W. Mountz Elementary School
Spring Lake, New Jersey, USA

Gino Sangiuliano
Elementary Teacher
Barrington Public Schools
Barrington, Rhode Island, USA

Susan Silverman
Instructional Technology Integration Consultant
Adjunct Professor, New York Institute of Technology
St. James, New York, USA

CHAPTER 1

Contextualizing the New Literacies of Information and Communication Technologies in Theory, Research, and Practice

Donald J. Leu, Jr., Marla H. Mallette, Rachel A. Karchmer, and Julia Kara-Soteriou

How do we best prepare students for the new literacies that will define their future? Quite possibly that is the single greatest challenge we face in literacy education today. This is ironic, because much of the attention in the literacy community is currently devoted to the *No Child Left Behind Act of 2001* (U.S. Department of Education, 2001) and the important challenges we face with assessment, beginning reading instruction, and comprehension instruction. If students are prepared only for the foundational literacies of book, paper, and pencil technologies, they will be unprepared for a future in which the new literacies are required by new information and communication technologies (ICTs). Thus, it is important to expand our definition of literacy, not limit it.

Many researchers and educators of literacy are studying the rapidly and continuously emerging new literacies required to effectively exploit new ICTs (Coiro, 2003; Karchmer, 2001; Kinzer & Leander, 2003; Labbo & Reinking, 1999; Leu, Kinzer, Coiro, & Cammack, 2004; Reinking, McKenna, Labbo, & Kieffer, 1998). New literacies emerge almost every day as new ICTs emerge. As a result, it becomes important to understand the new skills in reading, writing, viewing, and communication that these technologies demand. Just as important, it becomes essential to consider how effectively to integrate these new literacies into the curriculum. We believe that continuously emerging ICTs are an important literacy issue—they are not simply a technology issue. Moreover, as literacy educators, we have a responsibility to provide leadership in this area.

Literacy scholars such as Gee (1996) and the New London Group (2000) argue that our students must acquire *multiple literacies* so they may fully participate in the global community. These literacy scholars correctly point out that twin forces are prompting multiple literacies: (1) the many new modalities of communication forms that are now available as technology advances and (2) the increasingly global community in which we regularly encounter wider differences in languages and cultures. We, the authors, believe that multiple literacies will emerge in our future because of a third force: New technologies for information and communication will repeatedly appear and new envisionments for exploiting these technologies will be crafted continuously by users. Thus, it is not just that new modalities of communication forms have generated multiple literacies; even more important is the fact that new technologies for information and communication will appear repeatedly in our future, generating even newer literacies on a regular basis.

Each new ICT demands new literacies for its effective use. The Internet, for example, requires new forms of reading and writing skills that were never required with book technologies (Coiro, 2003); so, too, do other ICTs such as word processors, instant messaging software, presentation software, e-mail, virtual worlds, and many others. Moreover, each time a newer version of an ICT is created, it requires new literacies to fully exploit its new potential. Consider, for example, what happens each time you upgrade your word-processing, Internet browser, e-mail, or other software (something that many of us have done several times in the past decade). Each time you upgrade one of these software types, you need to develop new skills to take advantage of the new reading and writing potentials inherent in each. Perhaps you have recently upgraded to the latest version of Microsoft Word. If so, you probably have developed new literacies as you have learned to exploit its new potential. Although you might have learned how to save documents in different formats in an earlier version of this program, recent versions include the new composing skills associated with developing a webpage, such as including hyperlinks within a document. Subsequent generations of this single program will require even newer literacies that we must acquire to fully exploit its potential.

Networked technologies for information and communication, such as the Internet, permit the immediate exchange of even newer technologies and envisionments for their use. This speeds up the already rapid pace of change in the forms and functions of literacy, increasing the complexity of the challenges we face as we consider how best to prepare students for their literacy futures. Today, continuous, rapid change regularly redefines the nature of literacy as changing technologies regularly generate new literacies.

Theory

What are these new literacies? Leu, Kinzer, Coiro, & Cammack (2004) suggest the new literacies of the Internet include the skills, strategies, and dispositions necessary to successfully exploit the rapidly changing ICTs continuously emerging in our world for personal growth, pleasure, and work. These new literacies allow us to use the Internet and other ICTs to identify important problems, locate information, analyze the usefulness of that information, synthesize information to solve problems, and communicate the solutions to others.

The new literacies build on the foundational literacies we have always taught in schools to prepare students for the effective use of book, paper, and pencil technologies. However, the new literacies go beyond these foundational literacies to include the new reading, writing, viewing, and communication skills required by the Internet and other ICTs. Examples of the new literacies of the Internet and other ICTs include

- knowing the many new strategies for constructing and comprehending information on the Internet;
- effectively using a search engine to find the precise information that is saught;
- critically evaluating information encountered on the Internet by using clues on a webpage to infer who created the information, what stance the author takes, and how this stance shapes the information;
- sending an effective e-mail message in a variety of contexts and to a variety of individuals to obtain useful information; and
- effectively using a word processor and functions such as a spell-checking, inserting graphics, and formatting text.

It is too early to propose a comprehensive theory of the new literacies. Some researchers and educators, however, are beginning to define a *new literacies perspective*, identifying a set of principles so that these ideas might be subject to debate and empirical evaluation. Leu, Kinzer, Coiro, & Cammack (2004) have identified these principles of a new literacies perspective, which are discussed in the following paragraphs.

The Internet and other ICTs are central technologies for literacy within a global community in an information age. Although other technologies demand new literacies, the Internet and other ICTs are the most important ones, because they provide access to the most central information resources for learning and they provide the most powerful tools for communicating about newly constructed information.

The Internet and other ICTs require new literacies to fully access their potential. Just as older technologies such as book, paper, and pencil require certain skills to unlock their information and communication potential, so do the Internet and other ICTs. These define the new literacies. Further, new technologies require new and more sophisticated strategies for their use. The new literacies largely will be defined around the strategic knowledge central to the effective use of information within rich and complexly networked environments

New literacies are deictic. New literacies regularly change as new technologies require even newer literacies. Thus, because literacy is regularly redefined by even newer technologies, learning *how to learn* may become just as important as learning particular technologies.

The relationship between literacy and technology is transactional. Technology helps define literacy, but new envisionments of literacy by talented teachers also redefine technology.

New literacies are multiple in nature. Because there are so many new technologies requiring so many new literacies, we can no longer think in singular terms about literacy and literacy instruction; we must think in plural terms.

Critical literacies are central to the new literacies. Open networks such as the Internet allow anyone to publish anything. As a result, the ability to evaluate critically the information we encounter becomes even more important, and new skills are required to make these evaluations.

Speed counts in important ways within the new literacies. The speed it takes to acquire information is an important measure of success within various technologies. Quickly finding, evaluating, using, and communicating information is central instructional issues.

Learning often is socially constructed within new literacies. As technologies rapidly change, no single teacher can be expected to keep up with them all. We need to orchestrate classrooms to take advantage of the opportunities to learn from one another because different students possess different new literacies and are important sources of information. Moreover, meaning also is socially constructed as students share and exchange information rapidly with others around the world.

The theoretical construct of new literacies continues to evolve as technological advances appear at an unprecedented rate, even though empirical research that investigates new literacies involving the Internet is almost nonexistent (Leu, 2000; Leu, Kinzer, Coiro, & Cammack, 2004). However, studies exist that investigate aspects of these new literacies with other computer technology. For example, Labbo (1996) investigated the meanings young children attached to the pictures they created as they worked on computers in a kindergarten classroom. Using the metaphor of screenland, a place where children could play and explore, Labbo found that their expanding understanding of multiple literacies shaped young children's stances toward symbol making. Similarly, Baker (2001) explored the nature of literacy in a technology-rich fourth-grade classroom. The findings from her study suggest that literacy in this context was a fluid, public, and social process, thus supporting the idea that the nature of literacy is expanding to multiple literacies.

It seems that when talking about new literacies from a theoretical perspective, the conversation can become obscure and dense; and when trying to locate research that systematically explores new literacies, the number of studies is small. However, we believe that the Miss Rumphius Award winners are leading the way in understanding and experimenting with these new forms of literacy. Theory and research will only work to strengthen the knowledge learned from their experiences.

Research

What do we know about these new literacies, and how should we teach them? Unfortunately, we still know very little. Much of this is a consequence of our failure as a literacy community to play a leadership role in this area. We have focused our attention on foundational literacies, not new literacies. This is partly the result of the narrow focus of recent state and national legislation (e.g., the No Child Left Behind Act of 2001 [U.S. Department of Education, 2001]), which focuses on foundational literacy tested by paper and pencil designed to increase reading and writing levels in nations around the world and the assessment practices they have created. State and national assessments currently used to fulfill legislative requirements, for example, do not include any of the new literacies required for success with the Internet and other ICTs (Leu, Ataya, & Coiro, 2002). As a result, we have ignored them. Not a single state allows all students to use a word processor, if they wish to do so, on their state writing assessments, despite recent research suggesting that nearly 20% more students would pass their state writing assessments if they were permitted to use word processors (Russell & Plati, 2000). Not a single state in the United States assesses students' ability to locate, read, critically evaluate, and comprehend information in an online environment, despite our knowledge that these skills will be required of all citizens in an information age. Not a single state currently assesses students' ability to communicate clearly by e-mail, despite the fact that many of us communicate more frequently by e-mail than by any other written form.

Our intense focus to achieve higher test scores on foundational literacies has distracted us from noticing that the skills now required to read, write, view, and communicate are profoundly different from what they were just a few years ago. Our failure to pay attention to these changes cannot continue without great cost to our world and to our children. We may end up raising test scores on foundational literacies without preparing students for the new forms of reading, writing, viewing, and communication that will be required in their adult lives.

As previously stated, although we have little empirical research on how the Internet is used in school classrooms or its effect on literacy and learning, we do know quite a bit about the pervasive and rapidly escalating nature of the Internet and other ICTs. Consider just a few pieces of evidence:

In a single year, the use of the Internet at work among all employed adults, ages 25 years and older, increased by nearly 60%, from 26.1% of the workforce to 41.7% (U.S. Department of Commerce, National Telecommunications and Information Administration, 2002). If this rate of increase continues, nearly everyone in the workforce will be using the Internet at work within a few years.

Nearly 60% of all households in the United States reported that they had Internet access in 2002 (Lebo, 2003).

The percentage of U.S. households with Internet access has been doubling each year from 1998 to 2001, an adoption rate in households exceeding that of any previous technology, including telephones, color televisions, VCRs, cell phones, and pagers (U.S. Department of Commerce, National Telecommunications and Information Administration, 2002).

Internet users reported an increase in time that they spent on the Internet and a decrease in the time that they spent viewing television (Lebo, 2003). Internet users reported watching about 10% fewer hours of television per week in 2002 (11.2 hours) than in 2001 (12.3 hours). This pattern also holds true for U.S. children, where nearly 33% of children reported in 2002 that they were viewing less television than before they started using the Internet; this was up nearly 50% from just one year earlier (Lebo, 2003).

In only 7 years (1994–2001), the percentage of classrooms in the United States possessing at least one Internet computer has increased from 3% to 87% (National Center for Education Statistics, 2003). This adoption rate is unprecedented in schools for any previous technology, including televisions, radios, telephones, VCRs, and even books.

Given these data on the penetration of the Internet and other ICTs into our daily lives, the insights of the authors in this book are important to consider as we seek to understand the complex changes taking place in literacy. Indeed, in the years ahead, it is likely that teachers will assume a greater role in epistemological approaches to understanding the *best practices* on teaching the new literacies required by the Internet and other ICTs. Technology changes faster than we can study it in classroom contexts and report the results using traditional paradigms within print research journals. As a result, the effect of traditional, scientific paradigms for discovering knowledge may be more limited than reports of daily classroom experiences that are regularly shared and exchanged over the Internet.

It currently takes substantial time to design an important research or study question, develop a systematic design, complete data-collection procedures, analyze the results, write up a report, have it reviewed for publication, and eventually have it published in a traditional research journal. By the time a study is published, the technologies that were the focus of the study will have changed, making any generalizations problematic to newer technologies. This issue is central to researchers. Therefore, teachers who use new technologies with their students every day will likely become an increasingly important source of information about new literacies and how to teach them. They conduct informal classroom experiments through their instructional decisions, developing a body of wisdom that is invaluable. We need to pay closer attention to the insights of teachers about the new literacies of the Internet and other ICTs (Karchmer, 2001).

Practice

Most of us would be surprised to see all the exceptional work with the Internet and other ICTs taking place in classrooms today. You will see some of this work in the wonderful examples shared by the Miss Rumphius Award winners in this book. You also will discover the important instructional models these teachers are constructing and sharing via the Internet. These models include Internet Workshop, a research-based model that requires students to navigate a particular website and share their findings with classmates (Leu, 2002); WebQuest, an inquiry model where students use the Internet to uncover answers to questions (Dodge, 1998); Internet Project, a collaborative project-based model with classrooms working together on a common learning unit (Leu, 2001); and Internet Inquiry (Leu, Leu, and Coiro, 2004). You also may discover some highly innovative school districts such as the Oswego City School District, Oswego, New York, USA (www.oswego.org/staffdev_frameset.htm), a district with one of the finest professional development programs for integrating technology into the curriculum (www.oswego.org/staffdev_frameset.htm) and one that should be replicated in every district.

As you look for talented teachers and exceptional school districts on the Internet, you may discover Hazel Jobe, a vice principal in Lewisburg, Tennessee, USA, who has developed Hazel's Page (www.marshall-es. marshall.k12.tn.us/jobe). Here you will find a host of exceptional resources for teaching in your classroom, including a number of excellent scavenger hunts and useful information for conducting videoconferences over the Internet.

You also might discover Oz Projects (www.ozprojects.edna.edu.au), one of the finest central sites for project-based learning using Internet technologies. Oz Projects is part of the Educational Network of Australia, and it contains Project Registry, a database where teachers can find other teachers looking for classroom partners for collaborative learning experiences. Classrooms in Australia, Canada, Germany, Japan, and the United States might, for example, share their developing responses to a book via e-mail.

Finally, you might find links on many classroom homepages to American Memory (http://memory.loc.gov/ammem), which is a website being constructed by the U.S. Library of Congress as a primary source resource on the history and culture of the United States. More than 7 million items from more than 100 collections are now available for students to consider as they explore primary source documents and learn to evaluate the meanings behind these important artifacts. Many more important documents are digitized and placed here each year from the extensive holdings of the Library of Congress. It is easy to see that literacy instruction is changing when you journey through classroom websites and explore the links that you find there. The contributors to this book can enrich your journey with the special insights that they bring to this issue because they are educators who are widely recognized for their expertise at integrating new technologies into the literacy curriculum.

A Concluding Thought

During the 18th and 19th centuries in the United States, a common aphorism was "Many hands make light work." This phrase was created to capture the collaborative spirit of individuals who were new to an area and relied on one another to build a community. Individuals came together to raise barns, bring in the harvest, and help one another to understand a new environment. The same might be said of the new literacies we are discovering on the Internet and with other ICTs. At no time in the history of education has the potential expressed in this aphorism been more critical to our success. It will take a truly collaborative effort to respond to the fundamental changes we see taking place in literacy and learning. Fortunately, the Internet allows us to take advantage of the special perspective that each of us can offer each other, enabling all of us to work together more effectively. The challenge, however, is getting each of us to think in new ways about our work. This means thinking about how we can use the Internet to enrich the separate work we do by connecting us with others we have yet to meet and exchanging ideas we have yet to consider. We hope this book moves us closer to that reality.

REFERENCES

Baker, E.A. (2001). The nature of literacy in a technology-rich fourth-grade classroom. *Reading Research and Instruction, 40*(3), 159–184.

Coiro, J.L. (2003). Reading comprehension on the Internet: Expanding our understanding of reading comprehension to encompass new literacies. *The Reading Teacher, 56*, 458–464.

Dodge, B. (1998). *The WebQuest page.* Retrieved January 14, 2003, from http://www.webquest.sdsu.edu

Gee, J.P. (1996). *Social linguistics and literacies: Ideology in discourses* (2nd ed.). London: Taylor & Francis.

Karchmer, R.A. (2001). The journey ahead: Thirteen teachers report how the Internet influences literacy and literacy instruction in their K–12 classrooms. *Reading Research Quarterly, 36*, 442–466.

Kinzer, C.K., & Leander, K. (2003). Technology and the language arts: Implications of an expanded definition of literacy. In J. Flood, D. Lapp, J.R. Squire, & J.M. Jensen (Eds.), *Handbook of research on teaching the English language arts* (pp. 546–566). Mahwah, NJ: Erlbaum.

Labbo, L.D. (1996). A semiotic analysis of young children's symbol making in a classroom computer center. *Reading Research Quarterly, 31*, 356–385.

Labbo, L.D., & Reinking, D. (1999). Negotiating the multiple realities of technology in literacy research and instruction. *Reading Research Quarterly, 34*, 478–492.

Lebo, H. (2003). *The UCLA Internet report: Surveying the digital future.* Retrieved January 14, 2004, from http://www.ccp.ucla.edu

Leu, D.J., Jr. (2000). Literacy and technology: Deictic consequences for literacy education in an information age. In M.L. Kamil, P.B. Mosenthal, P.D. Pearson, & R. Barr (Eds.), *Handbook of reading research* (Vol. 3, pp. 743–770). Mahwah, NJ: Erlbaum.

Leu, D.J., Jr. (2001). Internet project: Preparing students for new literacies in a global village. *The Reading Teacher, 54*, 568–572.

Leu, D.J., Jr. (2002). Internet workshop: Making time for literacy. *The Reading Teacher, 55*, 466–472.

Leu, D.J., Jr., Ataya, R., & Coiro, J.L. (2002). *Assessing assessment strategies among the 50 states: Evaluating the literacies of our past or the literacies of our future?* Paper presented at the National Reading Conference, Miami, FL.

Leu, D.J., Jr., Kinzer, C.K., Coiro, J.L., & Cammack, D.W. (2004). Toward a theory of new literacies emerging from the Internet and other information and communication technologies. In R.B. Ruddell & N.J. Unrau (Eds.), *Theoretical models and processes of reading* (5th ed., pp. 1570–1613). Newark, DE: International Reading Association.

Leu, D.J., Jr., Leu, D.D., & Coiro, J.L. (2004). *Teaching with the Internet: New literacies for new times* (4th ed.). Norwood, MA: Christopher-Gordon.

National Center for Education Statistics. (2003). Internet access in public schools and classrooms: 1994–2002. Retrieved December 1, 2003, from http://nces.ed.gov/surveys/frss/publications/2004011

New London Group. (2000). *Multiliteracies: Literacy learning and the design of social futures.* London: Routledge.

Reinking, D., McKenna, M.C., Labbo, L.D., & Kieffer, R.D. (Eds.). (1998). *Handbook of literacy and technology: Transformations in a post-typographic world.* Mahwah, NJ: Erlbaum.

Russell, M., & Plati, T. (2000). *Mode of administration effects on MCAS composition performance for grades four, eight, and ten.* Retrieved December 15, 2004, from http://www.bc.edu/research/nbetpp/statements/WE052200.pdf

U.S. Department of Commerce, National Telecommunications and Information Administration. (2002). *A nation online: How Americans are expanding their use of the Internet.* Washington, DC: Author.

U.S. Department of Education. (2001). *The No Child Left Behind Act of 2001: Enhancing education through technology.* Retrieved January 12, 2004, from http://www.ed.gov/policy/elsec/leg/esea02/pg34.html

A Commitment to Social Change and Community Service

Section I focuses on how the use of the Internet and other information and communication technologies (ICTs) can lead to the development of projects that offer a true commitment to social change and community service. The first three chapters in this section describe how the Internet and other ICTs have helped three teachers reach a global community, while supporting the teaching and learning of literacy in their own or others' classrooms.

In chapter 2, Gino Sangiuliano describes Books on Tapes for Kids, an ongoing project he began several years ago with his second- and third-grade students and continues with every new class of students he has. As part of this project, students tape record themselves reading books they enjoy and then send the tape and other materials related to the reading of the books (i.e., students' illustrations) to patients in U.S. hospitals. Sangiuliano explains how this project had a positive impact on his students' reading development.

In chapter 3, Mark Ahlness describes the Earth Day Groceries Project and how students who participate in the project hope that their participation will make a difference and even save the Earth. Through the project, students "borrow" grocery bags from local stores and then decorate these bags with environmental artwork and motivational slogans to celebrate Earth Day. Students return the completed bags to the stores, which then use the bags to pack shoppers' groceries on Earth Day. Finally, students exchange information about their participation in the project with a larger community of participating students throughout the world. Ahlness explains that student participation in the project not only helps students build environmental awareness but also offers them authentic reading experiences.

In chapter 4, Cathleen J. Chamberlain describes how her design of a website for a professional preconference workshop evolved into a website that teachers can use to become more educated about the integration of technology in their instruction. Her website, World of Ideas, provides a wealth of resources teachers can use either to learn how to use certain software or to get more information to support their instruction. This website was only the beginning of more of Chamberlain's websites and projects for teachers who want to use the Internet to enrich literacy teaching and learning in their classrooms.

This section concludes with a chapter by Charles K. Kinzer. He comments on the previous chapters while discussing the importance of linking schools and communities. Kinzer explains that technology, especially Internet technologies, can support the outreach of schools to different communities and the learning of new literacies, even with primary-grade students.

CHAPTER 2

Books on Tape for Kids: A Language Arts–Based Service-Learning Project

Gino Sangiuliano

Children's Literature, Cassette Tapes, and the Internet: What's the Connection?

The gymnasium is full on a hot Wednesday evening in May. The school committee members are seated at the front of the gymnasium behind their nameplates and microphones. A video camera is stationed in the rear to capture the images for the local cable access channel. Each year, the school committee takes its show on the road to all the schools in the district and conducts open meetings. At each stop, the first item on the agenda is reserved for that school's annual report, presented at school report night, in which the principal and school improvement team share with the staff, parents, and general public all the wonderful programs and initiatives that are taking place in that school.

The meeting is called to order by the chair, and the school's principal is introduced. After some brief opening statements, the principal introduces the first of many speakers. The first speaker begins, "Good evening, and welcome to Sowams School. We are here this evening to share with you a project called Books on Tape for Kids."

The second speaker continues, "This is an ongoing community service project being conducted by the multiage classrooms at Sowams School in Barrington, Rhode Island." The reason these particular individuals were chosen to kick off the meeting is simple: It's a school night, and they need to get home and go to bed. You see, they are second- and third-grade students in a multiage classroom.

The audience watches in amazement as two students speak with poise and confidence, fully aware that all eyes are on them. Although their teachers had assisted them in cowriting the script, the students have rehearsed well and barely look at their notecards.

"Here's what we do: First, we choose our favorite children's books and practice reading them. Then, we record ourselves on cassette tapes reading the books. Finally, the cassette tapes; the pieces of artwork; the books; the photographs of us, the readers; and our letters are packaged and sent to children in hospitals across the United States. Our goal is to distribute two packages to a hospital in each of the 50 states!"

Another student stationed at the laptop computer projects the class's website onto the large screen. The main speakers, sensing their cue, resume. "This is a map of the United States showing the locations of hospitals where our Books on Tape for Kids have been donated. You can click on the red stars to find out the Books on Tape for Kids that were donated or scroll through the list. So far, 72 books have been donated to hospitals in 35 states. The list of books and states helps us keep track of all the tapes we've done. You can also click on the names and visit that hospital's website."

That scene took place following the first year of the Books on Tape for Kids project in Barrington, Rhode Island, USA. The motivation to share the students' work in such a public forum was partly to celebrate the accomplishments and partly to solicit funds to continue our endeavor. I am convinced that the ultimate objectives of reading instruction and community service would have been reached without the use of the Internet; however, a great number of learning opportunities along the way also would not have been realized.

In the Books on Tape for Kids project, students choose their favorite children's books and practice reading them over time. After the students develop a level of comfort, I record them reading the books onto cassette tapes. We then donate the tapes and a new copy of the book to children's hospitals across the United States. Also included in this package is a piece of student-created artwork inspired by the book, a pen-pal letter explaining each individual's role in creating the final product, a photograph of the readers, and a return-addressed postcard for the recipients to offer us feedback. As a result of the project's authenticity, the students are very motivated to take part and develop expertise in the process.

A project of this magnitude takes a great deal of preparation by the teachers and volunteers, motivation from the students and parents, and support from the community. In Barrington, all these factors have been successfully employed and have become the foundation of what we hope will be a longstanding tradition—a tradition that has been recognized as a

Miss Rumphius Award winner. As I write this chapter, I often refer to *we* in the spirit of the many participants who have helped and contributed to this tradition, including fellow teachers, students, parent volunteers, and administrators. The website (www.booksontapeforkids.org) is geared to help both children and adults learn more about the project while providing students the opportunity and forum to showcase their work.

Books on Tape for Kids

The three major components of Books on Tape for Kids are (1) literacy, (2) technology, and (3) community service. However, lessons relating to any content area are being derived and developed constantly. Variations continue to be explored, so Books on Tape for Kids is never really the same project twice. It has been extremely interesting to hear how teachers across the United States take the basic principle and personalize it to suit the needs of their students and the intended audience.

Literacy

In our grades 2 and 3 multiage classroom, children's literature is a common thread that weaves its way through the entire curriculum, and it touches all students. Hearing a good book; sharing a good book; and discussing, debating, and reflecting on a good book are universal themes that can be explored regardless of age, ability, or grade level. Every day, our students are exposed to quality children's literature because teachers know that in doing so they are providing models for students' writing as well as preparing them to be lifelong learners. Furthermore, on the road to becoming fluent readers, we want to provide enjoyable experiences. Oftentimes, to achieve reading fluency, young readers are exposed to repeated readings of familiar texts. When the piece has been rehearsed, inexperienced readers are better able to focus their attention on intonation and expression. It is common for teachers to give students the opportunity to listen to professionally recorded books either borrowed from the library or purchased as they follow along with the text. These opportunities offer early readers the benefit of developing word recognition and story structure (Marchionda, 2001). They also are able to listen to how readers use their voices and pace themselves throughout the text. These were the traits of reading we wanted the students to be aware of and exhibit. To help chart growth over time, we began to tape record the students reading short passages from their favorite books. We also used the recordings to assess and critique students' oral reading with both them and their parents at conferences. The students thoroughly enjoyed listening to themselves read, and the purpose was served. After many years of recording and collecting dozens of tapes of students reading, the idea of embedding student-recorded books into our schools language arts program was born.

Technology

Books on Tape for Kids was initially sparked by the technology component. During the summer of 1999, I had the wonderful opportunity to take part in the Rhode Island Foundation's Teacher Training Initiative, which was instrumental in providing the tools and support I needed to cultivate many thoughts and ideas about recording the students reading and, ultimately, to put these plans into action. It was through that training program and the technology made available to me that my class was able to create Books on Tape for Kids.

This professional development experience opened my eyes to the role that technology could play in my growth as an educator and my effectiveness as an instructor. I reflected on my practice and asked myself, What do students need to learn? I determined that students ought to be motivated to investigate the world around them, need to be able to communicate with that world and have an opportunity to contribute to it, and want to share their efforts with that world. Before the Internet entered my classroom, that world was limited. Technology changed that: Computers and related technologies can be tools of inquiry, communication, creation, and sharing. They can be tools of change.

Books on Tape for Kids has been the catalyst for the creation of our webpages designed for and by students (see Figure 2.1) and the complete integration of technology into my classroom. This project truly changed the way I view computers and the Internet and the impact they can have on student learning.

Community Service

Once the class established an authentic audience and a goal to create 100 packages and distribute them nationally, the momentum was unstoppable. It seemed that with every recording, the group of students became more creative. With every e-mail or postcard received, the motivation increased. And with every passing week, new twists and variations emerged. Readers worked in teams on the same book using sound effects and created more elaborate artwork with the help of the art teacher.

We had come full circle. I became keenly aware of the many benefits the project offered to both the creators and recipients. Obviously the hos-

Figure 2.1 Books on Tape for Kids

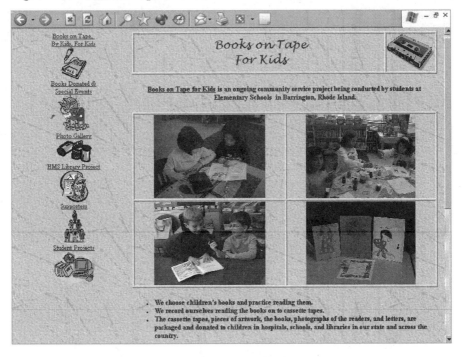

pital patients appreciate receiving beautiful gifts from distant strangers. It hopefully will encourage them to continue to find the joy in reading and writing. Yet the notion of community service has not only provided the students with opportunities to spread good will but also become a catalyst for them to become more introspective about their own reading development. Now students are looking at reading and writing in a completely different light. For example, previously reluctant readers now are rereading familiar texts countless times to master them. They beg family members to act as their audience so they can rehearse the reading time and time again. Students suddenly care deeply about self-assessing their oral reading for word recognition, pronunciation, enunciation, and pace. Self-selecting the texts they want to share with another youngster teaches them to identify the audience and the author's purpose. Matching a style or genre of writing to the intended audience is a skill that is useful when creating their own original pieces. Students have become intrinsically motivated to produce their best work not because their teacher has asked them to, but because they *want* to and have a clear understanding of why it is so important. Finally, teachers found that the students thoroughly enjoy listening to themselves read. During free moments and choice time, they clamor to the listening center to enjoy one another's tapes. The pride and self-confidence they feel is clearly evident.

Sharing the Torch: Using Technology to Inspire Others

From its inception, Books on Tape for Kids was meant to be a conduit for literacy instruction. As the months went by, my definition of *literacy* broadened to include the *new literacies*. The students used the Internet daily to research and locate audiences for the books. The class was sending e-mails to our supporters communicating our efforts, soliciting donations, and thanking them for their contributions. As word of what we were doing spread, we became inundated with correspondences from around the United States inquiring about what we were doing. We had become nationally recognized thanks to the power of the Internet. This realization only stimulated more buzz and excitement around our efforts. We wanted to do something to capitalize on the positive energy. With the help of two colleagues and a new mobile laptop computer station, we took the next step, introducing our projects to other schools with how-to technology-based presentations.

The culmination of the Books on Tape for Kids project was not producing any of the tapes at all. The attainment of our goal occurred when the students completed and delivered some very memorable presentations for students at a neighboring primary school (see Figure 2.2).

In preparation for our visit, my colleagues and I offered students an opportunity to learn about three computer applications: webpage design, PowerPoint, and brochure publication. The students then selected the format they wished to use to spread their message. The class formed three groups and worked cooperatively with their teacher to create their presentations. They met once a week for 10 weeks. Incidentally, this project also allowed me to collaborate with the school's librarian and enrichment specialist. We each were able to bring our areas of expertise to the process. The quality of the students' work would not have been as great as it was had we not communicated our expectations with each other. The final products were awesome. Groups of second- and third-grade students stood before an auditorium filled with children their own age and delivered PowerPoint presentations, shared webpages, and distributed colorful brochures. As a result of their efforts, more than 100 students at Primrose Elementary School were inspired to start similar service learning projects. In addition to using

Figure 2.2 Student-Created Projects

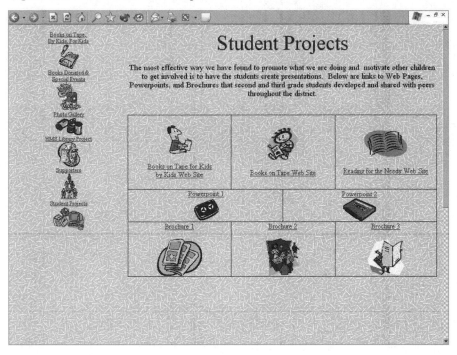

various modes of technology to spread their message, the students were able to refine their writing, reading, and public speaking skills.

As the Books on Tape for Kids project gained momentum, more and more opportunities to teach the new literacies naturally evolved. The ICTs that exist today are real and should be treated as such. By the time their schooling is complete, students will be accessing and sharing a great deal of information using these mediums. What I became conscious of was that authenticity mattered. If students did not use the technologies meaningfully in concert with the existing curriculum, and if students viewed computers simply as auxiliary equipment, educators would not realize the full potential of their effectiveness. Technology instruction should be presented in a manner that allows students to apply what they learn to real-world situations. The students need to be aware of that fact and buy into it as well. The best way to accomplish this is to provide students with genuine experiences that both meet existing curriculum guidelines and motivate students to realize their full potential.

There are powerful implications for students' work when it is authentic and has a broad audience. With the technology available today, teachers can share writing, thoughts, and talents with large populations. Computers, the Internet, printers, scanners, and digital cameras are tools that helped achieve specific goals the town of Barrington had established. In addition to the benefits the students received, the teachers gained valuable experience as I learned how to integrate these tools into the existing curriculum in a meaningful way and developed a model plan to replicate it in the process.

Rethinking the Teacher's Role—Rethinking Technology's Role

On a bulletin board next to my desk is a photograph of me taken when I was about the same age as my students. In it I am wearing a faded blue baseball uniform and a hat that is clearly too big for my head. The bat I am holding also would be considered large for a Little League baseball player. The photograph has followed me from classroom to classroom for more than a decade. Because it is obscured by notes and papers posted around it, only the most observant students notice it during the first week of school. Furthermore, only the plucky ones ever ask, "Who is that?" and "Why do you have that there?" The answer lies in the events that occurred that day leading up to the photograph. It was a bad day. I had lost my hat and was late for the first game of the season. To make matters worse, it was the day of the team photograph. I had never played sports on a team and did not know what to do or where to go. The coach that day gave me his hat and the closest bat he could find, so I could have my picture taken. As the years passed, I went on to be a pretty good athlete, playing many sports throughout high school and college. I will never forget how I felt that first day, however, confused, alone, scared, and ashamed. When students ask me about that picture, I tell them it is there to remind me of what it is like to experience those feelings and to persevere because things that once seemed so overwhelming have a way of becoming more manageable as time goes on.

When I made the decision to truly integrate technology into my curriculum, I did not know how to do it or where to begin. All the training I had gone through to become a teacher was not helping me keep pace with the advances in technology. Restructuring my educational practices by making a technology-based community-service project the focus of my literacy instruction was a huge gamble, to say the least. I realized that the best way to encourage students to become risk takers and lifelong learners was by modeling. As students created Books on Tape for Kids, it was clear that I did not have all the answers about how to maximize the potential use of the equipment that was being made available to me. *I was learning with them.*

As I think back to my first years of teaching with computers in the classroom, it is accurate to say that I *used* computers pretty well; the students had the opportunity to explore word processing, drawing tools, and basic skills games. I used the minimal technology as best I could. As I reflect on the role technology has in my classroom today, particularly in regard to Books on Tape for Kids, it can be described as central. The repercussions of teaching with technology have been widespread. Perhaps most notable has been how it has affected my style and delivery of instruction. I found myself encouraging and assigning cooperative groups of students to complete tasks more often. Coupled with the fact that the tasks were related to service learning, this unity cultivated an environment of togetherness and caring that was palpable. The youngsters had developed a sense of community within the classroom by working to benefit the community at large.

To keep them motivated, it was essential for the students to have a true understanding of the importance of what they were doing. Successful community-service learning projects depend on the students' belief that they are making a difference. It became my mission and responsibility to somehow demonstrate the impact they truly were having on the lives of others, and I wanted it to be authentic. The Internet helped me accomplish that.

In recent years, as I have developed a proficiency in using technology in the classroom, I have become adept at assisting others. Along the way I have encountered many teachers who feel the same way I did before I became comfortable with the new technologies. They are confused and scared about how to use the computers with students who may know as much or more about them than they do. Others feel alone and ashamed that they have not kept up with the latest innovations in technology. I have learned that the face of education is constantly changing and that it is impossible to be an expert on every new tool, strategy, practice, and approach. However, that should not stop educators from being innovative and taking chances. Persevere. What once seemed impossible will become very feasible with time.

Finding the Right Fit: Different Ways to Achieve Your Objectives

One factor that contributed to the ultimate success of this award-winning project was that it took place in the context of a multiage program. Older students, in this case third graders, grew into their roles as mentors to the second and third graders. Training younger students to produce the books on tape developed into somewhat of a class tradition. This is not to suggest that similar technology-based community-service projects would not succeed in classrooms with one-year placements or of different grades. It just means that the procedures may have to be tweaked to suit the needs of the intended participants and audiences. In fact, by transferring to a new school and grade, I was able to experience this firsthand. The following are some variations my students have experimented with.

The original idea was for young students to donate *picture* books to hospital patients who were about the same age as them. This way, the students could produce tapes efficiently and at the reading level of the second- and third-grade students who were reading them. However, as the readers became older and more capable, the entire class began to record chapter books. I divided the text into sections for each of the readers. The students illustrated what they read on an index-card sized piece of paper and arranged them to make a mini picture book. A variation of this project involved youngsters using the pictures to make a collage.

Another approach was to select books based on a specific genre, subject, or author. This approach gave the class a common theme to work from and was a perfect progression toward research projects. For example, when classes were studying reptiles, students needed to find nonfiction books to record, and their artwork had to be a diagram or illustration that included labels and captions sharing factual information. Recently, students conducted author studies based on the books we recorded. The assignment was to use the Internet to research authors and report their findings. The class compiled, printed, and distributed students' findings to faculty and students through the school library.

Producing musical books was a fun, creative way to share a piece of children's literature. Students used instruments to enhance the telling of the story. With the help of the music teacher, students experimented by using songs as part of the performance or adding sound effects to the reading. For example, the students and I recorded *Alexander and the Wind-Up Mouse* by Leo Lionni (1969) twice. Side one of the tape contained a traditional reading performed by two students. Side two, however, was produced by a group of eight students who accompanied the readers with sound effects for the mice and bells for the magic.

Perhaps the most special experience I have had to date with Books on Tape for Kids came on a Saturday morning in June. Students and family members joined us in putting together a Books on Tape for Kids package. The families had selected their books and rehearsed their parts prior to participating, and showed up at school on a weekend morning to record their tapes and illustrate a piece of artwork. It was truly a joy to see families sharing literature and applying their efforts toward creating something special for others.

As people around the United States contact me to get more information about the project, I am reminded of how many different audiences exist for such a project. Teachers for those who are blind have expressed interest in receiving a package from us. Another group who have appreciated our work are English as a second language teachers. They find that students who are learning English benefit from hearing the text while they read along with it.

The latest edition of our project finds us donating the books and tapes to our very own school library, with a bit of a twist. These packages not only contain the Books on Tape, but also an original story inspired by the book they recorded. Furthermore, students prepare writing tips and lessons to complement their pieces. These lessons are typed onto a template, printed onto an index card, and included in each package. These complete packages are sorted by writing themes based on the six-trait writing assessment (Spandel, 2001) and are currently being used by teachers looking for writing samples to share with their class.

Using Technology to Do Things Differently— To Do Things Better

At the inception of this journey, my colleagues and I were racing to keep up with the latest technology. Since then, an interesting transformation has occurred. From its meager beginnings, the project is now a catalyst for district-wide change regarding how our teachers use technology in the classroom. Teachers anxiously await upgrades to our Internet system that will enable efficient video streaming without interruption. This technology will give students anywhere who have computers the opportunity to see and hear their peers read a book. Video and audio devices are on the horizon that will make it possible for us to digitally produce recordings. Students are currently able to save the work they do on personal digital portfolios that will follow them throughout their school lives. Compact disk burners will allow them to take files home to share with family members. Constant communication with parents is made possible using e-mail and group lists. Parents have reported feeling connected to their child's school experience when they receive a message from me with an attached photograph of something special going on in the class. Also, it has been nice to send updates and photographs to individuals and organizations that support student projects. Members of the Parent-Teacher Organization, school committee, and various grant organizations that help fund our projects are very interested in knowing what we are doing.

The ICTs that we have today can truly influence learning in powerful ways. Instant access to information about virtually anything is astounding. Search engines help us find what we need, and fast. *Children-friendly* websites like Yahooligans (www.yahooligans.com) make it possible for students to learn more independently. Our school librarian has set up a webpage (www.hampdenmeadows.org) with links to helpful sites related to each grade's curriculum. Video streaming has emerged as another vehicle to introduce and reinforce concepts taught in the classroom. Websites such as United Streaming (www.unitedstreaming.com) offer teachers another way to share content with students. Individual class webpages created by students or teachers provide platforms to share unique class projects and events taking place with others and can act as an idea exchange for educators.

Often today, the news reports horror stories about the risks related to Internet use. Despite the many precautions educators take, there are inherent dangers associated with its use by children. Those concerns are valid and should be addressed. Parents and teachers need to be vigilant about providing appropriate supervision and guidance while kids are online, in addition to using any filters or locks their computers may have. Nevertheless, it should be noted that the Internet also can provide an avenue for community service and civic responsibility and, as such, be used to improve the user's lives and the lives of others. That is the approach teachers have taken with this project, and have been extremely pleased with the results.

Looking Back, Looking Ahead: What We Need to Succeed

I sometimes try to imagine what growing up today is like from my students' perspective, but it is very difficult. Like vinyl records, black-and-white television, and rotary-dial phones, the idea of a world without the Internet is completely foreign to them. This is the reality of today's world, and as teachers, we need to be prepared to embrace the challenge of learning new competencies alongside our students. This pedagogical shift can feel very uncomfortable and threatening. As professionals, we need to rise above our discomfort and recognize that our students are able to become as proficient, if not more so, than we are in the area of new technologies.

I am not sure how much longer we can refer to the knowledge of the Internet, computers, and other technologies as new literacies. In fact, as far as our students are concerned, they are anything but. That point was amplified for me one evening when my in-laws were baby-sitting my 3-year-old son, Michael. My father-in-law, who was an educator for 30 years and retired about 10 years ago, would be the first to admit that he does not know how to turn on a computer. He watched in amazement as Michael opened my laptop, connected to the Internet, opened the browser, found his folder, located the bookmark I had set of his favorite website, and proceeded to play a game. My son is not a child prodigy; he has seen me simply turn on the computer hundreds of times. I am sure that in 5 minutes, I could teach my father-in-law to do the same. Is my son computer literate? That's debatable; however, I know that when he begins school in 2 years, computers will not be a new literacy for him.

Teachers need to assume that most students are entering school with a level of prior computer experience and need to be prepared to use that knowledge to enhance existing curricula. When educators are open to this approach, that is, technology instruction in an authentic and integrated manner, learning and teaching will reach a new level. Teacher-guided instruction and prepared activities are good places to establish the basics; however, the larger picture cannot be ignored. A time will come when students will view these experiences as artificial and will not be invested in learning them. Teachers would be doing a disservice if they did not at times take a leap of faith and let their students create frameworks for their own learning experiences. I am fortunate to work in a district that recognizes and values this notion. For example, high school seniors complete a senior project to graduate. The students' self-selected projects, based on their interests, must complete research papers, do fieldwork with mentors, and present their final projects to a committee. A major component of that project must be based in technology.

The most challenging and perhaps most exciting change to my classroom in recent years has been the way that the Internet has affected my teaching and the role that computers play in my daily instruction. Although infinite in its applications in the elementary classroom, the Internet brings with it many factors that promote change in students' literacy learning, most notably its own vernacular. To successfully gather meaning from what is on the screen, students need to be able to do more than just decode the words. Furthermore, rules of etiquette that govern the Internet and questions of ethics inevitably arise. When they do, it offers teachers the opportunity to communicate the many perils of the Internet and how to use this tool responsibly. How this is addressed will manifest itself differently depending on the grade level of students. However, Barrington's school district has been very proactive in educating its teachers in this area. Through numerous workshops and informational meetings, teachers have developed a level of comfort governing Internet use in their classrooms. The school district also provides each building with a technology specialist whose role is to assist teachers in any way possible.

Earlier in my career, I struggled just to fit computer time into my daily plans. Today, it continues to play a more prevalent role throughout the curriculum. In regard to Books on Tape for Kids, the Internet has become a necessity. I have used the Internet as a tool to promote the wonderful work students are doing, communicate with organizations around the world, motivate and aid students in research, encourage students' creativity as they contribute to the class webpage, and authenticate literacy learning. In turn, many students who at home perceive the computer as simply a device used to play games—be it educational or otherwise—see it for something different in the classroom. To them, it has become the place they go to share their work, correspond with others, find answers, use their imagination, and learn.

Educational reform is often initiated by test scores and global competition. Standards, competencies, performance tasks, and assessments are constantly being created to measure students' learning and growth. According to a position statement published by the International Reading Association in 2002,

> Despite the fact that students will be expected to navigate complex networks of information technologies when they leave school, not a single state in the United States and no country assesses reading with anything other than paper and print technologies. Further, despite the fact that many children prefer word processors when completing writing assignments and approximately 20% more students will pass a state writing assessment when permitted to do so (Russell & Plati, 2000), not a single state in the United States and few nations assess writing by allowing students to use a word processor.

Our district continues to raise the bar for its students. Each teacher of the district is trained to create every lesson and activity with the standards in mind. In fact, administrators require specific goals and objectives based on the standards before time and money would be allocated to projects like Books on Tape for Kids. The notion of accountability is carried all the way from the elementary grades through the secondary grades, as shown by the example earlier in this chapter about the high school senior projects.

When these new literacies are viewed collectively as a separate entity, teachers run the risk of isolating them and teaching them out of context.

The positive influence they can have on all content areas will never truly be appreciated. However, policymakers continue to ignore the Internet and other ICTs and omit them from their definitions of reading and, therefore, are not reflected in their assessments.

Without question, the biggest change I have seen during my career has been the integration of technology in the classroom. If teachers are not equipped to deliver instruction that reflects these new literacies, teachers simply are not doing their job. One of the factors that make it difficult for educators to properly prepare students for a future inundated with these new literacies is that these literacies have been developing at an alarming rate and will most likely continue to do so. Another challenge is ensuring fiscal equity with regard to technology in all classrooms. Finally, teachers need to become familiar with how to integrate these technologies into their existing curricula. The burden of responsibility to address these issues falls on parents, educators, administrators, and policymakers. The International Reading Association offers recommendations to each of these groups that tell what can be done to make sure students are prepared for their literary future. A common thread among the recommendations revolves around funding, participation, and support for staff development. A major principle of teacher education programs and district-based staff development opportunities should be to integrate the Internet and other technologies into the literacy curriculum. It is only then that teachers will be preparing their students to succeed in the future and establishing the foundation that fosters a lifelong appreciation for learning.

REFERENCES

International Reading Association. (2002). *Integrating literacy and technology in the cirriculum. A position statement of the International Reading Association.* Newark, DE: Author.

Marchionda, D. (2001, September). A bridge to literacy: Creating lifelong readers through audiobooks. *AudioFile Magazine*, Retrieved January 11, 2005, from www.abcaudiobooks.com/Article2.aspx

Spandel, V. (2001). *Books, lessons, ideas for teaching the six traits: Writing in the elementary and middle grades.* Wilmington, MA: Great Source Education Group.

CHILDREN'S LITERATURE

Lionni, L. (1969). *Alexander and the wind-up mouse.* New York: Pantheon.

CHAPTER 3

Giving It Away:
The Earth Day Groceries Project

Mark Ahlness

Beginnings

Sometimes a little idea grows into a movement. It can even get out of hand. In the spring of 1994, I had a great idea and was looking for a way to put it on the Internet. I sent out a simple invitation and began what has become one of the largest and longest running educational projects on the Internet. The Earth Day Groceries Project, my Miss Rumphius Award–winning project, continues to this day. Here is the idea: A teacher borrows paper bags from a local grocery store that the students at the school then decorate with beautiful environmental artwork and motivational slogans to celebrate Earth Day (April 22). The school then returns the bags to the store, which uses them to bag groceries for amazed and appreciative shoppers on Earth Day. This activity is a wonderful way to integrate several curriculum areas (Ahlness, 1999), and it is a cost-free means of establishing a strong school–community partnership (Strangman, 2002).

The idea for the project came from a 1991 summer workshop I attended as a teacher in the Seattle School District. I was about to start teaching third grade after being a special education teacher for 10 years. I was looking for good ideas—any ideas, actually—to use in my new school and position. This seemed like an all-encompassing project: a great science activity, a great environmental education unit, and a great community-service opportunity. I tried it my first year in my own class, without technology, and my students and I had a wonderful time. My students were so excited about decorating bags that would eventually end up in someone's kitchen. The energy and care they put into their artwork and slogans were so amazing that I introduced the project to the whole school the next year. It was a huge hit, with nearly every classroom joining in and over 400 Earth Day grocery bags decorated. My classroom proudly carried the bags to our neighborhood grocery store. The store and the community loved the idea, and a partnership between the school and the store was established that continues to this day. And, at

Arbor Heights Elementary School (www.halcyon.com/arborhts), a new tradition was born.

The Project Grows

In early 1994, as spring and Earth Day approached, I was in the middle of the building excitement of the emerging Internet. E-mail, file transfer protocol (ftp), and gopher (a menu-based information archive) were opening possibilities for communication, and the World Wide Web (whatever that was) was on the horizon. I had been granted an e-mail account through National Aeronautics and Space Administration from the Quest program in 1993, and I was truly excited by the possibilities of using the Internet in education. I participated in two early listservs, Kidsphere (no longer in existence) and Ednet (www.umass.edu/ednet), which helped me to expand the boundaries of my classroom. These lists had a wonderful feeling of openness, sharing, questioning, and experimentation.

Having such a positive experience decorating bags for Earth Day at my school, I figured this was something that others ought to hear about. I wanted somehow to distribute the idea, but I still wanted to keep track of and manage it in some way. I struggled with how best to go about getting the idea out there. Finally, it was my wife who said I just ought to give the idea away—and just ask people to let me know if they participated. Out of that simple premise grew an enormously successful Internet project.

I sent the idea to Kidsphere and Ednet, along with a request that people send, via e-mail, a brief report to me if they tried the project at their school. I promised to share the results with everyone who participated. In 1994, the first year, 43 schools sent in reports. I saved the e-mails and sent them to all the participants. The following is an example of a report on the Earth Day Groceries Project (2004) from that first year:

> My 33 elementary enrichment (gifted) students took on your project with a whopping success.... The students who delivered the bags had their picture taken by the local newspaper and made the FRONT PAGE. I can't thank you enough for bringing this project to me. The students (and our community) have become much more aware of environmental issues, and the project was a lot of fun!

For the first three years, each school received all the reports from all the participating schools. As you can imagine, this quickly became unwieldy as the number of schools taking part rose rapidly from 115 in 1995 to 188 in 1996. Thank goodness the World Wide Web was up and running. The project continued to grow as reports arrived from around the world. I remember getting a report from Crete and looking with my third graders at digital pictures of grocery bags that said Happy Earth Day in Greek. What a great lesson in language literacy. Talk about breaking down those traditional classroom walls.

In the fall of 1994, I also created a website for my school. This was a truly exciting time to be on the Web. I still vividly remember the first time I connected to the school website and saw that simple graphic slowly appear. Because there were so few websites at the time (fewer than 10 elementary schools had websites), it seemed I ought to have a reason for the school to have a website. It was not just enough to be a school; you had to have something special to say. So, the school website was known as the Home of the Earth Day Grocery Bags (see Figure 3.1; www.halcyon.com/arborhts/ahold1.html) until 1998.

I eventually established an independent website for the Earth Day Groceries Project (see Figure 3.2; www.earthdaybags.org). Project partic-

Figure 3.1   First Homepage for Arbor Heights Elementary School

Figure 3.2 Website for the Earth Day Groceries Project

ipants were able to fill out Web-based forms to post their reports. In addition to this advancement, the American Forest & Paper Association provided financial support for further development of the website and a new database. I established a database that added reports to the website more easily and allowed users access to thousands of reports and pictures via active server pages. Schools also could e-mail digital pictures and put their own webpage on the website. Each school that sent in pictures had a webpage for those pictures. Through all of this, the project had become a huge investment of time for me because I spent hundreds of hours every spring adding new reports, creating webpages with digital pictures of students decorating bags, and so forth. In 2001, I established the project as a 501(c)(3) nonprofit organization.

As the project grows, I remain adamant about having it remain free, with no registration necessary. As time permits, I try to expand what reasonably still can be given away. Currently, the website offers a starter kit containing desktop wallpaper, PowerPoint presentations, drawing templates, clip art, and even screen savers. The list of free material grows every year for the project.

When I first started the Earth Day Groceries Project, I had no idea how large or how successful it would become. Today it has been done in all 50 states and dozens of countries, and millions of students and consumers have been affected in some way by this project. In 2004, the project celebrates a decade of existence and is still growing.

Lesson Learned From the Project

Besides being an environmental awareness lesson, the Earth Day Groceries Project can be a wonderful geography lesson. Every year, I have my students mark a large map with dots indicating the locations of participating schools. As students read the reports to find the location, they are often amazed to read what teachers have to say about their schools, how many bags the students decorated, and so on.

In recent years, I have been struck by the incredible artwork on the bags (see Figure 3.3). As more schools make this an annual event, the artwork seems to grow more sophisticated. Each of the hundreds of thousands of bags distributed every year is a unique work of art. I hope that

Figure 3.3   Earth Day Grocery Bags From Arbor Heights Elementary School, 2002

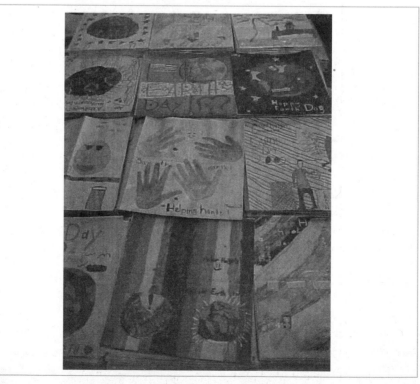

the people taking these bags home will take the time to really look at them. I believe this project is the largest art giveaway anywhere. The Earth Day Groceries Project contains thousands of digital images of beautiful bags on the website (www.earthdaybags.org/pictures.htm), and they are only a small fraction of the number actually given away.

But more important, the hope behind the Earth Day Groceries Project is that those grocery shoppers will read the comments written on the bags. The students who wrote on them did so with the intention that their bags would make a difference, could change an attitude, or might even save the earth. Sometimes students get very attached to the bags they have created. Some spend hours working on them, and they are very proud of their creations. Ultimately, despite teachers' reminders throughout the creative process that the art will be given away, students sometimes do not want to part with their bags. What a wonderful time for a lesson on civics. What a great opportunity to introduce at an early age the idea that students can make a difference. Naturally, the message from the teacher will be aimed at the developmental level of the child, but the opportunity created by this project is a real-life lesson that has an outcome that just might make a difference. And so, it is appropriate that the product of this project be something that is given away.

Giving It Away—Proceed With Caution

There is a difference between giving something away and having something taken from you. Despite the glowing reports and the lofty goals and accomplishments set forth here so far, there have been some challenges along the way. Developing my school's website, being among the first handful of schools with a website, and being on the cutting edge were thrilling accomplishments. Imagine my surprise when in the fall of 1995, a man from Germany sent me an e-mail with a congratulatory note about my school's website appearance in *The Road Ahead* by Bill Gates (1995). Wow, how exciting! I rushed out to buy the book the day it was released in the United States. There it was, a screen shot (one of only two in the book) of my school's homepage. The innovative design was entirely my own, parts of it created pixel by pixel on my little 386 computer at home. I was incredibly proud.

As all teachers of literacy know today, copyright and citing sources appropriately are currently very hot topics that are made more difficult to deal with as a direct result of the millions of documents available to students on the Internet. Ensuring that students create their own work—and motivating them in a positive way to do so—is an additional challenge for teachers, especially at the secondary level. However, this issue must be addressed when students are at a younger age. So, when my third graders produce a PowerPoint presentation, I require them to cite any sources that are not their own—from who took the pictures with the classroom camera, to the URL of a website where they grabbed some clip art, to ideas and peer feedback they used to complete their presentations. At their age, this new literacy skill is just as important as having a good title or using proper grammar and conventions.

So when the excitement of having my work used in a bestseller wore off a little, I naturally asked myself if the same expectations should not apply to everyone. I never received a request for permission for my work to be used in *The Road Ahead*. Perhaps this is why I am so happy when people ask permission to use some of my Web work. Material from the Earth Day Groceries Project has been used in several books and magazines and even in a standardized test. I have given permission wherever possible and have always thanked the authors for asking.

Part of the reason I established a separate website for the Earth Day Groceries Project was to maintain some sort of autonomy. The nonprofit status was a part of that. The sour taste in my mouth from that early experience made me much more cognizant of what money and business were capable of. I was very concerned in the first few years that people seeing the website might assume that the Earth Day Groceries Project belonged to a large supermarket chain, stamped with a commercial copyright. One year the grocery store Albertson's unveiled Albertson's Earth Day Groceries Project. Ralph's, a grocery store in California, has for several years coordinated a very large effort to get children to decorate its grocery bags. These stores also have encouraged teachers and students to participate in the online aspect of the project by printing the Web address of the Earth Day Groceries Project on their bags, for which I am very grateful. I did indeed copyright the website early on, actually paying the fee to do so. Nonprofit status now helps ensure the integrity of the project name and mission.

Many teachers have volunteered large amounts of time to work on technology in their schools. One of the tasks is developing and maintaining the school's website. I have been maintaining the one at Arbor Heights for 10 years now (as of August 14, 2004). A few years ago, I assembled a history of the development of the school's homepage at www.halcyon.com/arborhts/history.html. It is "dedicated to the thousands of educators who have built and maintained their school websites on their own time" (Ahlness, 2004). Unlike my school's website, which I maintain on my personal Internet account, most school websites are maintained on servers owned and operated by school districts. Ownership and copyright reside with the district. I only hope that the teachers who developed those websites on their own time will someday receive the proper recognition for their efforts.

Literacy Changes in the Classroom

When I moved out of special education into the world of regular education, I was extremely lucky to land at such a wonderful school, Arbor Heights Elementary. It has always been a place where students come prepared and are nurtured. It's a place teachers retire from, not transfer out of. Nestled in an out-of-the-way, blue-collar corner of the Seattle School District, this school has been preparing its students for the future by teaching the whole child—for many, many years.

Third grade is a wonderful age to teach. Teachers who have taught at the same grade level for many years often say their grade is the absolute best. Add me to that chorus. During third grade, 8- and 9-year-olds learn multiplication, are introduced to cursive handwriting (yes, still), and grow up so much during the course of the year. They are starting to be independent thinkers and "cool" social beings, but they are still entranced by my annual readings of E.B. White's *The Trumpet of the Swan* (1970), *Stuart Little* (1945), and *Charlotte's Web* (1952). A classroom discussion of the existence of Santa Claus walks a delicious line between fantasy and reality that the students enjoy talking and thinking about. The same sort of dicey exchange often happens after my reading of Chris Van Allsburg's *The Polar Express* (1985).

When I first started using the Internet in my classroom, times were quite different. In 1993, I tapped into the phone line (one of three in the building) in the staff room by running a phone wire to my classroom and plugging it into a little laptop with a 2400-baud modem. I hooked this up to my overhead projector with a liquid crystal display device on top and dialed into my Internet provider. Amazingly, there were words on the screen that my students could read. If I received a new e-mail, for example, of another report from a school participating in the Earth Day Groceries Project, my students and I would read the e-mail together and then all crowd around the classroom map, trying to find that school's location. The only catch was that if someone picked up the phone in the staff room while I was dialed into my e-mail account, we were disconnected. So I created a cover for the phone, which was a large cardboard box with a sign on the bottom that said, "Room 12 on the Internet, please do not use the phone. Thanks!" I would send a student next door to the staff room to put this box over the phone. I was not a real popular guy during this time.

Gradually, I built up a small group of computers that my students could use for Internet research, and the principal finally gave me my own phone line. Connection speeds (using a dial-up connection) were pretty slow, but the students' excitement of seeing amazing things such as the Mars Pathfinder website (http://mars.sgi.com) or paintings of Monet at the WebMuseum (www.ibiblio.org/wm/paint/auth/monet) kind of made up for it. Every week, I designed Web assignments for my students and posted them on our school's website—an early form of a simple webquest. Some people called these assignments task cards. Basically, they were one-page handouts instructing the students to go to a website, find information, and write down the answers. Some of the early assignments focused on researching Martin Luther King, Jr., writing to U.S. troops in Bosnia, exploring the Franklin Museum Institute in Philadelphia, PA, and learning more about Jane Goodall at the Jane Goodall Institute website (www.janegoodall.org). For many years, I posted these assignments on the Web in portable document format for other people to use. I often heard from teachers who were grateful for help in getting started using the Internet in their class. (The assignments are still on my school's website at www.halcyon.com/arborhts/rm12/assign.html.)

Designing these assignments certainly was not an exact science. First, I had to find an interesting website that would enrich what my students were already studying. Second, I had to be sure my third graders could handle the reading level at that website. (This was always the biggest challenge.) If I had to compromise anything, it was most often the curriculum, which simply meant that although I could find wonderful websites from which my students could learn a great deal, the content was not what they were studying, for example, following Seattle sports teams (see the Seattle Mariners at http://seattle.mariners.mlb.com and the Seattle Supersonics at www.nba.com/sonics), visiting Volcano World (http://volcano.und.nodak.edu) and White House for Kids (www.whitehouse.gov/kids), and watching webcams aimed at bird nests such as the King Falcon Cam (http://birdcam.xcelenergy.com/kingfalcon.asp). So although this early Internet experience enriched the curriculum, it also enhanced reading skills such as reading questions on a page, following directions (i.e., click on the link under the picture of the cow), and writing information down. These were lofty goals to achieve every week, but there were also assignments that were failures, usually because I overestimated what the students could handle. Occasional failures also occurred because of the website being down; the Internet connection failing; or our school district filter, designed to shield students from inappropriate material on the Internet, not allowing access to a particular website. But overall, these assignments became an important part of my literacy instruction.

My own web development skills and style were influenced by my growing awareness of reading levels on websites. This is not to say that I began writing everything at a third-grade reading level. Rather, I think the websites I have created over the years actually have contained more text and fewer graphics than most. As I saw my students struggle with reading on the Web, I tried, through my websites, to *make* my students read. That is, it was not enough that they figure out which icon would most likely lead to the goal; I wanted my students to read their way through a website. For example, whenever they were at a website I had designed, they would have to use their reading abilities.

With very few websites being written at a third-grade level and not wanting to limit Web exploration by reading level, I began to include the development of some new skills to my reading instruction. For example, I taught my students how to scan a page quickly and look for keywords. They learned to transition from reading on paper to reading on a computer screen, and vice versa. They increased their Internet vocabulary with the addition of words such as *scroll*, *document*, *link*, and the like.

As I worked with my third graders year after year in this new medium, I began to realize there was so much more they had to learn about reading than just continuing line after line, page after page. To be truly literate, they had to learn how to make sense out of and enjoy these new literacies.

Whole language and *literature based* are frequently heard buzzwords describing reading instruction. I would suggest there is an additional way to teach reading: using the Internet and computer programs. Readers must be taught the specific skills necessary to read efficiently in these new mediums, including how to use the new tools available. As much as educators have taught students how to read a table of contents or how to use an index, educators now need to teach them how to find a word or phrase on a website or document—and how to do an efficient Internet search. These, and many more new literacy skills, should be a part of a classroom teacher's reading curriculum, certainly not taught in the isolation of a computer lab by a technology specialist. This integration of new skills and content is one of the biggest challenges facing today's teachers.

Using the Internet to Share Knowledge and Create Partnerships

Educational listservs are some of the best resources for teachers who accept the challenge of preparing their students to use today's technology tools. In terms of making an impact, the listservs have a distinct advantage over other Web-based resources, at least for me: Websites have to be sought out, whereas with listservs, e-mail discussions arrive in my inbox. At the very least, I have to look at the message subject before I delete it. I might go to a website, but I have to remember to do so, set a time, and so forth. Teachers just have too much on their plates to remember to regularly check out a website.

Some of my favorite education listservs are Ednet (www.umass.edu/ednet), wwwedu (http://groups.yahoo.com/group/wwwedu), Edtech (www.h-net.org/~edweb), and The Reading Teacher (www.reading.org/resources/community/discussions_rt_instruct.html). I have been gratefully learning from the members of those lists for more than 10 years. When I published my school's website, the first book on hypertext markup language (HTML) was just going to press. At this time, there was a wealth of knowledge that list members, including me, were willing to share. I learned how to use ftp, gopher, and telnet, and build webpages, thanks to many early pioneers willing to share their knowledge and expertise. I also have moderated tictech (http://groups.yahoo.com/group/tictech), an ed/tech listserv in Seattle for several years. It is interesting to note that all these listservs, including mine, are moderated by volunteers.

From the crew at the University of Massachusetts moderating Ednet, to Andy Carvin moderating wwwedu on his own time, to this third-grade teacher moderating tictech, list moderators have continued to provide forums for the free exchange of information in the spirit of the *gift economy* of the Internet. This term comes from the early development of the Internet on university campuses and in educational institutions (Lehnert, 1998). Although freely sharing ideas without expecting monetary reward may seem to be naïve, it is this spirit that has built the framework of the Internet and that enriches its educational promise and diversity.

Louis Schmier, a professor of history at Valdosta State University in Georgia, has posted his Random Thoughts (www.halcyon.com/arborhts/louis.html) on educational listservs since 1993. These wonderfully inspirational e-mail messages speak from his heart and soul about the students whom all teachers are trying to reach. One classic example is this excerpt from a Random Thought called "To Be A Teacher":

If you want to be a teacher, you first have to learn how to play hopscotch, learn other children's games, learn how to watch a snail crawl, read "Yertle the Turtle," and watch "Bullwinkle." If you want to be a teacher, you have to blow "she loves me, she loves me nots" with a dandelion or pull the individual petals of a daisy, wiggle your toes in the mud and let it ooze through them, stomp in rain puddles, and be humbled by the majesty of a mountain.... If you want to be a teacher, you have to put aside your formal theories and intellectual constructs and axioms and statistics and charts when you reach out to touch that miracle called the individual human being. (Schmier, 1995, p. 240)

I am honored to maintain the complete archive of Louis Schmier's Random Thoughts on my school's website. With over 400 Random Thoughts at this writing, Louis is still going strong. He continues to inspire and to freely give away his insights, and I am very pleased to help.

Thousands of school websites have been created, maintained, and often funded by volunteers—most often, classroom teachers. This is not matched in any other organized profession. Why? The obvious answer is the lack of money. But the more important answer is that teachers have long recognized the educational potential of the Internet, and they have been willing to sacrifice to continue the gift economy.

Teachers are in the business of providing service and building lives and careers for others. If a need arises, a teacher will address it. I am not saying other professions are without those who selflessly give of their time. I just believe it is a part of the culture of being a teacher that leads in the direction of trying to make a difference, often with blinders obscuring their personal gain. From simple Web lessons such as those of the Room 12 Top Ten List (www.halcyon.com/arborhts/topten.html) to a wonderfully organized Internet Projects website by Susan Silverman (www.comsewogue. k12.ny.us/~ssilverman/2000/projects.htm) and Marci McGowan's First Grade website (www.mrsmcgowan.com), the spirit of the gift economy lives on.

A Webcam Story

In May 1998, I had six classroom computers connected to the Internet. My students and I were still using my dial-up connection, but we were able to share it using WinGate software. Speed was very slow by today's standards, but the excitement of having several computers on the Internet at once was exhilarating. The world was truly opening up!

Being an amateur bird watcher, I discovered the Xcel Energy King Plant Bird Cam (see the King Falcon Cam website at http://birdcam.xcelenergy.com/kingfalcon.asp), with a camera focused on a peregrine falcon nest box mounted on a power plant smokestack in Minnesota. The female falcon, called Mae, was sitting on eggs. The camera took a fresh picture every 5 minutes. I showed my students, and they were absolutely amazed.

Mae was one of the first offspring of the legendary MF-1, the first peregrine falcon raised in captivity to breed successfully in the wild. Mae became quite well known as the first peregrine falcon to nest at a power plant (Anderson, 2000). Through the efforts of the nonprofit Raptor Resource Project (www.raptorresource.org) and the Northern States Power Company (now Excel Energy), nest boxes were set up at several sites in the upper Midwest; the birdcam my students and I were watching was the first one.

My students and I spent lots of time running back and forth to the computer screen during the next month, as we watched the eggs hatch and then saw baby peregrines (eyasses) grow up and eventually fledge. I sent an e-mail to the Raptor Resource Project to let them know how excited my students and I were to be watching the nest, far away in Seattle. A couple of e-mails later, I was bursting with excitement as I told my class that we had been asked to name one of the eyasses. That night's homework assignment was to come up with a name and write a justification for why it would be a good name for one of the males and why it would be a good name for a falcon. The students submitted great names and wonderfully written explanations. The students and I voted to name the falcon Smoke (see Figure 3.4).

Figure 3.4   Smoke (left) and Prescott in the Nest Box, May 1998

Webcam image used with permission of Xcel Energy.

The folks at the Raptor Resource Project loved our name and published it on the website along with the name of his brother, Prescott, who was named by an elementary school in Montana. As the birds matured, my students explored the Web with purpose, reading as much as they could about peregrine falcons.

During the next month, our excitement was often difficult to contain. June approached, the end of school was in sight, and the birds were about to fledge. The final writing assignment of the school year was to write a story called Smoke's First Flight. The stories the students wrote were remarkable—so good that I sent the best to the Raptor Resource Project, where they were posted (with permission) on their website. As a thank you, and to share our experience with others, I created an online slideshow in HTML of 36 birdcam pictures I had managed to save on different computers in the classroom (www.halcyon.com/arborhts/falcon).

This is an example of a commercial enterprise (a power company) collaborating with a nonprofit organization and a school to create a free online experience. It was a time the students and I will never forget. Now, every year a new group of third graders gets to hear this story but with a very amazing ending.

Because my students and I knew that first-year peregrine falcons had a mortality rate of more than 50%, we worried about Smoke and Prescott. During the next school year, the previous year's third graders would come back and ask if I had received any news. No news, I told them. The following year's class watched Mae hatch another brood. In April 2000, I received an e-mail from the Raptor Resource Project that Smoke was alive and well. Incredibly, he had a found a mate and claimed a nest box—at another birdcam site. He has been at that site, with different mates, for the past three years. Usually it is the female who stays at the same site, but Smoke, as all alumni of room 12 know, is a special falcon. So now, when my new students in room 12 watch those birdcams (my students and I have 14 computers, with high-speed access), they watch both Mae's and Smoke's nests. The students also know that Mae, at the age of 16, is nearing the end of her expected lifespan. My students love to hear the story, and I love to tell it. They are excited to be a part of it—and they always ask if they can name a falcon this year.

Is There More?

There have always been philanthropists. There have always been volunteers. Yet this new medium of the Web provides opportunities like no other before. Where once only neighbors could share resources, now strangers share them across international boundaries. An idea that used to take decades to creep across a country now travels the world in seconds. Stories like Mae's, Smoke's, and ours would not exist without the Web. Relatively few people would have heard of Schmier's Random Thoughts without it. Ideas such as the Earth Day Groceries Project would have spread slowly and would exist only in isolated pockets were it not for the Web.

Will there always be those willing to share their inspirational thoughts and ideas? Will there still be those wanting to share their passions for the greater good? Will there still be those willing to donate their time to better the world? Will there still be teachers? Most certainly.

What can teachers and educators do to ensure that this attitude of giving and sacrifice will continue? Is there more to this idea of giving things away that needs to be explored to make sure it keeps happening? I think not. The world, thanks to the Internet, has had its doors opened. Those doors will never close, and there will always be teachers.

As long as teachers inspire their students by example and share their passions, students will grow to do the same. I certainly am carrying on the energy that my teachers brought to the classrooms of my childhood. The giving away of knowledge and passion is the very definition of what it is to be a teacher. Because the fabric of the world has changed forever, the potential for good is now so incredibly exciting. I am very lucky to be a teacher today.

I have a sad note on this story: Mae, the mother of Smoke and 36 other falcons, died. She was killed in a territorial battle on March 25, 2004, fighting another falcon for her nest box, something she had to go through each spring (Divine, 2004). I am incredibly saddened by her passing, but I will continue to tell the story of her and Smoke to my third graders. My students and I are watching a new falcon in Mae's nest box this spring, and I am happy to say that the magic and wonder is still there for my students and me. I am so grateful to the people who make it happen. And thank you, Mae.

REFERENCES

Ahlness, M. (1999). The Earth Day groceries project. *Science and Children, 36*(7), 32–36.

Ahlness, M. (2004). History of the Arbor Heights WWW site. Retrieved August 13, 2004, from http://www.halcyon.com/arborhts/history.html

Anderson, R. (2000). Bringing the Duckhawk home. Retrieved September 30, 2003, from http://www.raptorresource.org/pdf/mnbirding.pdf

Divine, M. (2004, April 17). Famed peregrine falcon perishes. *St. Paul Pioneer Press*, pp. A1, A4.

Earth Day Groceries Project. (2004). Pennsylvania Earth Day Groceries Reports—1999. Retrieved January 25, 2004, from http://www.earthdaybags.org/states/PA.html

Gates, B. (with Myhrvold, N., & Rinearson, P.). (1995). *The road ahead*. New York: Viking.

Lehnert, W.G. (1998). *Internet 101: A beginner's guide to the Internet and the World Wide Web*. Reading, MA: Addison-Wesley Higher Education.

Schmier, L. (1995). *Random thoughts: The humanity of teaching*. Madison, WI: Magna Publications.

Strangman, N. (March, 2002). Teachers voices: An interview with Mark Ahlness and Jean Carmody about the Earth Day Groceries Project. *Reading Online 5*(7), Available: http://www.readingonline.org/articles/art_index.asp?HREF=voices/ahlness_carmody/index.html

CHILDREN'S LITERATURE

Van Allsburg, C. (1985). *The polar express*. Boston: Houghton Mifflin.

White, E.B. (1945). *Stuart Little*. New York: HarperCollins.

White, E.B. (1952). *Charlotte's web*. New York: HarperCollins.

White, E.B. (1970). *The trumpet of the swan*. New York: HarperCollins.

CHAPTER 4

Literacy and Technology:
A World of Ideas

Cathleen J. Chamberlain

How I Created My Website

It never ceases to amaze me that I still rush to the computer to check my e-mail. I never tire of running that same well-worn path in my rug to the machine that holds those unknown and possibly exciting electronic posts. I sense it might stem from the realization that the unknown is awaiting. It might be analogous to the finely wrapped gift sitting on my table that I am not supposed to open for another two days. It creates a feeling of suspense. I want to know what lies within.

I vividly remember one such e-mail that almost simultaneously created excitement and trepidation. An old friend of mine, whom I dearly respect, asked me to fill in for him at a preconference session for the New York State Reading Association. The session was to be a three-hour session about using the Internet to enhance literacy. This e-mail created the possibility for new learning in my life and an opportunity I would rarely pass up.

During the next few weeks, I began to brainstorm the endless possibilities of how I might structure such a session. The question that kept going through my mind was, What could I provide for the participants that they would consider a valuable resource? Whenever I am given a task of this caliber, I always try to put myself in the participants' shoes. What would they want to learn that they would find exciting and useful when they left the session? After much consideration, I decided that if I were enrolled in a session like this, I would like to be shown the best resources for enriching the teaching and learning of literacy within my classroom. I wanted to open the teachers' eyes to a world of ideas. Many teachers who have just begun using the Internet are often not savvy enough about search techniques to find the types of websites that could help them in their own learning and teaching. My path was now clearly laid in front of me.

I began to make a list of the topics that are often sought in relation to literacy. See Figure 4.1 for the list that I created. Once my list was

Figure 4.1 Literacy-Related Internet Resources

1. **Literacy—www.oswego.org/staff/cchamber/literacy/literacy.cfm:** This website is included so teachers can find resources easily and glean information from them.

2. **Authors and Illustrators—www.oswego.org/staff/cchamber/literacy/authors.cfm:** This website provides teachers with links to almost any author that they would be studying with their class.

3. **Writing—www.oswego.org/staff/cchamber/literacy/writing.cfm:** This website includes links to various websites that focus on the writing process and other essential writing components. It also has websites where students can post their writing online.

4. **Poetry—www.oswego.org/staff/cchamber/literacy/poetry.cfm:** This website includes websites related to poetry and websites where students can post their own poetry online for others to enjoy.

5. **Online Portfolio—http://electricteacher.com/onlineportfolio/index.htm:** This website provides teachers with examples of online portfolios and the information they need to get their own classroom online portfolio up and running. This is where students can publish their writing and other samples of their work. Each student has an individual webpage to post work.

6. **Mrs. Chamberlain's 2nd-Grade Authors—http://electricteacher.com/bookpublishing/index.htm:** This website provides teachers with a model for students to display their written stories online. This is different from the online portfolio because it displays the story in book format, including the student's illustrations.

7. **Grammar—www.oswego.org/staff/cchamber/literacy/grammar.cfm:** This website teachers can use to gather ideas for instruction and students can use them to help with any grammar questions they might have.

8. **Internet Projects—www.oswego.org/staff/cchamber/literacy/internetproject.cfm:** This website provides links to the various projects that support literacy learning that are posted on the Web. These projects often revolve around a theme. Participating students get connected and share their writing, which gets posted to the website.

9. **Interactive—www.oswego.org/staff/cchamber/literacy/interactive.cfm:** This website provides links to literacy-based websites that include an interactive quality. The websites are often designed so students can engage in them and get feedback. Many are in the form of educational games that focus on literacy skills.

10. **Literature Guides—www.oswego.org/staff/cchamber/literacy/litguides.cfm:** This website provides teachers with free literature guides. Teachers often buy literature guides when reading novels or picture books to their students. These guides provide rich ideas about using the story to teach literacy concepts and additional information about the story, author, or illustrator.

11. **Mailing Lists—www.oswego.org/staff/cchamber/literacy/listserv.cfm:** This website provides lists of places to which teachers can subscribe to connect with other teachers who are interested in similar topics. There also are links where teachers can find connections for their students such as key pals.

complete, I was able to concentrate on the task of creating the website that the participants would use in the session. This task is often the one that takes the greatest amount of time but is the most exciting. I had to design a website—complete with background, text, and buttons—that would be easy to use and navigate. I knew that I wanted to have authentic images on the website, not pictures of models posing in photographs. I began looking for photographs of students engaged in literacy activities, but I could not seem to find images that completely fit my vision. Hitting this brick wall was not a novel occurrence for me. When this happens, I often assess whether I could create the images myself. That seemed to be the answer to my problem. I went into the classrooms in my school district, received permission from parents to photograph a few students, grabbed my trusty digital camera, and spent some time photographing those images that were floating in my mind. I was very happy with the photographs and quickly set out to incorporate them into my Literacy and Technology website (Figure 4.2), thus completing it. It is always a great feeling when you complete a website. I was pleased that the website would offer teachers a wealth of resources at their fingertips so that they did not have to search for literacy websites.

After creating my website, I felt ready to design the preconference session. I decided to go through the difficult task of picking my favorite websites to showcase. Knowing that the participants would have various levels of computer ability, I wanted to showcase well-known websites as well as more obscure websites. I chose one or two from each of these categories and planned on giving the attendants a whirlwind tour of some of the many ways that the Internet can enrich students' literacy skills. I knew that the Internet might be overwhelming for some, but I always like to show a variety of websites because the interests of the audience vary.

After selecting the websites, I was ready to build my session. Because the session was to be hands-on, I had the participants use their computers to test the websites that I had demonstrated. They could choose to take a deeper look at those websites that were most interesting to them. They also could venture further and visit the many websites that I did not showcase but were linked to my website.

During the planning process for the session, I realized that creating a website is really an essential learning component for the participants. It allows teachers to return to websites on their own time to glean more information or to just use the websites that best fit with their own instruction. This seemed much better than having them write down all the Web addresses. My website, then, would serve as a sort of one-stop shopping place. All the websites the teachers liked to use would be easily accessible from my website. I knew that I wanted them to leave the session with something useful that they could use when they returned to their respective positions, but I kept wondering whether there was more that I could provide for them.

Figure 4.2   Literacy and Technology Website

Knowing that I had a three-hour block of time to work with the teachers, I decided to go a step further: I taught the participants how to use Netscape Composer to create their own websites, where they could book-mark their top favorite literacy websites. This way, each would learn a little about website design and also walk out with a disk that contained a website that was truly customized to his or her needs. It also was a way to introduce them briefly to the sense of accomplishment of creating their own website. I hoped that this activity would entice the teachers to create their own websites for their students.

The session went very well, and the teachers seemed happy with their newfound websites and newly designed webpages. Teachers have little time to explore the Web, so I wanted the session to give them the time to peruse some great new Web-based materials to incorporate in their classrooms when they returned from the conference. They left with a new sense of the world of ideas the Internet provides for them.

After the conference, I found that I often was accessing the website I had created for my own use and finding it beneficial, so I decided that I should use it in my position as a district elementary technology integration specialist working with teachers of grades K–6. Part of my job was to work with teachers to seamlessly incorporate technology use into the classroom. I was also in charge of staff development, so I began using the website in some of my training sessions. From these sessions, I learned about the needs and wants of classroom teachers. The number-one complaint I hear from them is that they do not have enough time to do everything they are supposed to be doing. The job has added requirements that take up more and more of their waking hours. With this important piece of knowledge, I knew that one of my tasks would be to research and compile websites, saving teachers search time. I typically use Google (www.google.com), my favorite search engine, to look for exceptional Web resources. Using various combinations of keywords, I began to find the websites that matched my needs. For example, if I was looking for a lesson for my second-grade students on the sun and the moon I would not just use the keywords *sun* and *moon*. My keywords may be *lessons*, *grade 2*, *sun*, and *moon*. As I searched for websites, I weeded out the good ones (websites that provide a contact name, up-to-date information, and relevant content) from the bad. I planned to present teachers with what I had learned and provide links and lessons on how to use the websites as well as ideas for incorporating their new learning into their classrooms. It is wonderful to find these rich resources on the Internet, but what teachers do with them in their own classrooms is the key to using them to their fullest potential.

I was pleasantly surprised when I received word that my website had won the Miss Rumphius Award. The award not only validated the fact that others found my website useful but also held a deep and more personal meaning for me because *Miss Rumphius* (Cooney, 1982) is one of my all-time favorite children's books. It was one of those stories that I faithfully read every year to my second-grade students. I always followed up with writing activities that naturally seemed to fit the story and provided my students with additional opportunities to sharpen and develop their writing skills. The poignant message *Miss Rumphius* holds about making the world a more beautiful place is one that has resonated with me for a long time. Winning this award made me contemplate the fact that in some small way, I, too, could become a part of the legacy of making the world a better place. I could help teachers by providing them with the resources to enrich students' literacy experiences within the classroom. If I bring newfound knowledge and ideas to the classroom teacher, and thus touch the lives of children, it would be time well spent. The Miss Rumphius Award motivated me to stretch even further in my own learning about the Internet and the world of possibilities it offers.

The Internet: My Learning, My Teaching

I love using the Internet, and I always wonder how I ever lived without it when I was younger. Today, I rarely use the phone book. I am a smart shopper because I can quickly scan products and their prices from stores all over the world and pick the best bargain from online resources. However, searching for information on the Internet can take a great deal of time. I am not referring to the actual act of searching for a finite answer or piece of information, which can be relatively quick, but the myriad distractions that can arise. It is a common occurrence while using the Internet to realize suddenly that time has just melted away. This loss of time often occurs because there is so much to look at and learn about on the Internet. Often when I start looking for something in particular, I stray from my original focus and pursue other topics of interest that I may not have originally anticipated. This realization made me see that developing websites that provide links to the educational materials would help teachers by narrowing the field. Otherwise, if a teacher wanted to look for information about grammar for their second-grade students, for example, they would have to look through webpages and webpages of hyperlinks that may have unrelated websites such as book companies selling grammar books or a college professor's website explaining his or her grading expectations in relation to grammar. But with my idea, the best of the best would be in front of them so they would not spend time searching or straying off topic. My own journey of teaching and learning about Internet use in classroom instruction has taken me down many paths.

Webpage Development

One of the first paths I sauntered down was webpage development. The more I used the Internet as a resource, the more I became intrigued with creating my own websites, which I decided to pursue as I began conducting my staff development sessions. There were many websites that I could use as resources for my own learning and to guide teachers, but I often felt that I needed to create webpages with information that produced a better fit for my instruction. For example, when I would find websites about using Microsoft Word, they would often be geared to people in the business world. However, I wanted to create a website that would show teachers how to use the program with their students in the classroom. To do this, I would have to create the webpages that teachers could use in training sessions. This development has brought me through many stages of learning. I read books about Web authoring and design, and I scoured the Internet to learn more about not only how to create the pages but also how to make them pleasing to the eye and easy to navigate. With each new website that I created, my skills were enhanced.

When I look back at the first few websites I had created, I now see them though a different lens. My understanding of webpage design and usability has grown tremendously. I have become much more adept at using programs such as Adobe Photoshop to design my own backgrounds, text, icons, and the like. I can look at top-notch websites and still realize that my journey in webpage development and growth are by no means over. I still have so much to learn in the areas of design and usability, but I also know that I have come a long way in my quest.

Having the capability of creating my own webpages has helped me in many ways. My own literacy in the area of technology has grown through my Internet use and webpage development. I have found that I learn best by doing. This simple strategy is one I use to build my sessions. I truly believe that for teachers to get the most out of a session that I teach, which are geared at teaching new technologies and how they can be incorporated into the classroom, they have to participate actively in the learning. For example, if a teacher wants to learn how to use Microsoft FrontPage, which is Web development software, I would have the teacher use the program to create an actual website. My goal is that teachers leave my sessions with ideas and practice in using the software to enhance the teaching and learning practices within their classrooms. Many teachers create a classroom webpage when they take one of my sessions, and when they are finished the session, they have a complete website that they can use and share with students and students' parents. I also make sure at the end of the training session that all the teachers present their new websites to the group. In this way, teachers pick up creative ideas from their colleagues. Staff development needs to have strong, direct connections between technology and the classroom.

Project Development

Creating projects is certainly an important piece in the learning process for the teachers in my staff development sessions. However, the benefits do not stop there. Most teachers that I talk with are concerned about not being able to find time to share their ideas and practices with other teachers at their grade level. If more sharing were to occur, teachers could begin to incorporate the best practices from various colleagues. One way to make this possible, given teachers' time constraints, is to post teachers' projects online. Our district created a website that catalogs the projects in a searchable database so that any projects that teachers create in the staff development program are then put online for everyone to see and learn from. Teachers at the same grade level will most likely have a keen interest in viewing the activities on the websites that their colleagues created. They may choose to use ideas from the particular project, or it may stimulate new ideas for them in designing their own projects. They may even choose to use the project just as it is. The variety of projects—from graphic organizers to lessons to PowerPoint presentations to assessments—is quite impressive and serves as a rich resource for teachers.

Making Connections

CLASSROOM VISITS. Teaching teachers about the new literacies required for Internet use effectively necessitates a few additional components. An important component is the hands-on philosophy (e.g., visiting teachers in their classrooms and showing them the various websites and little tricks that they might not have known before). Many times when I use the Internet with a teacher sitting next to me, the teacher may say, "I never knew you could do that!" The same can happen as you watch teachers work. You can begin to get little cues about new things they might want to try. This strategy is powerful because teachers actually use the programs and computer while being shown new tips and techniques. They are much more likely to remember a new feature the next time they do a task because they have gone through the steps themselves.

Troubleshooting with other teachers is another way for both teachers and me to continue our learning. I have always felt that the more I am asked to troubleshoot, the more I add to my own book of knowledge. Each time I problem-solve, I build on my own resources for future troubleshooting experiences. One of the first things I typically do when I run into trouble with the computer or one of its programs is to go to the help feature that is built into the program. Nine times out of ten, I will find a solution to my problem there. If I do not find it there, then I go online to search for answers. Many times, if you search on the website from the company that made the software, you will find a section with frequently asked questions (FAQs). Being prepared with the answers from FAQs will help you when brainstorming with teachers about problems they may have as they work with new technology. I also learn a great deal by conversing with teachers and staying in touch with the realities of the classroom so I can continue working toward making realistic connections between the needs of the teachers and the resources I create to benefit teachers.

LISTSERVS. Technology and the Internet are expanding rapidly, and to keep in step with my own literacy in this area, I have to keep current with what is new on the Web. To do this, I stay connected in a variety of ways. One way is to join pertinent listservs. You can find listservs by searching the Internet using the keywords *listservs* and *educational*. I belong to listservs that have discussions about educational issues, such as The Reading Teacher listserv (www.reading.org/resources/community/discussions_rt_about.html). I also belong to listservs that send links to educational websites, which I preview and share with other teachers. Kathy Schrock, an administrator for technology for the Nauset Public School District in Cape Cod, Massachusetts, created the Sites of the School Days weekly listserv (http://school.discovery.com/schrockguide/sos.html). A subscription to Classroom Connect (www.classroom.com) keeps me in touch with all the hot websites with ideas to incorporate Internet use into the classroom.

ESTABLISHING CONNECTIONS WITH PEERS AND EXPERTS. Since creating my Literacy and Technology website (www.oswego.org/staff/cchamber/literacy), which won a second Miss Rumphius Award, I continue to strive to learn and grow through my experiences and projects. Attending and presenting at professional conferences are other ways to enhance one's personal and professional journeys. With so many educators breaking new ground and sharing their expertise, these conferences make it possible to glean information from the leaders who are making things happen in education. Even when I give my own presentations, I am often gaining a deeper understanding and broadening my horizons. I can begin to make connections with others and often keep in contact with them. My electronic address book grew to include experts in many areas such as curators of famous museums, children's books authors, and literacy specialists. These experts help me as I work with the Internet and continue to learn how to use it as a tool in my classroom and life. It opens up a world of possibilities. I also can offer ideas and suggestions to these same individuals when they find themselves in need of answers that I might be able to supply.

I have always found that one of the most exciting facets of the Internet is the way that a person can make connections with others that he or she might never have had the opportunity to make before. People have contacted me just because they visited one of my websites. For example, connections can be made with authors by using the e-mail addresses that are displayed on their websites. Students can even participate in writing e-mails. When authors reply, teachers can share these connections with students.

Communication has never been easier, and it can open many doors that teachers and students never dreamed were possible. There are so many ways to enhance the literacy skills of students while also augmenting their technological skills. Many Internet resources are available for teachers that both motivate and build on students' literacy skills. These resources include unique Internet Projects (http://comsewogue.k12.ny.us/~ssilverman/2000/projects.htm); an online version of Working with Words (www.oswego.org/testprep/ela4/wwords1.html and www.oswego.org/testprep/ela4/wwwords2.html), Online Portfolios (www.electricteacher.com/onlineportfolio/index.htm), and online books (such as Mrs. Chamberlain's Second-Grade Authors, www.electricteacher.com/bookpublishing/index.htm); and resources that link to education standards (such as the Elementary Test Prep Center, www.oswego.org/testprep/ela2.cfm). Each resource can provide enriching experiences for students that will enhance the literate environment teachers are creating in their classrooms.

Expanding the Resources: My Current Projects

NY Learns

School districts throughout the United States have begun to focus on the standards and core curriculum documents that their teachers are using. With the passage of the No Child Left Behind (NCLB) Act of 2001

(U.S. Department of Education, 2001), district administrators know that correctly aligning their curriculum with standards is one way to ensure that students are taught the content they will be exposed to on state-level tests. This is one reason why I became involved in developing a website that would allow teachers to see online their specific English language arts (ELA) curriculum—the skills and knowledge that each student in grades K–12 should master for that year. Having the curriculum online provides teachers, parents, students, and administrators with easy access to the most current version of the curriculum, which they can choose to view online or print. The website is called NY Learns, and it can be accessed at www.nylearns.org (see Figure 4.3). When teachers use NY Learns to search for grade-level curriculum, they will have access to skills or knowledge and view pertinent resources such as lessons, books, other websites, practice pages, interactive games, and the like (see Figures 4.4 and 4.5). The teachers can gather teaching ideas that they had not thought of before. NY Learns also provides them with resources that they can direct to their students and parents as a way of assisting students that have not been able to master certain literacy skills. These resources can expose students to the knowledge or skill in a new way or just provide the practice they need to acquire the knowledge or skill.

Figure 4.3   NY Learns Website

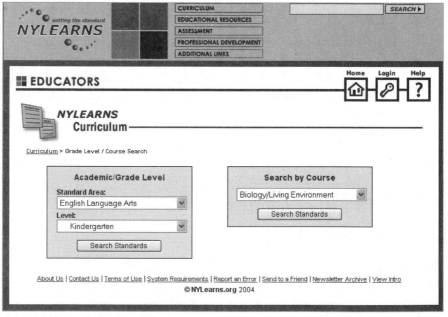

Printed with permission from NYLearns.org.

Figure 4.4   Sample of Curriculum Delineated for Each Grade Level by Subject at the NY Learns Website

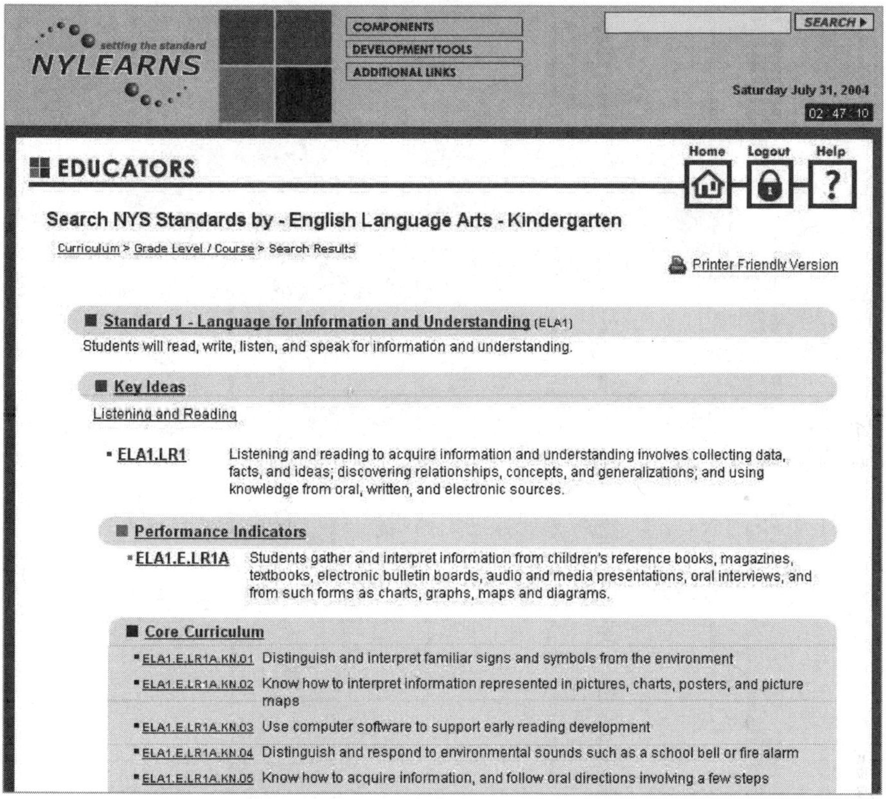

Printed with permission from NYLearns.org.

Some districts use NY Learns because they may not have reached this level in their curriculum development. Their curriculum may not be delineated to the skill or knowledge level and broken up by grade level. They also may not have it posted online. The NY Learns website shows how a free Internet resource for teachers can provide many valuable ideas that directly link to the curriculum they are responsible for teaching.

Study Zone

Our district created another website for teachers and students that provides grade-level literacy resources in the form of lessons, literature connections (books that relate to concepts taught in the classroom), practice

Figure 4.5   Sample Resource Directly Correlated With the Curriculum at the NY Learns Website

Printed with permission from Leeanne VanDurme.

pages, teacher resources, and interactive games. This website is called Study Zone (www.studyzone.org) and is divided into three grade levels: elementary school, middle school, and high school. Each grade level of the website has teacher-created resources that are aligned with the curriculum that is taught. A visiting teacher could select the subject—in this case, ELA—and click on the appropriate grade level (see Figure 4.6). The teacher would then be able to search for a type of resource, such as verbs, persuasive essay writing samples, story elements, comprehension strategies, and so forth. The resources that are only a click away will provide the teacher with a plethora of ideas and materials to build students' literacy skills. The lessons are designed for the students to use independently and are accompanied by a follow-up practice page (see Figure 4.7) where students can test their newfound knowledge. The practice webpages provide immediate feedback to students, so they know if they are on target. Students love the website because there are interactive pages that stimulate their interest while they are building a repertoire of skills. Students are used to a multimedia-rich world. These resources will provide teachers with

Figure 4.6   Sample Webpage at Study Zone's Elementary Test Prep Website

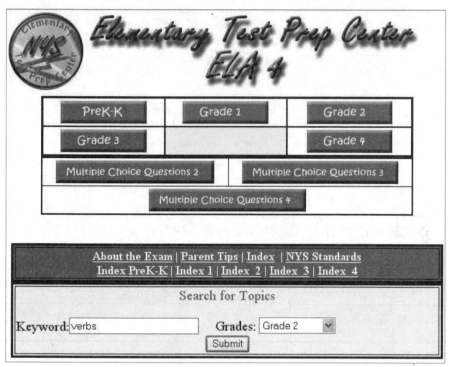

the interactivity that students crave (see Figure 4.8). With this website reaching more than 4 million hits per day, my district knows that they are fulfilling the needs of many teachers, students, and parents.

Internet Projects

Another favorite of mine for engaging classrooms in effective literacy activities are websites that contain Internet projects. Many websites exist that enable teachers to become involved in a project in which their students can actively engage in reading and writing activities with other students worldwide. One website that comes to mind is Susan Silverman's Internet Projects (http://comsewogue.k12.ny.us/~ssilverman/2000). (See chapter 7 for more information.) She has created literacy-based projects in which students read and write about familiar themes such as fall, owls, pumpkins, and apples. Students sign up for projects that often require them to read stories and then respond in various ways. Some choose to write stories, poems, and reflections,

Figure 4.7   Sample Practice Webpage at Study Zone's Website

Printed with permission from Marie Smith.

whereas others create projects and showcase them with digital images. Some projects involved the students drawing images using image editing software while others required the students to use software such as Kid Pix or Inspiration to create their images. There are often 25 classes from around the world participating in a thematic project. The clever component is that each classroom's project comes to life via the Web. Susan creates a webpage for each classroom and posts the students' projects online. Students are ecstatic that their work has been published online. It gives a whole new meaning to the last phase of the writing process. Students seem to work harder when they know that the final outcome will be true publication, and when their writing, thoughts, and ideas are shared with the world.

Susan is very selective about her choice of projects. They always relate back to the standards that are required by the participating class's state (which she posts online) so students have opportunities to work on au-

Figure 4.8   Sample Resource Link at Study Zone's Website

Printed with permission from Oswego City School District.

thentic tasks. When these students join the workforce, they will most likely be engaged in similar activities in which they are asked to share their ideas and thoughts in writing with others.

There are many online projects that teachers can use in their classrooms. It is important that they carefully look at each project and ensure that it aligns with their curricula. These types of projects are often ones that children do not forget, and that are a fun and creative way of building on students' literacy skills.

Online Portfolios

Keeping in step with the discussion on publishing students' work, another valuable resource is a classroom online portfolio, which is a website where teachers and students publish their work. Online portfolios involve a little more work because teachers have to create the website and maintain it themselves. However, these portfolios can be invaluable tools in enticing students to write and promoting high expectations. It is crucial to maintain criteria that students must master to post their work online. If you are working on the skill of descriptive language, for example, you need to ensure that before the work is posted it clearly demonstrates the use of that skill. Students also can use the website to post their best work throughout the year. Typically, at the elementary level, teachers set up the website as a classroom website with an individual webpage for each student to use for publishing. Because of the student's age at this level, the teacher usually does the publishing. There are several ways to set up the individual student pages. Students' writing, images, projects, videos, and the like can all be posted on their webpages to showcase their work. Think of the pages as a representation of the student's ability. The process does take some webpage development skill on the teacher's part.

If teachers create online portfolios, it is important to ensure that they have parents' permission to post student work and pictures. It also is a good practice to post only a student's first name and last initial. Some teachers even choose to give their students pen names.

Games

Children today also are intrigued by high-tech multimedia games. I vividly remember when my own son was 3 years old and played Nintendo games. It amazed me how quickly he knew the words on the screen. He did this through frequent use of the game and the high interest it held for him. As previously stated, students today are surrounded with rich multimedia experiences; therefore, teachers must provide engaging activities and learning experiences for the students to maintain their enthusiasm and interest in the subject.

The Internet is an avenue teachers can use to find and build interactive websites that will help enhance students' literacy skills (see Figure 4.9). You can access the websites at www.oswego.org/testprep/ela4/wwwords1.html and www.oswego.org/testprep/ela4/wwwords2.html. There are many interactive websites that companies have built, and many are free to use. I have included many links to these websites on my Literacy and Technology website. I would love to have the knowledge and skills to create many of these websites myself, but some involve a deep level of programming skills that I do not possess. I decided to hire a programmer to create an interactive version of an activity that many teachers across the United States frequently were using. This activity was created using Patricia Cunningham's concept of working with words and designed to build on primary-grade student's literacy skills. With this activity, teachers use either magnetic boards or cut up letters with the students. The teacher then thinks of a mystery word, which is created using all the letters that the student was given, and uses those letters

Figure 4.9 Working With Words Interactive Game, an Interactive Website

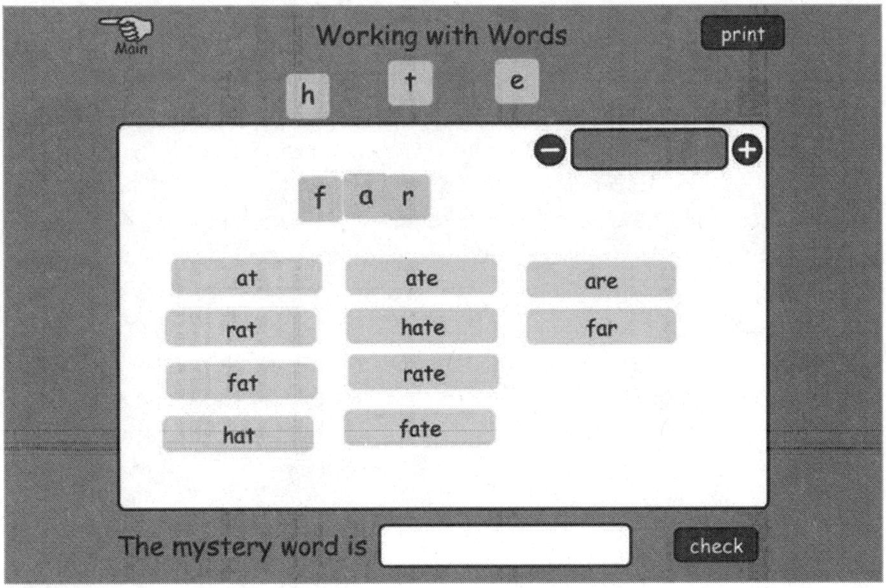

for the activity. The students find word families and create words using only the letters the teachers give them. The goal for students is to try to figure out the mystery word. I thought that if I created an online version of this activity, parents and students could continue working on it at home without having all the materials used in the classroom. Teachers also could have students working while they are on a computer.

Teachers to whom I introduce these websites are often very excited about the possibilities they afford. The website can be used in two ways. While one link leads to a website where the student would be working with an adult, as in the typical model, the other link allows students to work independently using common words that teachers would choose based on each student's ability level. If students are working alone, they can print out their final set of words to hand in to the teacher. Most children love to use the computer, which is just another way to use technology as a tool to enrich their teaching and learning experiences.

Children's Literature Authors

The last path that I would like to focus on comprises author websites. When I was teaching, my classroom presented a very literate environment. I found that if I introduced a particular author each month and got the students really interested in learning more about the author's writing style and life, I began to feed the students' hunger for books written by that author. Each author is unique, and learning about the authors makes them real for the children. I would create an author-of-the-month bulletin board with information about an author with a list of the author's books. I would use these books as part of my lessons to provide more exposure to the author's style. Soon after one such author study, the library received a sudden rash of sign-outs of books by that particular author. That hunger for knowledge is very contagious.

Today, most famous authors have websites where they often offer information about themselves and their books, such as where they can be purchased. One author's website that I find most impressive is Jan Brett's (see Figure 4.10, www.janbrett.com). Given the fact that Brett also is a phenomenal illustrator, her website offers reproducible materials that teachers can print for their students to use. The website also has videos that teachers can view online, and teachers actually can see her drawing some of her characters and talking about her life. Through her website, Brett comes alive in teachers' classrooms. She provides activity pages, bookmarks, calendars, bulletin board ideas, flash cards, postcards, and more. She also provides an address where teachers or students can write to her, which offers a great way for students to get in touch with the authors that they enjoy reading.

As a teacher, I know how difficult it used to be to access information about authors, such as photos and other tangible information that would help bring them to life in the classroom. Now, finding that type of information is so easy. Teachers can use a webpage, such as the one I created, to list links to many common children's book authors or to enter the author's name in a search engine, such as Goggle (www.google.com), and within seconds they will have resources to share with their students. It is truly amazing how much material teachers now have at their fingertips that is both free and useful in their field.

Final Thoughts

One similar trait that many teachers share is their love of learning. Even in their own lives, teachers strive to learn and have a deep passion for it. The Internet helps to quench this thirst. I am on various listservs that keep me abreast of current literacy issues and other learning as well. Listservs provide an opportunity to connect with other teachers who have similar questions or experiences. If teachers find a new educational topic being expressed or if they are having difficulty in a particular area when helping

Figure 4.10   Jan Brett's Website

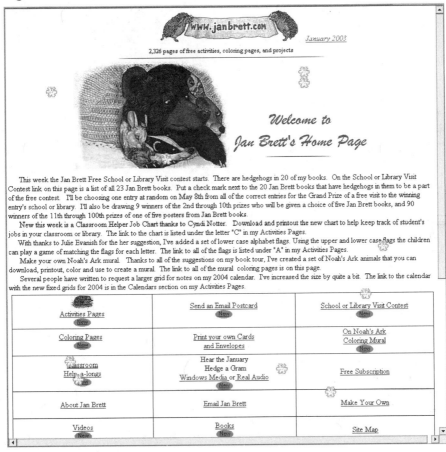

This week the Jan Brett Free School or Library Visit contest starts. There are hedgehogs in 20 of my books. On the School or Library Visit Contest link on this page is a list of all 23 Jan Brett books. Put a check mark next to the 20 Jan Brett books that have hedgehogs in them to be a part of the free contest. I'll be choosing one entry at random on May 8th from all of the correct entries for the Grand Prize of a free visit to the winning entry's school or library. I'll also be drawing 9 winners of the 2nd through 10th prizes who will be given a choice of five Jan Brett books, and 90 winners of the 11th through 100th prizes of one of five posters from Jan Brett books.

New this week is a Classroom Helper Job Chart thanks to Cyndi Notter. Download and printout the new chart to help keep track of student's jobs in your classroom or library. The link to the chart is listed under the letter "C" in my Activities Pages.

With thanks to Julie Evanish for the her suggestion, I've added a set of lower case alphabet flags. Using the upper and lower case flags the children can play a game of matching the flags for each letter. The link to all of the flags is listed under "A" in my Activities Pages.

Make your own Noah's Ark mural. Thanks to all of the suggestions on my book tour, I've created a set of Noah's Ark animals that you can download, printout, color and use to create a mural. The link to all of the mural coloring pages is on this page.

Several people have written to request a larger grid for notes on my 2004 calendar. I've increased the size by quite a bit. The link to the calendar with the new fixed grids for 2004 is in the Calendars section on my Activities Pages.

Activities Pages New	Send an Email Postcard New	School or Library Visit Contest New
Coloring Pages New	Print your own Cards and Envelopes	On Noah's Ark Coloring Mural New
Classroom Help a-longs New	Hear the January Hedge a Gram Windows Media or Real Audio New	Free Subscription
About Jan Brett	Email Jan Brett	Make Your Own
Videos New	Books New	Site Map

Printed with permission from Jan Brett.

a student learn to read, they can turn to the Internet to find answers. This is especially true when teachers do not feel comfortable sharing with others what they consider their lack of knowledge. Knowing where to look and making sure that the sources are reputable also are important whenever teachers access information from the Web.

The Internet has opened the doors for many people and has revolutionized learning. People have more opportunities to read when they are on the Internet. Teachers must seize this opportunity to learn the skills that will make it easier for them to use the Internet in their quest for learning and for creating learning opportunities for students. Children today have been brought up with this technology. It is second nature to them, and they clearly see technology as a tool that can help them in a variety of ways. We, as teachers, must look deeply and begin to see the wide range of opportunities that technology provides as we work with our students to strengthen their literacy skills. If teachers are unfamiliar with the types of activities and the websites that I have described, then I suggest they begin slowly and start to look at the varied resources that are at their disposal. If teachers are avid users of technology, then they must seize the resources and take them to a whole new level. Often when working with technology, teachers begin to brainstorm new ways of doing things and might even venture to create their own websites for their students and other teachers as well. The Internet provides connections and a way to promote reading, writing, speaking, and listening. There is a world of ideas out there for teachers to use.

REFERENCES

Brett, J. (1996–2005). *Jan Brett's home page: A great place for Ideas.* Retrieved January 10, 2005, from http://www.janbrett.com

Silverman, S. (2000). *Mrs. Silverman's site.* Retrieved January 10, 2005, from http://www.comsewogue.k12.ny.us/~ssilverman/2000

U.S. Department of Education. (2001). *The No Child Left Behind Act of 2001: Enhancing education through technology.* Retrieved January 12, 2004, from http://www.ed.gov/policy/elsec/leg/esea02/pg34.html

CHILDREN'S LITERATURE

Cooney, B. (1982). *Miss Rumphius.* New York: Viking Press.

CHAPTER 5

The Intersection of Schools, Communities, and Technology: Recognizing Children's Use of New Literacies

Charles K. Kinzer

The three preceding chapters in this section include wonderful applications of technology to enhance literacy teaching and learning in primary-grade classrooms. In chapter 2, Sangiuliano's description of Books on Tape for Kids shows how he developed specific elements of students' literacy—including fluency, reflection, writing, and presentation of ideas—in second- and third-grade students by using technology. As he notes, the ultimate objectives of reading instruction and community service could have been reached without the use of the Internet; however, a great deal of learning along the way would not have been realized. Thus, even more than the *traditional* and *new* literacies that were developed as part of his project, the learning opportunities that the technology provided—the value-added component of the technology—make a compelling argument for integrating technology into the literacy curriculum.

Mark Ahlness's Earth Day Groceries Project (chapter 3) takes place in a third-grade classroom and incorporates elements of civics, environmental awareness, authenticity, global outreach, technology, and multiple aspects of literacy. While I was reading his chapter, I was awed by how limited resources were considered a challenge to be overcome by a teacher who was committed to his students' success and who was convinced that much could be accomplished in teaching and learning literacy—integrated with other content areas—through the use of technology.

Chapter 4, by Cathy Chamberlain, shows how technology can provide support and resources for teachers, not only to enhance instruction for children but also to help teachers learn about technology and its possibilities.

Her chapter provides a window into how websites of resources can be created and shared with others, shows a range of websites and activities that can help teachers in their efforts to facilitate children's literacy success, and links 19 topics that are integral to the literacy curriculum with Web-based resources and activities.

Although the three chapters approach technology use in the primary grades from somewhat different perspectives and describe different implementation and integration projects, two aspects across the chapters appear seminal and can inform us all: (1) the intersection among schools, communities, and technology results in enhanced literacy teaching and learning opportunities, and (2) the use of appropriate technology in the primary grades supports the learning of what some have called *new literacies* and others have called *multiliteracies* (Kinzer, 2003; Lankshear & Knobel, 2003; Leu & Kinzer, 2000; New London Group, 2000). The remainder of this chapter discusses elements of these two important aspects.

The Importance of Linking Schools to Communities and How Technology Can Help

One cannot help but be struck that technology can extend the boundaries of classrooms. Much has been written about Internet projects and keypal activities (penpal activities using e-mail) that link students and classrooms worldwide and how these activities can benefit learning (Garner & Gillingham, 1996; Leu, Leu, & Coiro, 2004; see also the scope of available projects at the Internet Projects Registry: www.gsn.org/gsh/pr/_cfm/index.cfm). Technology has indeed extended children's worlds. When praising the opportunities that technology provides for interaction across classroom boundaries, we sometimes forget that these boundaries are achieved at intersection points between communities, schools, and technology.

Figure 5.1 illustrates three fundamental components that are encompassed in the chapters in this section: community, school, and technology. Of course, these broad areas include many subparts. Communities include not only the local communities in which schools are located, but also the businesses, parents, and others in the community who have a vested interest in education. However, the special nature of technology is resulting in a redefinition of communities. Definitions of *community* now must include global areas that schools, teachers, and students can reach through technology and cannot focus only on what is geographically local. Castells (2000), for example, looks at communities as influenced by and bounded by a "space of flows" (p. 408). He makes the point that communities are

Figure 5.1   The Intersection of School, Community, and Technology

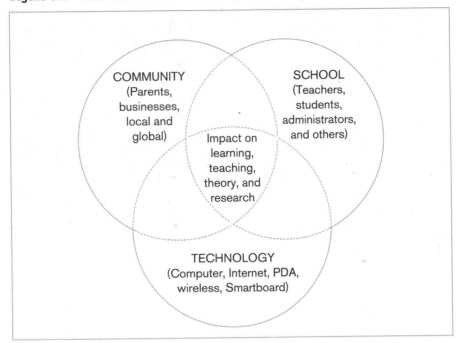

both virtual and real, but that children who are growing up with technology tend to make less of this distinction than do adults. These children see the virtual and real as intertwined and may not understand why some people make a distinction between the two. Because both virtual and real aspects of the community are parts of these children's lives, authentic, community-based projects are, in essence, redefining community through the use of technology. Consider also that when online activities become the norm—a part of every-day life—then a distinction between online and offline realities may become blurred. In this way, children who see their lives as including technology may view discussion of technology-mediated communities as somehow artificial, as a foreign concept.

Communities coalesce around interests and experiences and are fostered by communication that allows sharing of these interests and experiences. When projects such as the Earth Day Groceries Project begin to bring together children and teachers from around the world, a new form of community is being built—one based on common interests and goals, but one that transcends the specific geographic space in which schools are physically located, compressing distance as never before. And it is the school-based nature of projects, such as the Earth Day Groceries Project and Books on Tape for Kids, as enhanced by technology, which made these communities come into being in ways that support the teaching and learning of literacy. Within this new global community, children are interacting with their school and local communities in ways that previously were not possible. Through the use of technology, teachers and students increase their reach, learn in new ways, and use tools that allow literacy to be learned in new ways (see Garner & Gillingham, 1996, for a discussion of how schools and classrooms in locations ranging from Alaska to Pennsylvania created communities across geographic boundaries).

Schools and classrooms do not exist in a vacuum. Schools—including teachers, students, administrators, and others—are important in both local and global communities. Locally, parents often make decisions about where to live based on school zoning districts. They look to schools to provide education and life-enhancing opportunities for their children. Businesses, too, know that schools are important parts of the community. Businesses depend on schools to educate children so that as adults they can become valuable employees with appropriate skills and lifelong learning abilities. Yet links between schools and communities can sometimes be difficult to achieve. Through the use of technology, however, links can be created between local and global communities in ways that enhance the literacy skills that are valued by schools, parents, and communities.

As literacy educators, we often speak of the benefits of providing authentic learning contexts for our children, implying that learning in authentic contexts results in motivated learners and enhances both learning and application of what is learned (Bransford, Brown, & Cocking, 2000). Sangiuliano, Ahlness, and Chamberlain describe multiple authentic contexts in their chapters. In each instance, however, the motivational aspects of using literacy skills and technology for real purposes are clear. Sangiuliano's Books on Tape for Kids and Ahlness's Earth Day Groceries Project enable students to experience a visible impact and recognition of their work. Similarly, Chamberlain's World of Ideas is motivational because it creates online resources that actually are used by colleagues, and thus it indirectly influences children's literacy learning. All three projects incorporate theories that we know are beneficial to learning. These include theories related to motivation, authenticity of audience, consequence for communication, and teacher beliefs and understanding about the components of the reading process.

To date, many of technology's benefits to education have been discussed from perspectives that are shown in one of the circles in Figure 5.1. From a community perspective, we often hear of businesses that donate equipment or provide expertise to schools in ways that facilitate technology uses. Or we hear about how schools are using technology to further their teaching and learning goals or about how technology can benefit instruction through its capabilities or enhancements. However, the optimal uses for learning literacy appear to be in the overlap among community, school, and technology. The projects described in this section are in this overlap, and this is what makes them compelling.

Part of what links schools and communities has to do with what a society at large expects from schools. This expectation often has to do with teaching children the skills and abilities that will allow them to fully participate in their personal and professional worlds after they leave school, a goal that is often strongly linked to literacy abilities. In today's world, and perhaps increasingly so in the future, the literacy abilities related to using the Internet and other information and communication technologies (ICTs) will influence communication and quality of life (see Leu, Kinzer, Coiro, & Cammack, 2004, for a discussion of the relationship between societal demands regarding literacy abilities and the new literacies). Chamberlain's chapter remarks on how the Internet is becoming embedded in our lives. As Chamberlain notes, she rarely uses the telephone book and instead uses an electronic address book and database of experts' online resources for comparative shopping and other purposes.

The literacy practices described within this section reflect the practices that children and teachers need to function in what Reinking (1998) has called a post-typographic world. Several theorists have argued that children need to acquire new literacies to be considered fully literate today (Kinzer, 2003; Kinzer & Leander, 2003; Lankshear & Knobel, 2003; Leu, Kinzer, et al., 2004). Indeed, Leu, Kinzer, and colleagues (2004) have argued that the new literacies of the Internet and other ICTs will become more important in the future, especially because we cannot foresee all the new technologies and capabilities that will evolve. Thus, it becomes important to conceptualize definitions of literacy in ways that encompass new literacies as well as alphabetic literacies and the attendant comprehension processes that accompany both (Kinzer & Leander, 2003).

The literacies demonstrated by Chamberlain as she created websites for teachers and the literacies demonstrated by the children who participated in Sangiuliano's and Ahlness's projects show how traditional and new literacies can act in harmony. The synergistic effects of blending literacies—broadly defined—are what facilitate the overlap of community, school, and technology and result in enhanced teaching and learning. The overlapping area of the three circles in Figure 5.1 is more than the sum of its parts.

The following section describes how second graders are demonstrating a blend of new and old literacies. It does so by drawing on my recent visits to a second-grade class to illustrate the literacies that can be learned in technology-rich environments.

Technology and Children's *New Literacy* Abilities

Recently, I have visited classrooms that incorporate high levels of technology. Although these classrooms are not *normal* in the sense that they include technology resources beyond what is typical, they are helpful in examining what is possible in such environments. One school in New York City, which teaches students in grades K–4, is a case in point. All the classrooms are equipped with Smartboards (whiteboards on which a computer's desktop can be projected that allows touch interaction between the board and the computer), projection capabilities, and tables rather than desks. The school provides laptops for each student, along with requisite applications and communication software. The laptops are recharged each night so the students can use them throughout the day. The entire school is wireless.

Technology is used throughout the day in all subject areas. It is not unusual to see pairs of students sitting on the floor in coatrooms or hallways accessing the Internet or working on joint projects. As I interact with teachers and children in this environment, descriptions of what children do with the technology seem to become less important—they do what their knowledgeable and committed teachers have incorporated into the curriculum, much as we see in the descriptions of technology integration in chapters 2–4 of this volume. In addition to descriptions of what the children are doing, related questions about how technology in such an environment can influence how the children think about communication and literacy become important as well and include the following questions:

> What do young students talk and think about as they read and write using technology?
>
> Is the technology moving children toward abilities that demonstrate multiliteracies?
>
> Do children in technology-rich school environments develop and use abilities related to the new literacies of the Internet?

Those questions are yet to be answered definitively, but in reading the chapters in this section I immediately thought of my recent interactions with Mina (a pseudonym), a second-grade girl, while visiting her classroom. My interactions with Mina provide hints about the multiliteracies that young children are becoming familiar with and can help answer the questions. Thus, I share four vignettes, along with commentary that I believe shows the importance of what Mina overtly and implicitly told me.

The vignettes were part of a discussion that Mina and I had about her class project, which was a PowerPoint presentation about Hinduism. The presentation was the result of Mina's research and composition both in and out of class. The teacher provided support to the second-grade students as they worked on their projects, and Mina's parents also provided her with feedback. It was clear from our discussion, however, that the presentation was Mina's own work. She had a comprehensive grasp of both the content she presented and the literacies she used to create the presentation, which included text, photographs, graphics, and audio.

Mina explains her project to me while she presents her PowerPoint title page and then continues paging through her presentation. Figure 5.2 shows her third slide, which has three icons down the left side and a brief paragraph beside each icon. I ask Mina where the items on the page come from, and she responds as follows:

Mina: I copied them [points to the icons] from the Internet. I right-clicked, and then I clicked paste. Same thing here [points to text]. I did this text box.

Charles: Did you copy the words from the Internet, also?

Mina: I copied it [text] from the Web, and I put it in my own words and deleted the Internet's words.

I immediately noticed how sophisticated this 8-year-old's response was and how facile she was at describing what she does. Her response showed that she understands the concepts of copy and paste, the left and right mouse button functions, and the difference between and uses of text and graphic boxes. Mina also understands the basic elements of research and writing—gathering information, thinking about it, and synthesizing it with what she knows and stating it in her own words. Initially, Mina looks for information around her central idea. She incorporates graphics and text, and she understands word processing and the tools that make her computer powerful. All these aspects of literacy are in addition to the

Figure 5.2   Mina's Third Slide

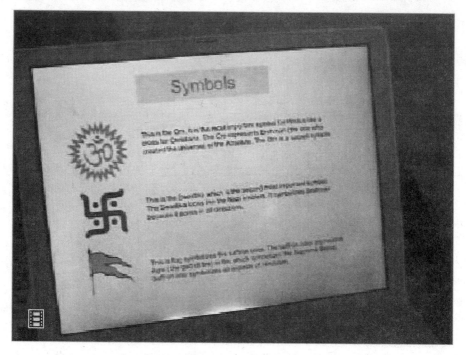

literacies that Mina used to write the text-based parts of her PowerPoint presentation. Her presentation also incorporates different font sizes and highlighting functions, such as the box around the slide's title, which uses a different color and has been centered at the top of the page.

In short, many of the literacies Mina used to compose and present her thoughts require fluency of the tool functions that are a part of using technology. The following vignette reinforces this idea of fluency in new literacies.

Mina shows me a PowerPoint presentation slide of a timeline showing key points in the history of Hinduism (Figure 5.3). The timeline consists of a line, a narrow box filled with black, and arrows pointing from text-box descriptions to specific dates on the timeline.

Note the various design elements that Mina used to impart information and that merge both new and alphabetic literacies. For example, she centered and used a different color and larger font for the title, and offset it from the body of the text to indicate its special function. Mina also indented the paragraph and included the conventions that are part of alpha-

Figure 5.3   Mina's Slide of a Timeline

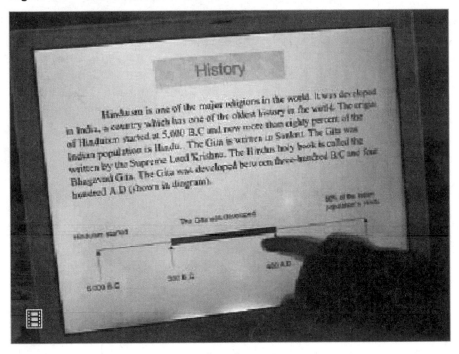

betic literacies: words bound by white space, correct spelling, and grammatical sentences with good punctuation.

The elements of layout and design on the page also are part of the communicative aspects of new literacies, but I was most curious about how Mina created the timeline and her knowledge of the literacy tools and techniques that allowed her to do so. After all, knowing how to use communicative tools is a part of being fluent in literacy practices and an important aspect of one's ability to communicate. I asked Mina to talk about the slides and the timeline.

Charles: Tell me what this is [points to the timeline] and how you made it.

Mina: This timeline I created in PowerPoint. This is my history. I created the box [points with her finger to the filled-in black box on the timeline] from the auto shapes and made the line from the line tool down there [points to where the toolbar would be located if the screen were not displaying the full slide view].

> You click the line and then drag and make the arrows and text
> box.

Charles: ...Why did you decide to use arrows? Why not something else?

Mina: It can point like really *sharply*, it can point *exactly*...You go down
        there [points to the toolbar] and click the arrow thing and then
        drag from top to [pauses] bottom to top, because if you drag it
        from top to bottom, then the arrow will be pointing that way
        [points to indicate away from the timeline].

Clearly, Mina understood how to use the tools within PowerPoint effectively to get her message across and meet her goals; she had the literacy tools to communicate and compose in this environment, using both alphabetic and other representational systems and tools. Her goal was to make a timeline that included descriptive information and linked text and graphics. Notice how this second grader used vocabulary such as autoshapes, line tool, click and drag, text box, and so on in her description of her actions, showing that these terms are a fluent part of her literacy-tool vocabulary.

Some researchers have noted that perhaps the most common use of the Internet is research (Leu, Kinzer, Coiro, & Cammack, 2004; Leu, Leu, & Coiro, 2004). Yet being able to find information requires knowledge of multiple search strategies and literacy knowledge related to keywords and tool functions. Such knowledge is specific not only to the technology being used but also to the particular search engine that is chosen to carry out the search. To continue Mina's example, I noticed that she had chosen specific pictures for her presentation. I wanted to know (a) whether she could find these pictures again if needed, (b) how she first found them, and (c) what her search strategies were.

Figure 5.4 shows one of her PowerPoint slides containing three pictures and a bulleted list. I begin by asking Mina if she could find the pictures again if needed. She answers yes. Then, Mina responds to my additional question:

Charles: Where did you find the pictures?

Mina: All of the pictures I found with a little help from my encyclope-
        dia. I just go to www.dke-encyc.com and then I typed in the key-
        word *Hinduism* and then it gave me a lot. A lot of different
        links...I researched on those sites...and Google also helped
        the encyclopedia.... I thought Google would have a lot more
        searches so I went to Google and typed in *Hindu temples*. It gave

me a lot of sites and that's where I collected these two from [indicates the left two pictures]. This one [indicates the picture on the right] was from the website, the encyclopedia website.

As in the previous example, note the many features of layout, design, and alphabetic literacy conventions present in Mina's work, such as the centered, highlighted heading using a larger font; the bullets (not numbers, dashes, or another signifier) to highlight each paragraph; and the use of boldface text within paragraphs to draw attention to important concepts. In addition, note the conventional literacy practices around the use of graphics, such as the centering of the three pictures, the equal white space between them, and the centered text underneath them; the visual layout of the tallest image being placed between the other two images, and so on.

Part of the effective force behind a communicative act is its impact. In oral and written language, this communicative impact encompasses vocabulary choice, sentence structure, paragraph length, and so on. In electronic environments, these literacies include visual impact and

Figure 5.4   Mina's Slide Containing Pictures and a Bulleted List

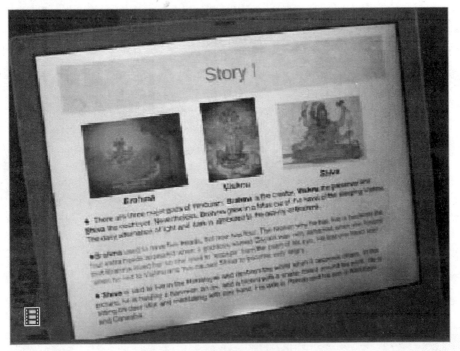

appropriate use of tools to create a message that is accepted because of its look. Mina had mastered the tools and the design principles necessary for her work to have communicative appeal and impact and used elements of an expanded definition of literacy that moves beyond only alphabetic notions.

Mina also has mastered strategies for finding information. As our conversation continued, she said that she almost always followed the strategy outlined in the above dialogue by first looking at the encyclopedia website and then using Google. She was aware that Google is more wide-ranging and may have more information than the encyclopedia website, but she also told me that she thought the encyclopedia might be more "truthful." The awareness of the need to critique and evaluate information relative to its source is important in a world where anyone can post information on the Internet in a relatively unchecked manner. Developing these skills in the early grades provides children with critical literacy abilities that become increasingly important as they move to higher grade levels.

Figure 5.5 shows a PowerPoint slide containing two pictures and a block of text. I ask Mina why there are two pictures on the page and why she decided to use them. Mina specifies reasons for choosing the first (upper) and then the second (lower) picture telling me, "First it was only that picture [points to the upper picture], but then I thought we should have a close-up because that one doesn't really show the whole thing because it goes from white to black so I decided to get this picture [points to the lower picture], also."

Mina had used the first picture to illustrate the text. After deciding that a picture would benefit a reader's understanding of the text, she found an appropriate picture through Internet research. Mina applied skills related to new (rather than alphabetic) literacies and audience awareness. Mina realized that although the first picture was valuable to a degree, its small image and low contrast would make the focal aspect hard to perceive. Thus, Mina found a close-up of the central image and added it beneath the first picture. She then had to reformat the slide's layout to provide both a contextualized image with details that are hard to make out and a close-up that provides the reader with additional, detailed information. What occurred in Mina's decision-making process is a sophisticated outcome based on the application of literacies that range across knowledge of images, audience awareness, and positioning of images and text in a correlational sense on a slide.

Figure 5.5   Mina's Slide Containing a Close-Up

Throughout the vignettes on pages 71–75, Mina demonstrated the application of multiple literacies to facilitate composition and communication using visual design, text, graphics, color, links, symbols such as bullets and lines, and so on. In other PowerPoint presentations, Mina has demonstrated her ability to create and use audio and video together with the representational systems just noted. My interactions with Mina and other children from her school imply that the availability of technology, coupled with knowledgeable teachers, result in students' mastery of the new literacies for communicative purposes.

Conclusion

Communicating through websites, PowerPoint presentations, and other electronic means requires literacy abilities that encompass but extend the notions of literacy that have defined our field. Leu (2000) and Leu and Kinzer (2000) have noted that literacy can be viewed as a deictic term—a term that has meaning only relative to its embedded context. Thus, what it means to be literate now, in the present-day context, is different from what it meant to be literate 20 years ago and is different from what it will mean to be literate in the future. At present, being literate means having the ability to compose and understand messages not only in textual forms but also in forms that include text as well as graphics, audio, color, links, icons, and so on. Being literate means being able to search for information, synthesize that information, and use it as needed. It means being able to use metacognitive knowledge—knowledge that allows one to monitor understanding (one's own as well as potential understanding of one's audience) in constructing a message. It also means being able to blend, merge, and use multiple sign, symbol, and representational systems in a synergistic way so that each system supports an author's intended message. The two points of (1) applying metacognitive knowledge and (2) synergy across multiple sign, symbol, and representational systems to impart and support a message are important aspects of new literacies that are represented in the first section of this volume.

Metacognitive knowledge (Brown, 1977; Flavell, 1987; Scardamalia & Bereiter, 1985) also helps individuals monitor understanding and select strategies consciously to increase their understanding. It allows readers to notice consciously that their comprehension has broken down and helps them decide to reread, to look quickly at a heading, or to use other strategies to enhance comprehension. Similarly, metacognitive knowledge allows readers to put into play audience awareness, which allows them to predict the support that a reader might need to understand the author's message. When students understand what might make a message more or less difficult, it helps them decide how much background to put into a message, what vocabulary to use, and how redundant to be. When students use metacognitive skills in electronic environments, they know when to add information, insert hyperlinks (if material might need additional information to make it comprehensible), highlight text, vary the typeface, animate something, use audio or video, and how to layout a page to include graphic and textual elements. In short, students know when to use the tools available in whatever medium they are working to make their message understandable to their intended audience.

Metacognitive skills allow the conscious application of strategies and tools to meet one's goals, which presupposes that the tools are available and the goals are explicit. If one does not know that PowerPoint has a line tool, then a strategy for its use cannot exist. One may want to draw a line, and hope to draw a line, but without knowledge of the existence and capabilities of the appropriate tool the line cannot be drawn. Similarly, if one does not know that hyperlinking is possible within a text or that one can compose a document to include audio files and animation, strategies for such compositions will not be developed. Thus, teaching students about the tools related to new literacies is important. Providing opportunities for children to develop both the knowledge of compositional tools and strategies for their use within authentic contexts is important at even the youngest grades.

Often, however, I hear from teachers, parents, business leaders, and others that technology uses in schools should be implemented later in the curriculum—generally in the middle grades and above. In most cases, this comment stems from a feeling that technology is a tool to be used within traditional literacy boundaries, as a search tool for research projects or only as a connection to the Internet, which is viewed merely as a vast encyclopedia. Such views, however, ignore the essential premise of the chapters in this section: Technology and its uses move well beyond tool functions, technology encompasses literacies, and the development of literacy as defined in current societal contexts requires the implementation and teaching of technology within the literacy curriculum from the youngest ages.

Labbo (1996) and Labbo and Kuhn (1998) have documented technology-related learning and activities that teachers can use with preschoolers and kindergarteners. In reading Mina's comments, it seems clear that the availability of technology in the primary grades results in acquisition and use of new literacies without detrimental effects to alphabetic literacy. Without the availability of technology, children will not develop and practice the communication necessary for their future success. The optimal uses of technology—as shown in the chapters by Sangiuliano, Ahlness, and Chamberlain—are in the overlap of community, school, and technology, as discussed earlier.

In reading the preceding three chapters in this section, I am once again struck by what has previously been noted about the implementation of technology into literacy instruction: Often, the best uses of technology in literacy instruction do not wait for research results or testing of findings before being implemented (Leu & Kinzer, 2000; President's Committee of Advisors on Science and Technology, 1997). Also, I am struck by how teachers who understand how literacy develops support this development through a wide range of technology and technology tools. Taken together, the chapters show how knowledgeable educators and technology can make a difference. In each project, committed educators persevered and overcame challenges to implement a vision. In short, I was struck by how many principles of effective reading instruction were encompassed in Sangiuliano's, Ahlness's, and Chamberlain's chapters through activities that were facilitated through technology.

The past decade has seen several visible efforts at documenting effective practices, for example, as seen in work by the National Reading

Panel (2000) and by Snow, Burns, and Griffin (1998). Also, Schrader and colleagues (2003) and Teale, Leu, Labbo, and Kinzer (2002) describe 12 principles of effective practices related to reading. These principles are the result of a review that incorporated the findings of the National Reading Panel and additional literature that was published since the panel's report appeared. The 12 principles are as follows:

1. *Teacher knowledge, insight, and orchestration of instruction.* The teacher's knowledge, ability to make principled, insightful, instructional decisions for individual children, and the ability to orchestrate effective instruction for the group of children being taught are more influential factors in student literacy achievement than knowing particular procedures for instruction or following scripted lesson plans.

2. *Language, culture, home background, and literacy instruction.* Providing school reading instruction that builds on young children's language, culture, and home background enhances their chances for success in learning to read and write.

3. *Emergent literacy foundations.* Basic early literacy concepts, skills, and positive attitudes that form the foundation for subsequent reading and writing achievement are developed by immersing young children in literacy-rich classrooms.

4. *Phonemic awareness instruction.* Instructional activities that develop children's phonemic awareness increase reading achievement, when individual children have not acquired this important knowledge.

5. *Decoding instruction.* Instruction in the sound–symbol correspondences of language (often called phonics instruction) is positively related to student achievement in reading.

6. *Comprehension instruction.* Instructional activities that develop children's abilities and strategies for comprehending written language enhance reading achievement.

7. *Independent reading.* The more young children read a variety of texts that interest them, the more likely they are to achieve well in reading.

8. *Fluency instruction.* Fostering the development of reading fluency through appropriate instructional activities and extensive opportunities to read fluently is associated with higher reading achievement.

9. *Integrating writing and reading.* Providing writing instruction linked to reading instruction enhances achievement in reading as well as in writing.

10. *Technology and early literacy development.* Integrating computer and Internet technologies into literacy instruction in the early grades of school provides the foundation for continued learning of both conventional and digital literacies as children proceed through school.

11. *Early assessment and instructional intervention.* Monitoring children's early literacy development through ongoing classroom as-

sessment and providing instruction based on the diagnostic information obtained, including appropriate instructional intervention to
children who fall significantly behind, enhances the chances that children will achieve satisfactorily in reading and writing.

12. *Enthusiasm for reading and writing.* Teaching in ways that foster young
children's enthusiasm for and engagement with reading and writing enhances the likelihood that they will learn to read and write successfully
and become lifelong readers and writers. (Schrader et al., 2003, p. 317)

The chapters in this section range widely, yet have teaching, learning,
and technology as their common cores. They describe technology to involve students, businesses, parents, and teachers and do so within authentic contexts that often had social consequences. Although applauding
the innovative uses of technology that were described, we should not forget the aspects of literacy that these projects developed. Therefore, I ad-
vocate that readers closely examine the literacy activities described by
Sangiuliano, Ahlness, and Chamberlain together with the 12 principles of
effective reading instruction. Doing so clearly shows that technology can be
used in the primary grades to develop the range of literacies that children
will need throughout their lives. Sangiuliano, Ahlness, and Chamberlain
have done us a service by showing how they are doing so on a daily basis.

REFERENCES

Bransford, J.D., Brown, A.L., & Cocking, R.R. (2000). *How people learn: Brain, mind,
experience, and school* (expanded ed.). Washington, DC: National Academy Press.
Brown, A.L. (1977). Development, schooling, and the acquisition of knowledge about
knowledge. In R.C. Anderson, R.J. Spiro, & W.E. Montague (Eds.), *Schooling and
the acquisition of knowledge*. Hillsdale, NJ: Erlbaum.
Castells, M. (2000). *The rise of the network society* (2nd ed.). Oxford: Blackwell.
Flavell, J.H. (1987). Speculations about the nature and development of metacognition.
In F.E. Weinert & R.H. Kluwe (Eds.), *Metacognition, motivation, and understanding*
(pp. 21–29). Hillside, NJ: Erlbaum.
Garner, R., & Gillingham, M.G. (1996). *Internet communication in six classrooms:
Conversations across time, space, and culture*. Mahwah, NJ: Erlbaum.
Kinzer, C.K. (2003). The importance of recognizing the expanding boundaries of liter-
acy. *Reading Online*. Retrieved January 19, 2003, from http://www.readingonline.
org/electronic/elec_index.asp?HREF=/electronic/kinzer/index.html
Kinzer, C.K., & Leander, K. (2003). Technology and the language arts: Implications of
an expanded definition of literacy. In J. Flood, D. Lapp, J.R. Squire, & J.M. Jensen
(Eds.), *Handbook of research on teaching the English language arts* (2nd ed.,
pp. 546–566). Mahwah, NJ: Erlbaum.
Labbo, L.D. (1996). A semiotic analysis of young children's symbol making in a classroom computer center. *Reading Research Quarterly, 31*, 356–385.

Labbo, L.D., & Kuhn, M. (1998). Electronic symbol making: Young children's computer-related emerging concepts about literacy. In D. Reinking, M.C. McKenna, L.D. Labbo, & R.D. Kieffer (Eds.), *Handbook of literacy and technology: Transformations in a post-typographic world* (pp. 79–92). Mahwah, NJ: Erlbaum.

Lankshear, C., & Knobel, M. (2003). *New literacies: Changing knowledge and classroom learning.* Buckingham, UK: Open University Press.

Leu, D.J., Jr. (2000). Literacy and technology: Deictic consequences for literacy education in an information age. In M.L. Kamil, P.B. Mosenthal, P.D. Pearson, & R. Barr (Eds.), *Handbook of reading research* (Vol. 3, pp. 743–770). Mahwah, NJ: Erlbaum.

Leu, D.J., Jr., & Kinzer, C.K. (2000). The convergence of literacy instruction with networked technologies for information and communication. *Reading Research Quarterly, 35,* 108–127.

Leu, D.J., Jr., Kinzer, C.K., Coiro, J.L., & Cammack, D.W. (2004). Toward a theory of new literacies emerging from the Internet and other information and communication technologies. In R.B. Ruddell & N.J. Unrau (Eds.), *Theoretical models and processes of reading* (5th ed., pp. 1570–1613). Newark, DE: International Reading Association.

Leu, D.J., Jr., Leu, D.D., & Coiro, J.L. (2004). *Teaching with the Internet K–12: New literacies for new times* (4th ed). Norwood, MA: Christopher-Gordon.

National Reading Panel. (2000). *Teaching children to read: An evidence-based assessment of the scientific research literature on reading and its implications for reading instruction.* Washington, DC: National Institute of Child Health and Human Development, National Institutes of Health.

New London Group. (2000). *Multiliteracies: Literacy learning and the design of social futures.* London: Routledge.

President's Committee of Advisors on Science and Technology (PCAST): Panel on Educational Technology. (1997). *Report to the president on the use of technology to strengthen K–12 education in the United States.* Washington, DC: Executive Office of the President of the United States. Retrieved November 18, 2004, from http://www.ostp.gov/PCAST/K-12ed.html

Reinking, D. (1998). Introduction: Synthesizing technological transformations of literacy in a post-typographic world. In D. Reinking, M.C. McKenna, L.D. Labbo, & R.D. Kieffer (Eds.), *Handbook of literacy and technology: Transformations in a post-typographic world* (pp. xi–xxx). Mahwah, NJ: Erlbaum.

Scardamalia, M., & Bereiter, C. (1985). Fostering the development of self-regulation in children's knowledge processing. In S.F. Chipman, J.W. Segal, & R. Glaser (Eds.), *Thinking and learning skills: Current research and open questions* (Vol. 2, pp. 563–577). Hillsdale, NJ: Erlbaum.

Schrader, P.G., Leu, D.J., Jr., Kinzer, C.K., Ataya, R., Labbo, L.D., Teale, W.H., et al. (2003). Using Internet delivered video cases to support pre-service teachers' understanding of effective early literacy instruction: An exploratory study. *Instructional Science, 31*(4–5), 317–340.

Snow, C.E., Burns, S.M., & Griffin, P. (Eds.). (1998). *Preventing reading difficulties in young children.* Washington, DC: National Academy Press.

Teale, W.H., Leu, D.J., Jr., Labbo, L.D., & Kinzer, C.K. (2002). The CTELL project: New ways technology can help educate tomorrow's reading teachers. *The Reading Teacher, 55,* 654–659.

A Commitment to Collaboration

Section II focuses on collaboration through the use of Internet technologies and celebrates the collaboration that students and teachers build among themselves as they use the Internet to support literacy instruction and learning. The first five chapters of this section describe teacher-based collaboration by Miss Rumphius Award winners, such as when a teacher develops an Internet project and invites others to participate and share their learning, when a teacher designs a webpage and publishes resources for other teachers to use, and when teachers publish students' writings on the classroom's webpage for other students and teachers to view and use according to their instructional and learning objectives. These same forms of collaboration are celebrated and analyzed by a university scholar in the last chapter of the section.

In chapter 6, Marci McGowan discusses how an unsuccessful Web search for fall poems motivated her to develop a collaborative Internet project—the Fall Poetry Project—in which her students write their own fall poems to be published online. McGowan also talks about her second collaborative Internet project, My Town Is Important, as well as other Internet resources she has been using to enrich her instruction and her students' literacy learning.

In chapter 7, Susan Silverman takes readers on a journey into the world of collaborative projects and reveals how this small world grows bigger and bigger over the years. Silverman describes several of her collaborative projects, such as An Apple a Day and Frosty Readers, and shares information on other Internet resources teachers can use in their literacy classrooms.

In chapter 8, Dale Hubert describes the Flat Stanley Project and other classroom applications of technology. He stresses the importance of using authentic learning experiences when integrating technology in the curriculum.

In chapter 9, Mary Kreul outlines the many different learning experiences she offered her students by integrating the Internet and other information and communication technologies (ICTs) in her teaching. Kreul describes how she and her students first attempted to use technology by simply participating in basic e-mail and Internet projects. She then explains how they gradually advanced to sponsoring keypal projects, participating in collaborative projects, using software and other digital technologies, and designing and maintaining the classroom webpage.

In chapter 10, Tim C. Lauer describes his journey in the world of Internet technologies from teacher to principal. He discusses his webpage *The Buckman School Room 100*, which became an avenue for his students to share their classroom experiences and work with an authentic audience. Lauer also targets the use of the weblog publishing software, which makes it easier for teachers to publish and share materials online.

This section concludes with a chapter by Linda D. Labbo. Labbo discusses fundamental qualities of effective Internet literacy instruction, while drawing examples from actual classroom observations and from virtual visits to the websites of the Miss Rumphius Award winners, including authors from this section. In particular, Labbo analyzes four characteristics of teachers who are effective in integrating the Internet and other ICTs in their instruction and three qualities of successful student Internet collaboration.

CHAPTER 6

My Internet Projects and Other Online Resources for the Literacy Classroom

Marci McGowan

Why would any teacher want to sort through a couple hundred e-mail messages and download, resize, and post numerous images, along with 90 poems, to a webpage? I asked myself that same question when I felt very weary at the end of one Internet literacy project. Then I received an e-mail from a teacher 3,000 miles away that lifted my fatigue. The following e-mail replaced this fatigue with thoughts about my next project, along with much professional satisfaction:

> My class and I loved doing the Read a Winter Book...Write a Winter Poem project (www.mrsmcgowan.com/winter2003/index.html). For many of the students, this was an introduction to poetry writing and they were fascinated by the process we used to create our acrostic poem for *Snow Riders* by Constance W. McGeorge [1995]...we will be continuing our poetry writing this year using the project page as "real world" examples of the types of poetry we can write.
>
> We are also using the webpage as a reading activity. My students love it when I display the poems on our "big screen." The poetry examples are fun to read and the books that were used as springboards are many of the same ones we know and have enjoyed reading. The students are making wonderful, meaningful connections as we read the poems that the other classes have so beautifully written. I'm looking forward to the transfer of the reading and modeling and writing showing up in Writing Workshop as my students experiment with writing poems as a format-of-choice....
>
> Thank you...for hosting this project and for providing the "World Wide Web" with a great resource of poetry writing models. (J. Filer, personal communication, February 15, 2003)

The Internet offers many opportunities for students to engage in authentic reading and writing experiences. One such opportunity is the collaborative Internet project. Collaborative Internet projects are learning activities between two or more classes at different locations using the Internet. Students work on similar problems or topics and share their findings and activities through the Internet. This purposeful, authentic, and engaging work begins to prepare today's learners for new literacies in the technological world of today and tomorrow. Teachers can use collaborative Internet projects to integrate Internet use in the classroom and promote the learning of both traditional and new literacies (Leu, 2001).

The Fall Poetry Project (http://myschoolonline.com/folder/0,1872, 34898-119831-38-35031,00.html) and My Town Is Important (www. mrsmcgowan.com/mytown.html) are my earliest attempts at creating and hosting Internet projects. These projects continue to be resources for online thematic reading material and community information as well as models for collaboration between classes via the Internet. My story shows how Internet integration can be achieved and used on a regular basis in the classroom, how I use technology today, and how the Internet has changed literacy instruction and learning in my classroom.

Fall Poetry Project

The Fall Poetry Project of 2000 was the first official collaborative Internet project I hosted. I created a webpage to provide my first-grade students with additional reading material on a seasonal topic (see Figure 6.1).

The project was a direct result of my unsuccessful Internet search for fall poems that my young students could read either independently or with some assistance. Regie Routman's (2000) enthusiasm for writing poetry with young children inspired my focus on this genre. Her examples of free verse lessons and childrens' writing in her book for first-grade teachers provided me with ideas on how to integrate poetry into my own teaching. I selected an acrostic poetry format for my project so students would not have to be concerned with sentence writing or word rhyming. In the past, my first graders had written acrostic name poems early in the school year so I knew this format could be used successfully by both novice and more experienced writers.

Once I decided on the project's format and objectives, I registered it on the Global Schoolhouse website (www.globalschoolnet.org/GSH). This website provided a convenient standard template for describing project objectives and requirements. It also offered an e-mail (newsletter mail to:gsn-hilites-list-subscribe@topica.com) to notify teachers of various projects. It also offered a listserv that I could use to announce my project to all list-

Figure 6.1 Screen Shot of Fall Poetry Project

serv members (send e-mail to gsn-hilites-list@topica.com). This listserv, called GSN Project Hilites Anouncements, provides its members with e-mail announcements of all registered collaborative Internet learning projects. Next, I designed a webpage to post student work, in the hope that other teachers would share a similar interest in fall poetry written by young children. A total of 60 grade K–6 classes from the United States, Canada, and South Africa signed up to participate in the Fall Poetry Project. Teachers sent by e-mail a class-written poem and illustration or photo about the fall season to be published on the project webpage. The project requirements were minimal and were designed to encourage poetry writing by young children. The project ran for 3 months and generated a rich body of student poetry. These poems, almost all written in acrostic format, continue to be available as a resource for student reading and teacher instruction. A few examples are provided (Figures 6.2, 6.3, and 6.4).

In my classroom, we visited the project's webpage often and read a few of the poems together each time. Different students took turns navigating the website and using the mouse or arrow keys on the keyboard to locate poems. We printed some poems and added them to our fall collections of leaves and pictures. I also added them to my resources for seasonal instructional materials.

Figure 6.2   A Student Poem From Nova Scotia, Canada

> **FALL**
>
> **F** alling leaves,
> **A** corn collecting,
> **L** ittle children smile...
> **L** ots of fun!

Figure 6.3   A Student Poem From New Jersey, USA

> **FALL**
>
> **F** rosty mornings,
> **A** time for sweaters,
> **L** eaping into leaves,
> **L** eaves need raking.
> We Love Fall!!

Figure 6.4   A Student Poem From Arizona, USA

> **FALL IN ARIZONA**
>
> **F** alling leaves
> **A** pples.
> **L** eaves all over the place.
> **L** iving in the desert.
> **I** t is Fall!
> **N** inety degrees.
> **A** sking questions.
> **R** unning in the rain.
> **I** guanas sleep.
> **Z** ig zag
> **O** wls hoot.
> **N** ights are cool.
> **A** rizona in the fall is awesome!

We used our classroom maps and found the country or U.S. state where classes were located. That, in turn, created opportunities for my students to share what they knew about geography. To further students' learning, I set up a classroom shelf for books about these new places for my students to browse at their leisure.

We received e-mails from other teachers about the experiences they had writing acrostic poems in the classroom. Some teachers had never attempted poetry writing with their students, and this project gave them the impetus to try. Others used this experience as an opportunity to work on writing process with their students:

> We finished our poem today. It was quite an experience! We chose one of two topics to write about, then when we finished we weren't sure we liked it. So then we wrote about the second topic, and were quite pleased with how it turned out. What a great time going through the writing process together! (Mrs. Burrows, personal communication, October 22, 2000)

> We traced our hands in lots of fall colors to make piles of leaves to play in...then glued tumbling leaves on paper to display with our poems. Thanks for the chance to be part of this! (K. Barrow, personal communication, October 30, 2000)

Some teachers sent in class webpage addresses to share all their student poems. Linking to class webpages was a special way to extend the scope of this project and a feature I used in projects from that point forward.

Although I had not intended to use images on the project webpages, one teacher sent photographs showing how she displayed the poems in the hallway of her school. I created a special webpage (www.myschoolonline. com/page/0,1871,34898-119831-38-44756,00.html) for showcasing this wonderful poetry display.

Poems about autumn and spring came from sixth-grade classes in a South African school. Their spring season had started in September, and naturally, the students elected to write about it. I was very pleased that they wanted to join in celebrating the change of season with poetry and our project. I use the project work as a resource when I teach how different seasons simultaneously take place in other parts of the world.

I altered the original project to include older students (the original design was for K–2 students), to change project requirements (use spring poems in a fall project), and to allow varied poetry formats to demonstrate the need to be flexible. An important lesson I learned from the Fall Poetry Project was that I had to be willing to change my plans.

As the project coordinator, I also learned to make changes that improved my future projects. I chose a different Web server to avoid viewing pop-up ads, used larger fonts to make the poems easier to read, required images as part of the project, created a separate webpage for comments or feedback about the project, created links to individual class pages to improve navigation, and used a Web editing program to save me much time and effort. However, the most important task was to establish a consistent plan that could be used for all of my future projects. To accomplish this, I viewed many other Internet projects that were available by winter 2001. What I considered to be the very best projects included a homepage with easy navigation to information about the project as well as a page to showcase student work. Some projects offered online resources, that is, lists of related literature for students and teachers, and encouraged feedback that could be published. The model I use is credited to Susan Silverman (for more on Silverman, see chapter 7). Silverman's Webfolio (www.kids-learn.org) lists her exemplary collaborative Internet projects.

My Town Is Important

The My Town Is Important project incorporated all the technical improvements previously mentioned and had quite a different look than the Fall Poetry Project (see Figure 6.5).

An essential component of a good Internet project is its relevance to curriculum and alignment with state educational and International Society for Technology in Education standards. This project integrated a communities theme with poetry to meet literacy, social studies, and technology standards. For example, through their participation in this project, students were expected to meet New Jersey's core curriculum standards for language and literacy and social studies.

3.2 Listen actively in a variety of situations for information from a variety of sources.

3.3 Write in clear, concise, organized language that varies in content and form for different audiences and purposes.

3.4 Read various materials and texts with comprehension and critical analysis.

3.5 View, understand, and use nontextual visual information.

6.7 Acquire geographical understanding by studying the world in spatial terms (www.state.nj.us/njded/cccs/s3_lal.htm).

Figure 6.5   Screen Shot of My Town Is Important

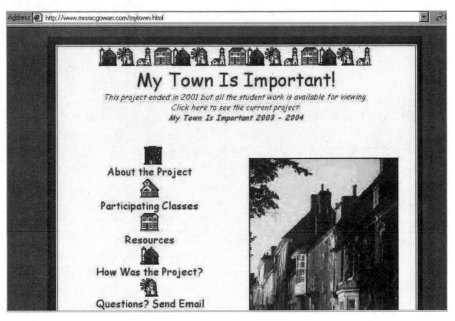

The project also met technology standards of National Educational Technology Standards for Students (NETS, www.iste.org/standards):

Use technology communications tools.

Use telecommunications to collaborate, publish, interact with peers, experts, and other audiences.

Learning about their towns is a common curricular objective for students in many primary-grade classes. Traditionally, they use books from their local libraries, photographs of special places in the town, and ideas about their own community favorites. Students might create oral and written reports, maps, drawings, or models of buildings using cardboard or paper bags.

In planning for this new collaborative Internet project, I wanted to provide an opportunity for students to write about their town without requiring skills beyond a 6- or 7-year-old level. My Town Is Important included a writing activity using a specific poetry format that allowed novice writers as well as more experienced writers to participate. This simple format consists of stating something important about a topic, listing a few more comments about it, and ending by repeating the first line. *The Important Book* (Brown, 1949), one of my personal favorites, offered this unique opportunity. It is as engaging today as when it was published, as illustrated by the following excerpt:

> The important thing about rain is that it is wet. It falls out of the sky, and it sounds like rain, and makes things shiny, and it does not taste like anything, and is the color of air. But the important thing about rain is that it is wet. (p. 5)

Brown makes readers think of everyday things as special and worthy of comment. Classroom teachers have enjoyed reading these words to new audiences of students over and over again. I thought Brown's poetry format would be just right for My Town Is Important.

Before opening the project to registration, I created a webpage (www.mrsmcgowan.com/feedback.html) to explain the project's requirements in detail. In particular, I asked participating classrooms to send an e-mail of their completed project work to me by a specific date and include one student writing sample for posting on the project webpage, one image (student drawing or photo taken by student or teacher), and a description of any additional activities. I also included suggestions for extension activities. Some of these activities included illustrating features of the town, interviewing local government officials, drawing a town map, writing a song about the town, mapping locations of other class towns, writing a response to a participating class about its town and sending it to the class via e-mail, or creating a slide show for webpage viewers. I created another webpage about the project and provided a resource page for teachers. The resource page included examples of other writing activities using *The Important Book* and links to websites containing background information about the author. Once again, I registered my project with Global Schoolhouse.

Teachers registered for the project and obtained copies of Brown's book to read to their classes and use as models for their students' writing. Each participating class submitted illustrations or photos of their town and a class-written poem using the suggested format. The following examples from first graders in Connecticut highlight the unique variations possible even within a structured project.

> The important thing about Weston, Connecticut, is that it has an AWESOME school system.
> The schools are close together. It has a great library and nice teachers. There are 21 busses to drive us to school. It has a firestation and a policestation to keep us safe. You can see the families spend time with

their friends at the Lunch Box. People in Weston, Connecticut are VERY nice. Weston has beautiful plants and trees. We also have special animals like a Pilated Woodpecker. It has GREAT backyards to play in.

But the important thing about Weston, Connecticut is that is has an AWESOME school system.

Fourth graders from Missouri sent in a link to a webquest, Major Missouri Cities Webquest (www.schoolweb.missouri.edu/central.k12.mo.us/looney/mocitywebquest/index.html), created by their teacher. The webquest task was to design and develop a travel brochure highlighting a Missouri city. In the brochures, students promoted and enticed visitors to the city by highlighting its important features. This activity extended my project because it included another form of writing and learning about other cities while using the Internet. It also demonstrates how an Internet project such as My Town Is Important can be adapted for various grade levels and student learning.

A third-grade class from British Columbia, Canada, extended their project by completing an extra writing activity based on the book-length poem *If You're Not from the Prairie* by David Bouchard (1998). Students wrote,

If You're Not from Port Alice
You don't know the rain.
You can't know the rain.
If you're not from Port Alice,
you won't know the rain...

Go to www.mrsmcgowan.com/mytownclass4.htm to view their work.

In my classroom, students read or listened to the poems sent in from the other 24 classes that registered for the project, and we tried to locate all the places on our maps. The project enriched our community study and gave the students a glimpse of student life that was similar to or different than their own.

Feedback about the project was very positive, as the following messages sent to my class reveal:

Our class has been able to use the poem format for other learning areas. It's been great. All the kids have been able to achieve some success in poetry writing using this method.... (K. Shilling, personal communication, April 4, 2002)

I'm hooked on Internet projects. My class got so much out of it. We are going to vote on our favorite town and graph the results. Loads of great extensions! (D. Richie, personal communication, September 12, 2003)

A unique aspect of Internet projects is that the shared work can be read days, months, and years after it was created. Thus, its impact can potentially be never-ending. For example, two years after My Town Is Important was completed, I received the following e-mail from a Pennsylvania company's representative:

> September 2003: The President & CEO and the Vice President of Finance have a business trip planned to Park Hills, MO, next week. They asked me to gather some information about that town of Park Hills for them to get them familiar with the area. I will print out My Town is Important! for them as part of their information packet. Great job! Keep up the good work! (D. Shupp, personal communication, September 12, 2003)

Using Technology in My Classroom

When I began creating collaborative Internet projects, I was in my sixth year of teaching first grade. It also was the year I created a class webpage. Before that, I used the Internet very tentatively, including a few websites related to my students' lessons, while favoring software such as Encarta (an encyclopedia) and Kid Pix (a drawing program). However, when I found two special collaborative Internet projects that were created by classroom teachers, my focus shifted to the Internet as the technology resource I wanted to be important in my classroom.

Tammy Payton created the Surfing For ABC's Project (www.siec.k12. in.us/~west/proj/abc). Kindergarten and first-grade students searched for topics beginning with every letter of the alphabet. The students used the Yahooligans search engine (www.yahooligans.com) to find their ABC topics. Hazel Jobe's The Earth Day Challenge (www.marshall-es.marshall. k12.tn.us/jobe/earthday99/main.html) was also very impressive. I recall visiting every page of Jobe's website project, selecting the activity links that I could use or adapt for my young students. Being very timid about using the Internet for instruction, I printed each of Jobe's webpages to guide me through the screen changes. Each day, my students and I all gathered around one little computer screen and visited a new website for a few minutes. Luckily, I opened the webpages beforehand, so we did not have to wait for graphics-heavy pages to load. We learned about energy and natural-resource conservation and used the Internet to complement traditional classroom resources such as books, magazines, posters, and pictures. I was hooked, and so were my students.

Over several months, I viewed many teacher-created websites, improved my search skills, and began building a list of online resources to use in the classroom. Eventually, by taking advantage of several tutorials for learning hypertext markup language (HTML, the code used to create webpages), I was able to create my own class webpage. Finding Internet projects my students and I could join was an exciting learning adventure for me. Our first collaboration was a winter weather project testing the proverb "March comes in like a lion and goes out like a lamb." We recorded weather conditions for our area during March and sent the information via e-mail to the project host. My students were thrilled to see their five lines of weather data on the computer screen.

At the same time, I joined a listserv (RTEACHER listserv: wwwreading. org/resources/community/discussions_rt_instruct.html) and mail rings (e-mail discussion groups focused on topics of interest to members) at teachers.net (www.teachers.net). These internet tools changed my once isolated classroom learning environment, which now was supported by global communication with many other teachers, all interested in sharing ideas to make instruction better for students and to expand personal and professional development. My personal experience confirms Karchmer's (2000) statement:

> The Internet has changed the way we communicate with one another. This is especially true for educators. Until recently, most staff development took place in school buildings, during or immediately after school hours. Today, teachers share instructional ideas, strategies, and questions over the Internet 24 hours a day. (p. 101)

Class Webpage

With this new learning, I was able to expand our class webpage and regularly post student work to share with families, other students, and teachers. Four and a half years later, my classroom webpages, Mrs. McGowan's First Grade (www.mrsmcgowan.com; see Figure 6.6) and Mrs. McGowan's Second Grade (www.mrsmcgowan.com/2nd/index.htm) contain over 500 webpages and have at least 200 visitors every day. The webpages highlight student work; Internet projects; and online resources for families, students, teachers, and other visitors.

The main purpose for the webpages is to provide authentic communication opportunities for my students. They are the home base for all our daily Internet activity. Students turn on the computers when they arrive for class and then navigate to the Internet and their respective grade's webpage. The students access information from various websites that I have previewed and posted on our site. A morning weather report that students can link to from an image link on our homepage is a good example. Several

Figure 6.6 Screen Shot of Mrs. McGowan's First-Grade Webpage

seasonal, thematic, and subject webpages are available through this linking procedure.

Students also get information about other places in the world through class e-mail, our website guestbook, and participation in other collaborative Internet projects. For example, one class communicated with e-mail pals in a Western Australia school. My students learned what it is like to have a school built on stilts in case of flooding and what it is like to ride a horse to school instead of a car or school bus!

However, the main way my students and I communicate with other classes and the general public is by publishing student work on our website. The students love to see their drawings and writing on screen, as do their families. Some of the most appreciative responses to our website have come from grandparents living far away. Knowing that so many people will be seeing their work helps motivate the students to do their best.

In addition to hosting collaborative Internet projects, I also use the class webpages to extend specific classroom lessons. The webpages include online quizzes and activities using compound words, math riddles, and spelling words. Some activities I create myself, and some are developed by other teachers who send me links to their online activities to post on my website. All activities are shared by teachers from all over the world.

Our website has become a supermarket of resources for parents and other teachers. It is a convenient place to find tips on reading at home with students, critical thinking questions using New Jersey state standards, website development, holiday puzzles, math projects, rubrics, booklists, and links to other teacher websites—just to name a few.

More Internet Projects and Other Online Resources

Following My Town Is Important, I created and hosted several other online collaborative projects. Figure 6.7 shows projects published through the 2000–2004 school years.

The concept of Internet projects as useful, relevant online resources for teachers and students has developed with each new project. All of the Internet projects have suggestions for extension activities, lists of trade books, and several Web links. I specifically design my projects to entice teachers into using the Internet with their students and to encourage experienced teachers to do more. I include a variety of activities for students to do online in response to the project. The project Read a Winter Book… Write a Winter Poem 2004 had students writing poems in response to literature they had listened to or read. To continue improving my projects, I continue to learn more about webpage development—my own personal new literacy.

Lessons I Have Learned

I have learned some important lessons about the new literacies of the Internet and teaching with the Internet in my classroom. Web safety continues to be an issue. Young students need adult supervision when using the Internet. Teachers need to check and recheck websites that they recommend for student use. I recommend only the websites that I post on my own website. At school, my first- and second-grade students do not type Web addresses in the Internet browser, to avoid accidentally reaching an inappropriate adult website. Instead, they click on an image or text link that I have made that takes them directly to a specific website. As another safety precaution, I preload the webpages I know we will be using on a given day. This precaution allows me to check the webpages and reduces student-loading time because the webpages are in our computer's cache for that day.

Figure 6.7   Collaborative Internet Projects, 2000–2004

PROJECTS	GRADE RANGE
Fall Poetry Project (2000)* (www.myschoolonline.com/folder/0,1872,34898-119831 -38-35031,00.html)	K–5
My Town Is Important (2001)* (www.mrsmcgowan.com/mytown.html)	K–4
Oh, the Places We'll Go! (2001)* (www.mrsmcgowan.com/places.htm)	K–4
Read a Book—Write a Poem (2002)* (www.mrsmcgowan.com/winterpoems/index.html)	1
That's What Happens When It's Spring (2002)* (www.mrsmcgowan.com/spring/index.html)	K–4
A Patchwork of Places and Poetry (2002) (www.mrsmcgowan.com/quilts/index.html)	K–4
Junie B. Jones Favorites (2002–2004) (www.mrsmcgowan.com/junie/index.html)	K–6
Read a Winter Book...Write a Winter Poem (2003)* (www.mrsmcgowan.com/winter2003/index.html)	K–4
My Town Is Important (2003–2004) (www.mrsmcgowan.com/town/index.html)	K–4
Read a Winter Book...Write a Winter Poem (2004) (www.mrsmcgowan.com/winter2004/index.html)	K–4

*Miss Rumphius Award–Winning Project, www.reading.org/resources/community/
links_rumphius_links.html.

Lesson planning usually includes visiting several websites to preview the information or activity. However, the greatest website may not be available when teachers go back to use it. Unlike retrieving a reference book from the same library shelf every time you use it, the Internet is constantly changing. As teachers, we need to be flexible and be prepared for an unavailable website. Having alternative websites or traditional resources ready saves teacher time and alleviates student disappointment or time off task.

Along with using the Internet in my classroom comes the job of preparing students to use new literacy skills. First, my students learn how to use the mouse, as well as find letters, numbers, and command keys on a keyboard. Working with a partner helps students learn to share computer time and, more important, to collaborate on the basic tasks of reading the screen and appropriately using the mouse. I try to pair students who can help each other—a better reader with someone who can use the mouse accurately. Classmates working together share the mouse and help reinforce one another's learning. Internet projects foster collaboration on a much larger scale and can lead to later collaborations for problem solving. Second, they learn to read different kinds of webpages. Some are easier than others to figure out, whereas webpages with frames, text boxes, and pop-up advertisements are more challenging for early readers. Third, they learn to use links to navigate between webpages and open windows.

This last skill mentioned has important implications for later student learning in the area of reading comprehension. Teachers need to teach students how to read and evaluate a webpage (go to www.siec.k12.in.us/~west/edu/rubric3.htm for an example of a webpage evaluation tool), navigate between webpages and windows, and find the information they are trying to obtain. In describing a webpage filled with several links that have different purposes, Coiro (2003) writes, "Readers need a new type of inferential reasoning to anticipate these differences and decide whether or not each hyperlink will enhance or disrupt their search for meaning" (p. 459). I prefer to teach these skills informally by modeling or directly guiding a student using a mouse. Likewise, students will need to learn how to evaluate the information found on a webpage and use critical thinking to successfully undertake Web-based inquiries such as webquests (go to http://webquest.sdsu.edu for an example). When creating webpages, teachers need to focus on meaningful content, ease of navigation, and minimal distraction. Flashy graphics and trailing cursors can make a webpage excessively distracting for students and increase the time it takes to load the webpage.

Using the Internet often as a classroom resource with young students helps them view it as an information source rather than a place to play games. Recently in my second-grade class, we were trying to name an instrument one of the students brought in for show-and-tell. A student immediately suggested using the Internet to find this information. I was thrilled to hear her say that so easily.

Changes in Literacy Instruction and Learning

The Internet is a fantastic information and communication resource not only for my students but also for me. When I needed to make webpages to publish student work, for example, I learned HTML and eventually became acquainted with the Web editor FrontPage. Centering text became easier when I learned how to use tables. My students' illustrations were easier to publish when I learned how to use a photo editor and scanner.

Connecting with other teachers through e-mail and webpages continuously adds to my professional development. I have learned about Readers Theatre and found many scripts online (www.mrsmcgowan.com/reading/readerstheater.htm). Participation in an Internet book study of *On Solid Ground: Strategies for Teaching Reading K–3* (Taberski, 2000) one summer with other first-grade teachers was more meaningful to my understanding of the text rather than reading it alone (for more information, go to www.mrsmcgowan.com/osg.htm).

Another important change in my literacy knowledge has to do with student's literature. Before using the Internet, I relied on trips to the library to find storybooks or informational texts that complemented lessons I was planning. Now I perform Internet searches with much greater success and can preview book contents and read reviews at websites that sell the books. I have compiled my own lists of thematic or seasonal books from titles teachers share on mail rings and, in turn, share the lists by posting them on my own website.

As much as professional development for literacy knowledge has been enhanced by the Internet, I think publishing student work is even more significant.

My students' audience is much larger now, which pushes the classroom walls far and wide and can be very motivating to students. See Figure 6.8 for the different kinds of student writing published on my website. A first-grade boy sitting at the computer commented, "I like to see my work on the screen. It makes me feel good!" His classmate responded, "I want to do some more and we can read it together!"

Conclusion

Teaching young students how to use technology is necessary. No longer can teachers excuse themselves from this aspect of their professional roles. As teachers, we need to integrate the Internet within regular classroom curricula to support students' learning. Leu (2000) writes that literacy teachers, teacher educators, or researchers should not leave this job to those who specialize in technology because "to do so would marginalize the important insights about literacy instruction each of us possesses" (p. 425).

On a personal note, my own grown children, similar to many adults in the workforce, use the Internet and computer technology as a regular part

Figure 6.8   Types of Published Student Writing

Traditional Writing Assignment (a written response to a reading selection or writing assignment done by McGowan's students)

> Guess Who? "All About Me" riddles
> (www.mrsmcgowan.com/2nd/guesswho/index.html)
>
> Story Retelling Acrostic Poem
> (www.educationworld.com/a_tsl/archives/02–1/lesson039.shtml)

Writing From Collaborative Projects (several classes from different schools participate in the projects or collaboration is with 1–3 other classes at the same time or of varied grade levels)

> Stranger in the Woods: Poems and Activities 2002
> (www.mrsmcgowan.com/frosty2002/index.html)
>
> A Collaborative Snowman Story
> (http://myschoolonline.com/folder/0,1872,34898-119831-38-66374,00.html) written with another first-grade class using e-mail and webpages.
>
> Collaborative Projects with a fourth-grade class and preservice teachers on *Tales of a Fourth Grade Nothing* (Blume, 1972)
> (www.mrsmcgowan.com/projects/tales/index.html)
> and *Pippi Longstocking* (Lindgren, 1950)
> (www.mrsmcgowan.com/projects/pippi/index.html) related to literature circles

of their work and personal lives. Simply stated, they use it to get information, solve problems, and communicate with others. Plenty of help is available for teachers to get started with new literacies integration, so let us all log on, learn together, and make a difference like Miss Rumphius did.

REFERENCES

Coiro, J.L. (2003). Reading comprehension on the Internet: Expanding our understanding of reading comprehension to encompass new literacies. *The Reading Teacher, 56,* 458–464.

Karchmer, R.A. (2000). Using the Internet and children's literature to support interdisciplinary instruction. *The Reading Teacher, 54,* 100–104.

Leu, D.J., Jr. (2000). Our children's future: Changing the focus of literacy and literacy instruction. *The Reading Teacher, 53,* 424–429.

Leu, D.J., Jr. (2001). Internet project: Preparing students for new literacies in a global village. *The Reading Teacher, 54,* 568–572.

Routman, R. (2000). *Kids' poems: Teaching first graders to love writing poetry.* New York: Scholastic.

Taberski, S. (2000). *On solid ground: Strategies for teaching reading K–3.* Portsmouth, NH: Heinemann.

CHILDREN'S LITERATURE CITED

Blume, J. (1972). *Tales of a fourth grade nothing.* Ill. R. Doty. New York: Dutton.

Bouchard, D. (1995). *If you're not from the prairie.* Ill. H. Ripplinger. New York: Atheneum Books for Young Readers.

Brown, M.W. (1949). *The important book.* Ill. L. Welsgard. New York: HarperCollins.

Lindgren, A. (1950). *Pippi Longstocking* (F. Lamborn, Trans.). New York: Viking.

McGeorge, C.W. (1995). *The snow riders.* Ill. M. Whyte. San Francisco: Chronicle Books.

CHAPTER 7

Getting Connected: My Experience as a Collaborative Internet Project Coordinator

Susan Silverman

I was the first teacher in my school district to integrate Internet use into my classroom, and although it was exciting to explore uncharted territory, at times I felt rather lonely. How I wished there were other teachers who shared my passion. I longed to brainstorm technology integration ideas with others and discuss my Internet experiments in a supportive environment.

Then one day, I received an e-mail congratulating me on having won a Miss Rumphius Award. "Who is this Rumphius?" I wondered. Well, after a quick Internet search, I found myself on the International Reading Association website (www.reading.org) and learned that this award is presented by members of the RTEACHER mailing list (listserv) (www.reading.org/resources/community/discussions_rt_instruct.html) to educators who develop and share exceptional curricular resources on the Internet. I immediately subscribed to the RTEACHER listserv, and in no time, I had connected with a community of like-minded educators. Finally, I was no longer alone.

The RTEACHER listserv has been invaluable to me as a place for networking with other teachers; finding new teaching theories; discovering best practices; and, in particular, locating participants for online collaborative projects. I have developed valuable friendships with RTEACHER listserv members, and I cannot imagine where I would be without this talented and knowledgeable online community.

As for the Miss Rumphius Award—well, I now appreciate how actors feel when they win an Oscar! It is so rewarding to receive recognition from your peers. Sure, it is great to get positive reinforcement from students, their parents, and administrators, but nothing can compare with acknowledgment from innovators in the new literacy field.

Over the years, I have learned a great deal from reading stories and ideas posted on the RTEACHER listserv. I hope that you will find these reflections from my six-year tenure as an online project coordinator similarly engaging. If you would like to visit any of my past or current projects, you can view them all at my website (www.kids-learn.org). I also hope that after reading this chapter, you will consider joining one of my online collaborative projects or hosting one of your own.

The Journey Begins: An Apple a Day

My odyssey into the world of project coordination began on the bus ride home from the 1997 Classroom Connect Conference, a professional conference sponsored by Classroom Connect, with several sessions on the integration of technology in the curriculum. As the bus pulled out of Atlantic City, New Jersey, and headed toward the interstate, I thought about all the lectures I heard, the people I met, the freebies I collected—my mind was flooded with information overload. During that long drive home, I sifted through my mental notes. One particular thought kept occurring to me: Although I did not really know how to go about it, I felt an overwhelming desire to coordinate my own Internet project. After listening to teachers describe their technology projects, I wanted to create one as well. At the time, however, I did not feel that I had enough technology skills to do that.

In the 1970s, the Internet was not part of my college education. I had to learn everything about Web publishing on my own, but I had lots of help from family and friends. In 1996 every classroom teacher in my school district received two classroom computers and was expected to use them. I had no computer skills and felt very inadequate, but when I saw the potential of technology integration, I spent all my free time at home acquiring new skills. In considering how to host a collaborative Internet project, I decided that rather than start from scratch, I would draw upon my 27 years of classroom experience—to perhaps integrate the Internet into a thematic unit I would normally teach without computers.

At the start of each school year, I would traditionally conduct an autumnal poetry unit with my second-grade students. So I decided to introduce Internet technology into the mix and narrow the focus to apple poems, and that is how my very first collaborative Internet project—An Apple a Day (http://kids-learn.org/a/apples2nd)—was born. Though quite unintentionally, I set many precedents with An Apple a Day, including the basic model I would use in each of my future collaborations. My model, The Online Thematic Showcase, is quite simple: Participating classes work on a thematic unit and send me samples of students' creative work via e-mail. Teaching suggestions, a timeline for the unit, and a list of books and related websites are included on the website where the work will be showcased. Registration information also is included on the website, along with the project's objectives, resources, and assessment.

As previously mentioned, I had never acted as a project coordinator so I did not really know how to go about it. I was, however, familiar with the online education community thanks to my participation in other projects, such as Dale Hubert's Flat Stanley Project (see chapter 8, www.flatstanley. enoreo.on.ca) and the I Have a Dream project (www.kidlink.org/dream). Plus, I already had a network of cyberfriends from chat rooms, listservs, and e-mail conversations. Therefore, I announced my project at a variety of Internet chatrooms I was familiar with. In the announcements, I invited educators to have their students write apple poems, following established formats, and to publish the poems online. I was surprised and delighted when more than a dozen teachers rapidly responded that they would love to participate.

At that time, my Web development skills were very limited. I was not even comfortable uploading images. So, out of necessity, I kept the design basic. I invited participants to submit as many poems as they wanted but only one student's illustration of his or her poem. I quickly discovered that I was not the only newbie around. Many of the teachers who participated in the project were still trying to find their footing in this strange new electronic landscape. One teacher from Australia, for example, had no idea how to send a picture via e-mail so she sent me an adorable crayoned picture through snail mail. At the time, all of the Web terms—now part of my vernacular—were new and exotic.

Looking back at An Apple a Day with a more critical eye, I can see that many of the pictures are distorted because I did not have a clue about design fundamentals like aspect ratio (when resizing an image, there is an option to retain aspect ratio so the smaller image can look the same as the original without any distortion). Yet nobody complained. Perhaps none of the participants themselves even noticed; after all, for many it was their first online project.

Then again, perhaps no one complained about how the website looked because the content itself was so appealing. Consider the following example of an apple poem from the website:

Drinking apple cider
Yum! Yum! Yum!
It looks like liquid gold
Tastes so fruity

The Australian student participants decided to take a tongue-in-cheek approach to writing their poems. Relying on a keen sense of humor, they submitted witty verses, such as the following poems from a school in Western Australia:

A camel
dribbled on Janelle's hand
when she fed it an apple
at the zoo
because camels have no table manners.

My apple
comes with me
everyday [sic]
to school in my lunchbox
because I like him too much to eat him.

The project participants were delighted, and it began to occur to me just how powerful international classroom collaboration could be—how the Internet was actually delivering on its promise of a new small world. It seemed quite obvious and enormously exciting that this simple poetry unit had become a genuine multicultural experience for the teachers and students involved. Through this project, I discovered how online student-centered activities enabled my students to learn at their own pace and level while I helped as needed. They love this dynamic and have become more mature, confident, and motivated. An added bonus is that having students create poetry and read student-created poems ties into state curriculum standards.

Well, that was it for me. I was hooked. Now neither my academic workload nor any other distractions would keep me from conceiving and coordinating a second collaborative Internet project.

The Journey Continues: Winter Wonderland

Anyone who knows me will attest to the fact that I complain bitterly each year when trees lose their leaves and the temperature drops. Skiing, ice-skating, sledding—none of these have any appeal for me. So I was more than happy to spend the winter of 1998 in my warm house clicking away at my computer.

Feeling slightly more comfortable about coordinating projects, thanks to the success of An Apple a Day, I decided to organize a more elaborate unit for my second project, Winter Wonderland (http://kids-learn.org/a/winter2nd/index.htm), a website that includes a page of age-appropriate winter-related books. Every participating class chose a book with a winter theme. I asked the students to participate in literary activities such as writing a book review, interviewing fictional characters, or creating new endings for stories. By now, I had discovered the hypertext markup language (HTML) editor FrontPage, which did the tedious website coding for me and allowed me to add graphics easily so participants were no longer limited to one graphic per webpage.

Seasoned teachers know that January can be a particularly challenging month in the classroom. Students and teachers often lose momentum after the long winter holiday, and getting up early on cold, winter mornings is no easy task. This project generated so much enthusiasm that it proved to be the perfect anecdote to the January blues.

In observing my students exploring the website, I discovered that Winter Wonderland appealed to Howard Gardner's theory of multiple intelligences. In this theory, Gardner expanded the concept of intelligence to include seven intelligences. Among them are linguistic intelligence, music intelligence, and bodily-kinesthetic intelligence. For example, auditory learners enjoyed hearing the music and audio clips, whereas visual learners enjoyed viewing the student-created graphics and typography. As for tactile learners, they liked using the mouse to point and click their way through the website and particularly enjoyed the interactive games such as Dress Frostina (www.comsewogue.k12.ny.us/%7Essilverman/frosty2001/game/imagecollage.htm), where students are instructed to mix and match some of Frostina's outfits by using the mouse to drag the pictures.

School media specialists also love this project because it motivates students to visit the library and check out the winter books featured on the website. Teachers adore the lesson plans and supplementary, interactive activities. The teachers in my school found this project especially handy on bitter cold days when students were not allowed to play outside during recess. The teachers would tell the students that they could explore the website during their free time, and students did not mind being stuck indoors when they could escape online.

Research suggests that performance improves when students write for authentic audiences. When students perceive that the teacher is the sole audience, the result is an "arid wasteland of purposeless sentences and paragraphs" (Dollieslager, Thompson, & Pedersen, 1993, p. 12). I have seen how writing becomes much more meaningful for students when they know real people will be reading their work. My students were extremely quick in picking up the smallest grammar or spelling mistakes in the showcased texts. I could not believe how they naturally assumed the roles of editors and critics, spontaneously performing close readings of texts. Not to mention the fact that they were having the time of their lives!

My students and I decided to evaluate the Web work created by other students more formally by creating and using a rubric. Together, we worked on a sample rubric and used it to evaluate other websites. The students then created and applied their own rubrics in collaborative groups. Beyond the usual writing issues of clarity and mechanics, we realized that Internet publishing also demands basic skills in typography and graphic design. As the students evaluated other student work published online, they gained awareness of the challenges in writing for electronic publication, making comments such as "He should have colored darker" and "I can't read with the font she picked." After looking at various websites, the students noticed that even adults frequently made mistakes, such as using dark background and font colors. In evaluating sites, students gained insight into the characteristics of high-quality web content and constructed their own knowledge about new literacy skills.

One teacher who asked to participate in Winter Wonderland hailed from Pushkin, Russia. I was delighted for her class to join our project. As it turned out, she and her students misunderstood the project guidelines and, rather than choose a book and submit related activities, they simply wrote, in their best English, why they liked the winter season. For example, one student named Vanya offered, "I like the winter of themes, that I can go for a drive on sledge, to trench and to jump in snow-drifts, I love to play snow-drifts." I showed the submissions to my second-grade class, eager about what my ultracritical students would say. I was both touched and impressed when they unanimously expressed the sentiment, "Wow! They write English much better than I could write Russian!" Not a single student made fun of the broken grammar or complained that the Russian students had not followed the project's guidelines.

Winter Wonderland underwent the New York Academy of Teaching and Learning State Peer Review in Albany, New York, and my class was awarded a Model Schools grant for a US$1,000 color printer. I was really surprised because my collaborative project did not conform to the state's more traditional educational model. But Winter Wonderland did meet state standards, and it was accepted by the academy as legitimate. This acknowledgment was incredibly rewarding for me, and I felt that my work had resulted in a real pedagogical achievement.

One More Journey: Frosty Readers

In winter 2000, I had developed a collaborative Internet project that was so popular it has become an annual event: Frosty Readers (http://kids-learn.org/frosty). Designed to meet New York state learning standards in the English language arts (Levine, 2005), the project's objectives were to develop literature appreciation, language skills, and creativity and to encourage a higher level of thinking among lower elementary-grade students.

In Frosty Readers, I asked the participants to select books with winter themes and to conduct related activities for Web publication. Some activities included creating a new ending to a story, rewriting a story as a play, writing a poem about a book or a book character, and writing a paragraph about a favorite or least favorite character. I also gave students the option to create illustrations on paper or on the computer. To include a variety of winter stories, I requested that no more than two classes work on the same book. A book list was provided on the website, and participants were invited to select their own books, which were added to the list. Whenever I think about Frosty Readers, the first book that comes to my mind is *Thomas' Snowsuit* (Munsch, 1985) and the activity done by one of the project's participants, Mrs. Gialdini's third-grade class at Warwick School in Fremont, California. I continue to share exemplary creative work accomplished by this class at technology conferences and with children in different classrooms.

In *Thomas' Snowsuit*, Thomas does not want to dress appropriately for the weather. One student sympathized with his plight and shared a story of her own fashion woes, along with an illustration she created using Kid Pix software (see Figure 7.1):

My Worse Clothes

I do not like wearing this pink dress. I do not like the color pink. It is itchy inside. I try to sit a different way but my mom will say, "Sit properly." When I wear it my mom says it looks pretty on me. I don't think so!

Although other second-grade teachers I know who were not participating in online projects would complain that they were begging their students to write, my students were begging me to let them write. What was my secret? I would simply share the work created by other students in classrooms from around the world. For example, after reading Mrs. Gialdini's student samples, my students wanted desperately to read *Thomas' Snowsuit* and to write their own worse clothes stories. In my opinion, there is nothing like the Internet for motivating students and providing them with a place to investigate, collaborate, and create within a global community of learners.

Figure 7.1   Illustration Titled "I Do Not Like the Color Pink"

Some teachers commented (see http://kids-learn.org/frosty/participants.htm) about the impact Frosty Readers had on their teaching and students' learning:

> Comments: Each year Frosty Readers gets better! I absolutely love the addition of the on-line games and activities by lots of the participants. My students like to read the books showcased on the site and then find the games to play after their reading. Frosty Readers gives me lots of new activities to use in my classroom—there are so many creative and awesome teachers throughout the world. Thank you to all who shared your activities with us—we'll definitely be "borrowing them"! Susan and Pattie, what can I say, you continue to impress me—thanks for all of your hard work on this project! (A. Madden, personal communication, February 9, 2002)

> Comments: Wow!! This was my first time as a Frosty Participant....What a super experience! My second grade class had a ball creating our Snowman Recipes for this project! I thoroughly enjoyed visiting all of the other activities and learned a great deal of super projects that I can implement in my classroom! My students "beg" to go and "check out" the Frosty activities and absolutely love doing the online activities! I thank you for giving me the opportunity to be a part of Frosty Readers 2002....It made a very mild winter, full of "frosty" fun!! (D. Marshall, personal communication, January 31, 2002)

Frosty Readers actually became a problem for me because of its popularity. The growing number of participants made it difficult to find the time to create all the webpages to showcase work from many classrooms. Fortunately, my friend and colleague Pattie Knox (technology support specialist for North Canton City Schools in Ohio) volunteered to help me host Frosty Readers 2001 and 2002. Several teachers who participated in the project were fortunate to have technology integration specialists in their buildings for technical support. In some cases, teachers sent e-mails to me and other project participants for technology solutions.

Pattie and I wanted to encourage Frosty Readers participants to include more technology integration in their project activities, so we launched Kidspired Frosty (www.northcanton.sparcc.org/~ptk1nc/Frosty2003/index.html). In this improved version of the original website, we asked the participants to plan activities using Kidspiration software, which can be shared as an online resource for everybody. Kidspiration offers several options for students to present their ideas, such as illustrations and Venn diagrams. The results of Kidspired Frosty were fantastic. One class used Kidspiration to create Venn diagrams, comparing how a student is similar to a snowman (Figure 7.2). The result is completely unlike any diagrams students are likely to find in a textbook.

Figure 7.2 Venn Diagram Comparing a Student to a Snowman

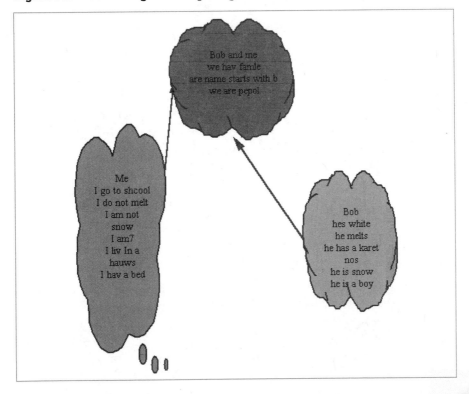

Figure 7.3   Illustration of a Chinstrap Penguin

Many classes took the initiative to use Kid Pix to illustrate characters from the books they read. Judging from the results, I suspect some of the students are future graphic designers and digital illustrators in the making (see Figure 7.3).

When we advertised Kidspired Frosty, Pattie and I invited participants to create their own online games and activities to share. We stumbled on a marvelous staff development incentive: Participating teachers rose to the challenge and, in doing so, learned how to use new online tools to create educational activities. Participants created their activities in Quia Corporation (www.quia.com). This website offers a tool that teachers can use to build various interactive activities easily without knowledge of computer programming.

A Student-Directed Journey: Stellaluna's Friends

By this point in my professional journey, I had become a collaborative Internet project proselytizer, and frequently was accused of being a Web junkie—someone who is addicted to surfing the Internet, writing e-mail, and basically attached to the computer all the time. Yet I was caught off guard when one of my students came up with an idea for a collaborative Internet project. We were studying bats right before Halloween. The book

Stellalluna (Cannon, 1993) motivated my student Deanna to dispel the bad reputation of bats. Although the students asked if we could do a collaborative project on bats, we already were involved in an online project and would be involved with Frosty Readers in the winter. So I told the students to remind me in February, and if they were still interested, we would do the bat project in the spring. The students made no mention of the bat project until February 1, when Deanna reminded me about it. Of course, I could not refuse, and it turned out to be a wonderful project.

In the online collaborative project Stellaluna's Friends, students helped improve the reputation of bats through scientific research, field trips, and online investigations. In particular, participating classrooms were asked to research a bat in their environment. If there were no bats in their area, the students could choose a bat that they would like to study. Students would then write reports, draw pictures, write poems and stories about bats, and send their projects to me to publish on their own webpages. The illustration in Figure 7.4 and the following excerpt capture the spirit of the project:

> Don't be afraid of bats because they won't bite you. Bats won't hurt you. Don't wake up a bat in the winter because they can die because they can't find food. There are about 1,000 kinds of bats in the world. Bats come from around the world. Bats eat different food. They eat fruit, flowers, fish and insects.

In coordinating this project, I discovered that students adored reading nonfiction writing produced by other students. Even students who usually disliked science lessons wanted to read the articles written by other students. I noticed that the students who usually struggled with reading were

Figure 7.4   Illustration Titled "Don't Be Afraid of Bats!"

not experiencing frustration, and I did not need to provide as much scaffolding as usual. The material the students read was written by students on or near their reading level and included familiar vocabulary words and definitions of new words. Without having to decipher the complicated scientific writing usually found in textbooks, my students could enjoy simply absorbing the bat information. Then, highly motivated to add to the online resource, it was so much fun to integrate English language arts activities such as writing poems and performing puppet shows with our newly acquired information about bats.

One of the highlights of Stellaluna's Friends was when two of my project participants, Shirley Crawford of Kikutaia Primary School, Paeroa, New Zealand, and Greenie Greenberg of Francis W. Parker School, Chicago, Illinois, met each other and decided to organize their own travel buddy project (www.geocities.com/EnchantedForest/Dell/8662/kiwikidz6hik.html). It was so exciting to see my project bringing educators together, encouraging further collaborations, and fostering new friendships.

A Multicultural Journey:
Cinderella Around the World

I have discovered that the trick to hosting a popular collaborative Internet project is to find a theme that fits into the curricula of many different school districts. The collaborative Internet project Cinderella Around the World (www.northcanton.sparcc.org/~ptk1nc/cinderella) ties into many subject areas and has such universal appeal that it attracted teachers from around the world.

In this project, I invited participating classrooms to read multicultural versions of Cinderella. Teachers were welcome to choose a Cinderella story from the recommended book list on the website or contribute a book to the list. After reading the story, students had to engage in language arts, social studies, math, or science activities that would be showcased on the website. Some of the activities were as follows:

- Compare the traditional Cinderella story with a different version.
- Write a book review.
- Create new endings for the story.
- Rewrite the story as a play.
- Explore the fauna and flora, geography, history, culture, and customs of the region where the story takes place.

■ Write a poem about the book or a character in it.

■ Create graphic organizers.

■ Feel free to select your own activity.

Although almost every child is familiar with the basic Cinderella story, this project introduces students to multicultural versions of this story, such as *Fair, Brown and Trembling: An Irish Cinderella Story* (Daly, 2000) and *Smokey Mountain Rose: An Appalachian Cinderella* (Schroeder, 1997). In fact, Cinderella Around the World featured books from at least 16 different countries.

Cinderella Around the World supports various New York state learning standards for English language arts (NYLearns, 2005) at the elementary level, such as,

> Standard 2: Students will read, write, listen, and speak for literary response and statement. Write in order to respond to text to describe characters, setting, or events. Listen to imaginative texts and performances in order to appreciate and enjoy literary works, and identify character, setting, and plot.
>
> Standard 3: Students will read write, listen, and speak for critical analysis and evaluation. Write to express opinions and judgments in order to compare characters, settings and events within and between stories. Listen in order to recognize differences in two or more versions of a familiar story.

Cinderella Around the World also easily integrates in other subject areas, such as social studies, art, and foreign languages. Consider, for example, how Michele Sowa of Clinton Avenue Elementary School, Port Jefferson Station, New York, used this project to create a rich, multidisciplinary learning experience for her second-grade students:

> Our class read *Domitila*, a Cinderella Tale from the Mexican Tradition. It was adapted by Jewell Reinhart Coburn [2000] and illustrated by Connie McLennan. The children had a wonderful time with this book, and it tied in so nicely to our Mexico/Chocolate Unit. We compared and contrasted *Domitila* and the regular version of Cinderella. The students learned many Spanish vocabulary words and created their own Domitila picture dictionary. We made Spanish/English counting books. We located Mexico on the map and learned a lot about the Mexican culture. We also found out that chocolate was discovered by the Aztecs in MEXICO! To culminate our unit, we practiced the new Spanish words as we made our own game boards for La Loteria. This game is the Mexican version of BINGO, and we can't wait to play it! OLE! (Sowa, 2001, n.p.)

I certainly cannot take credit for all the wonderful work the project participants accomplish, but I do take pride in having created a venue to showcase their inspiring activities. With the advent of digital camera technology, teachers who participate in my projects are now documenting their exciting activities with photos, allowing both teachers and students to enjoy vicariously some of their fun. After reading *The Korean Cinderella* (Climo, 1996), Mrs. Weber, a first-grade teacher at Greentown Elementary in North Canton, Ohio, and her class celebrated with a Korean feast of mandu (dumplings), kimchi (a vegetable pickle), and fried rice.

In my school district, a group of students were so excited by a script of *Smokey Mountain Rose* (Schroeder, 1997), which was adapted by Roxie Ahlbrecht's class in South Dakota, that they wanted to read Schroeder's original story for themselves. Unfortunately, the school library did not have the book. I told the students that if anyone went to the public library and found *Smokey Mountain Rose*, I would visit their class again and read it to them (at the time, I was the instructional technology integration specialist of my school district). Sure enough, one student tracked it down. After I read the book to the students, they decided to write their own script of *Smokey Mountain Rose*. I then sent an e-mail it to the class in South Dakota to thank them for their inspiring work. Well, the class in South Dakota then videotaped a production of their adaptation and sent it to the class in New York. Talk about a magical collaboration with a very happy ending.

Lessons Learned

Being a classroom teacher and project coordinator at the same time is a real opportunity. As teachers, we can choose a collaborative topic that ties into our curricula. This connection provides a chance to involve colleagues in the same building and will often generate excitement throughout the entire school district. When parents and administrators hear the buzz about a collaborative Internet project, they usually offer their support, which can help to make the project a success. One of the Frosty Readers project participants from Georgia told me that to have her students experience winter, the parent-teacher association paid for ice to be delivered to the school playground so students could build snowmen. My students were so proud to know that the project was hosted by Mrs. Silverman's Second Grade Class (www.kids-learn.org/class98). It gave them a real sense of ownership.

As we worked on our Internet projects, students learned new literacies such as how to navigate webpages, use the keyboard, save files, create graphics, scan images, and use e-mail. Children love computers and are not intimidated or easily frustrated by them. I usually had to teach the students one specific skill at a time, and if they needed help, their classmates were ready, eager, and willing to assist. Some former second-grade students volunteered to spend their recess in my classroom helping my new students. This peer mentoring was a wonderful experience for the younger students, who at the end of the school year asked if they could return in September to help my new students. These student volunteers were called technology mentors.

Teachers do not need many technology resources to participate in my collaborative Internet projects. Access to a computer with an Internet browser and e-mail enables a class of students to become successful participants. If there is only one classroom computer, students can take turns enjoying the showcased work. A projection devise is very helpful in this situation.

My advice to teachers who have never participated in a collaborative Internet project would be to join one that has a timeline they can work with and that supports their curricular goals. They also should make sure the project coordinator is easy to contact if they have any questions.

My Current Internet Projects

These days I am incredibly busy. I retired from the Comsewogue School District of Port Jefferson Station, New York, in June 2004. I currently am an adjunct professor at the New York Institute of Technology (NYIT). As an independent educational consultant I conduct professional workshops to their staff on technology integration.

As a technology integration consultant for Comsewogue School District, I find Internet resources for teachers and post them on the district website. I continue to coordinate online global cross-curricular projects. I am currently exploring ways technology can enhance literature circles. My most recent project, Literature Circles Extension Projects, will showcase projects created by students in grades K–12 and will include college students. All of my projects will remain online (http://comsewogue.org/~ssilverman/litcircles/index.htm) to be used as a resource for years to come.

As an adjunct professor, I am teaching a graduate-level course entitled Language Arts and Technology, offered through the NYIT distance learning program. I designed this course to make students aware of the many opportunities that technology can offer to enrich the language arts curriculum and provide students with the skills they need to be literate citizens of the 21st century. Students review and analyze how teachers use technology in their curricula and design activities based on the New York state and International Society for Technology in Education standards (www.iste.org/standards) to use in their own classrooms. This course has been so successful that I am now teaching it for the fourth time. Many of my students are pursuing a master's degree in technology integration, a degree that did not even exist when I started integrating technology into my own classroom.

Technology and Internet Resources I Currently Share With Teachers

I have found that it is not enough just to provide teachers with new technology; they need to learn how to integrate these tools meaningfully into their classroom learning. For example, whenever I teach computer software programs, I show teachers examples of how educators use these programs in the classroom. I have found that by introducing them to Miss Rumphius Award–winning sites, for example, teachers can learn from models of classroom-tested, teacher-approved technology integration.

Another resource I helped to develop in 2003–2004 is the ReadWriteThink calendar (www.readwritethink.org/calendar/index.asp), which resides on the website created by the International Reading Association, National Council of Teachers of English, and MarcoPolo Education Foundation. Teachers of all grade levels can find lesson plans, Web links, and suggested texts for each calendar day of the school year. My hope is that even the busiest educators will be able to integrate technology into their curricula thanks to this timely webpage. The ReadWriteThink website also provides interactive student materials that support literacy and learning. The interactive activities are perfect for students to use as a learning center activity. Also, the activities are so user friendly that students will want to use them at home if they have Internet access.

The Changing Face of Literacy Instruction

How times have changed since I started teaching more than 20 years ago. Teachers are no longer expected to be the "sage on the stage" but the guide on the side whose role is not to drill correct answers into students but to help them become critical thinkers. As educators, we need to teach our students traditional literacy skills along with new literacy skills. With so much data available to us at the click of a mouse, we need to help students learn how to make sense of it all. Students need to learn how to access, evaluate, and interact with information online.

When I first became an educator, I used only print materials for my lessons. Students had their textbooks, and the teacher's guides were always much thicker than textbooks because the teacher's role was to know all the answers. With the amount of information available on the Internet, students have access to as much information as educators. During my last few years as a classroom teacher, I assumed the role of facilitator and encouraged my students to create their own knowledge. I specifically prompted students to ask their own questions about a topic we were exploring and helped them find and evaluate information online. I remember when one class of second graders was doing a unit on bears and found conflicting information from a book and a website. When the students asked me what the correct answer was, I suggested that they send an e-mail to an expert in the field. My second graders sent an e-mail to a reputable authority, and within an hour, they received an answer.

As I mentioned before, it is very important to teach students how to evaluate information. They need to be taught that just because something is on the Internet, it is not necessarily true. Evaluating the credibility of a website is an essential skill for today's literate citizens. Further, students should be able to interact with the information they find. Teachers encouraged students to be creative and use this information as a learning resource for others to learn from.

Eight years ago, the only Internet connection my school district had was in the school media center. Today, all elementary classrooms in the Comsewogue School District are wired. Seven years ago, most teachers in my school district were using computer software for information because our Internet connection was too slow. Today these schools have faster connections and even have video conferencing. Today's students will be interacting in a highly technical world, and it is our job as educators to provide them with the skills they need to be considered literate citizens in the 21st century.

Nine years ago, when I embarked on this wonderful journey, I had a vision of opening up my classroom to the world. At the time, there were few connected computers in my school and I was a pioneer in my community. Many parents, teachers, and administrators were not convinced computers even belonged in the classroom.

The question is no longer "Should we have computers?" but "How should we be using computers?" Well, it seems to me that collaboration is one of the most exciting uses for Internet technology, and I hope that with faster Internet connections and more access to computers we will continue to learn from one another across time and space.

REFERENCES

Dollieslager, R., Thompson, V., & Pedersen, C. (1993). Exciting them to excellence: Publishing student work. In *Proceedings of Southeastern Conference on English in the Two Year College* (pp. 1–12). Chattanooga, TN: National Council of Teachers of English.

Levine, C. (2005). *English language arts.* Retrieved January 13, 2005, from http://www.emsc.nysed.gov/ciai/ela.html

NYLearns. (2005). *Standard area ELA: English language arts.* Retrieved February 25, 2005, from http://www.nylearns.org/standards/standard_tree.asp?StandardID=8&lev=sn

Sowa, M. (2001). *Domitila: A Cinderella tale from the Mexican tradition.* Retrieved February 28, 2005, from http://www.comsewogue.k12.ny.us/cinderella/sowa/sowa.htm

CHILDREN'S LITERATURE CITED

Cannon, J. (1993). *Stellaluna.* San Diego, CA: Harcourt Brace Jovanovich.

Climo, S. (1996). *The Korean Cinderella.* Ill. R. Heller. New York: HarperCollins.

Coburn, J.R. (2000). *Domitila: A Cinderella tale from the Mexican tradition.* Ill. C. McLennan. Auburn, CA: Shen's Books.

Daly, J. (2000). *Fair, brown and trembling: An Irish Cinderella story.* New York: Farrar Straus Giroux.

Munsch, R.N. (1985). *Thomas' snowsuit.* Willowdale, ON: Annick Press.

Schroeder, A. (1997). *Smoky mountain rose: An Appalachian Cinderella.* New York: Dial Books for Young Readers.

CHAPTER 8

The Flat Stanley Project and Other Authentic Applications of Technology in the Classroom

Dale Hubert

Dale,

    I have to tell you that your Flat Stanley Project, that I just happened to have stumbled on, has been one of the best things that has happened to me! I have taught for 23 years now, and this project has really sparked a new interest in learning for me! My kids know more about geography, letter writing, journaling and other cultures than they have ever before. I am so glad that I found your site. Thanks for all the hard work that you do to keep it current. I know that isn't easy. (Patty Rutenbar, personal communication, March 29, 2001)

The Flat Stanley Project (www.flatstanleyproject.com) that Rutenbar mentions had more than 6,000 classrooms from 37 countries taking part during the 2003–2004 school year, but it grew from very humble beginnings. I was making plans to switch from teaching grade 6 to grade 3 the spring of 1994, and I was looking for a way to involve technology to develop literacy. I was showing my grade 6 students how to use a search engine by typing in their last names to show them the results. When I entered one student whose name was "Stanley," a reference to *Flat Stanley* (Brown & Bjorkman, 1964) resulted in the search. I was intrigued by the title and at the end of the day I found a summary of the book. In the story, a falling bulletin board flattens Stanley Lambchop. At one point in the story, Stanley wants to visit his friends in California. In a stroke of creativity, his parents fold him up, put him in an envelope, and mail him there. This particular adventure greatly interested me and became the impetus for my project. My idea was to have students make paper Flat Stanleys and exchange them with a few other classes. The next day I went to my local bookstore and ordered a copy of *Flat Stanley*.

Although the Flat Stanley Project has evolved over the past 10 years, the underlying principles have remained the same. Students make paper Flat Stanleys and mail them, along with blank journals, to other classes on the Flat Stanley Project's list of participants. The receiving students involve the visiting Stanleys in their everyday lives and record in their journals Stanley's activities. After a short time, the students return the Flat Stanleys and the journals to the sender.

There is no fee to join the Flat Stanley Project and, apart from postage, no cost to take part. Some teachers participate all year long, year after year, whereas others are involved only for a few weeks. I had no guidelines apart from making paper figures and sending them along with introductory letters and blank journals. Some classes create one Flat Stanley per class; some create one per small group of students; and in some classes, where time permits, each individual student makes a Flat Stanley. Classes may use different approaches, but the common element in each project is that the students write about their Flat Stanleys as if they were real people. The Flat Stanley Project is an open-ended literacy activity with few rules, and teachers can modify it to suit their needs. It can be applied to virtually every area of the curriculum—from estimating distances between cities for math to learning about maps for social studies to writing poetry for language arts. For example, when a Flat Stanley returns from a trip, many teachers choose to read aloud the accompanying journal to the class and then plot his journey on a map. When I started this project, the Internet still had a lot of growing to do, and my hope was that the Flat Stanley Project would be part of this growth.

Beginning My Journey

I clearly recall how I became involved with computers. I was a first-year teacher at a special education school, and the vice principal brought in a computer for the students to use. It was an inadequate device with software that did not suit the needs of the students. For example, one student was eager to use the computer and had the reading skills that the programs required, but his cerebral palsy prevented him from using the standard keyboard. The keyboard in the PET computer was mounted on the case beneath the monitor, unlike today's keyboards that are attached to the computer by a cable, so it was very difficult to move this student's wheelchair close enough to the computer for him to use it. I eventually cut away part of a study carrel so he could move his wheelchair into position. Other students who had the fine motor skills did not have the reading skills, and the Commodore PET essentially was a text-based unit with limited graphic capabilities. Without waiting to be asked, I expressed my views. The response from administration was if I had so much to say about what was not right, then maybe I would like to show them how to do it the right way. They offered to send me to a computer workshop. My first thought was that I was the very last person who should be taking a computer course. I did not like computers, I could not type, I did not have the time nor the patience for computers, and I was not about to get on the computer bandwagon just because it happened to be popular. However, I was a first-year teacher and eager to please the administration. So I went to my first computer class because I felt I had to. I remember everyone sitting in front of their computers busily creating graphics and entering text. After a few minutes of sitting in front of my computer, I said to myself, OK. There's got to be a way to turn it on.

I gradually took an interest in computers and taught myself how to program using Beginner's All Purpose Symbolic Instruction Code (BASIC). I used BASIC to make programs more accessible to my special needs students. I removed time limits on games and reduced the complexity of math questions. In fact, I became so enthused that I invented an adaptive computer keyboard, wrote supporting software for it, began my own computer software company, and was even able to sell some software. It was certainly a learning experience, beginning with an idea, taking it through the prototype stages, refining it, redesigning it, and ending up with a professional looking product.

While I was working on my keyboards with the idea of making my fortune, I created the Flat Stanley Project as a volunteer with no intention of it amounting to anything very big. Today my software certainly takes a backseat to the Flat Stanley phenomenon.

In 1994 it was almost impossible to find websites that were motiviating, rewarding, and curriculum-related for students. After all, Tim Berners-Lee did not make his World Wide Web browser and Web server software available until 1991, and in 1993 Marc Andreessen first posted Mosaic, the predecessor to Netscape, for download. Even then, the Internet was not the visual smorgasbord it is today.

In the summer of 1994, before I began teaching grade 3, I began developing the Flat Stanley Project and posted messages on various bulletin boards inviting teachers to participate in my new initiative. My goal was to have perhaps 10 other classes to exchange Flat Stanleys with my students. When school began in September, I received quite a few reluctant writers in my third-grade class. They had poor literacy skills and were not interested in doing traditional remedial work to improve their skills. The majority of students had satisfactory ability, but the students' written work often did not match their potential. I felt that a project that connected my students to other students might increase their motivation to write because it would provide a real audience for their writing.

When I introduced the Flat Stanley Project to my class, the most interesting part for the students was creating the Flat Stanleys. The students enjoyed working by themselves or in small groups to create interesting-looking representations. However, some students would create many Flat Stanleys but not write the accompanying letters. I introduced the rule that before these students could make another Flat Stanley, they had to create a letter for the one they already had created and mail it to someone. This encouraged students to focus more on the writing component.

For the first few years of the project, my students and I used a low-tech approach. The students would simply take their own Flat Stanleys home every evening and write in their journals. After a week or two, each student would exchange his or her Flat Stanley with another classmate's, take that classmate's Flat Stanley home, and write in the classmate's journal. I usually assigned journal writing as homework anyway, so having a Flat Stanley to write about made it easier for the students.

When I was satisfied that the students could successfully complete Flat Stanley journals within the classroom, I decided it was time to involve other schools. I did not have the necessary computer skills to post my project on the Internet; however, Daryl Hunt, a former sixth-grade student of mine, gave me some guidelines in hypertext markup language (HTML) coding. In 1995, I posted the Flat Stanley Project on the Internet for the first time and invited other teachers to participate. I used my local dial-up account and was able to persuade the owners of the service to let me use space on their server for a reduced fee. Because there was only one computer in my school that could send and receive e-mail, students had to take turns. At the end of the first year, a total of 13 classes were involved in my Flat Stanley Project: 7 from Canada and 6 from the United States. While that is only a portion of the number of classes involved today, at the time I considered it a huge success. In fact, that initial participation exceeded my expectations. During the following summer, I received e-mails from many teachers asking that I sign them up for the next year's Flat Stanley Project. Until then, I had not decided whether to try it for a second year, but that positive response encouraged me to continue to run the Flat Stanley Project.

The Flat Stanley Project Today

The Flat Stanley Project has continued to evolve and expand. For the last few years, it has been hosted by the Educational Network of Ontario (ENO;

www.enoreo.on.ca), an educators' resource website and one of Ontario, Canada's, largest Internet service providers. The Flat Stanley Project not only resides on ENO's server, but ENO offers technical support to users and has developed an automated application form. Prior to ENO's support, I had to enter manually each participant's name and mailing and e-mail address one at a time. In the early days of the project when there were only 500 participants, I was still able to enter manually every participant's information even though it was very time consuming. Last year when there were 6,000 classes from 37 countries on the list of participants, manual entry would not have been possible.

The Flat Stanley Project is open-ended, motivating, able to address a wide range of ages and abilities, and adaptable to almost any curriculum. The teachers can start from scratch and do everything on their own, or they can use the sample documents on the Flat Stanley website. For example, I developed a cover letter template that students could use to introduce the project to others. It includes examples of the kinds of information students might write in their journal when discussing Stanley's adventures, such as,

> Dear Friends:
> I am a Grade 3 student at Wilfrid Jury School in London, Ontario, Canada. I am sending you a Flat Stanley and his journal. (Please add extra pages to the journal.) I would like you to write down some of the things you do with Flat Stanley.
> What is Flat Stanley? Well, about 30 years ago Jeff Brown wrote the book *Flat Stanley* and in it Stanley Lambchop was squashed flat by a falling bulletin board. When he wanted to visit his friends in California his parents folded him up and mailed him. In this Flat Stanley Project the students in my class send paper Flat Stanleys all over the place. My teacher created this Flat Stanley Project and you can visit it at www.flatstanleyproject.com.
> We hope to learn about how people are the same and how they are different. For example, the population of London is 300,000. We are 200 kilometers from Toronto. Wilfrid Jury School has over 800 students. We have two teachers and 51 students in our class.
> In the autumn in southwestern Ontario where we live the temperature gets down to freezing at night sometimes. In the winter it can get as cold as −30° Celsius and in the summer it can get as hot as 34°.
> I hope Stanley enjoys visiting with you.
> Your friend,

In addition to the cover letter, the website includes examples of structured journals that may help students just learning to include detail in their writing as well as a sample cover letter that teachers of participating classrooms may send to a celebrity.

The blank journals that accompany the Flat Stanleys take several shapes. Some teachers simply send a blank school workbook, although the increased weight entails extra postage. A better idea is to make a booklet out of sheets of paper, with a box for pictures and some title suggestions such as "On the first day, flat Stanley and I...," "On the second day, flat Stanley and I...," "I had fun visiting with flat Stanley because...," and "This is a picture of what we did together." Of course, teachers and students may modify the journals, as well as everything else in the Flat Stanley Project, to best meet their needs.

Classes apply online to appear on the list of Flat Stanley Project participants (flatstanley.enoreo.on.ca/list_map.htm). Teachers and students then are able to contact other participants and make arrangements to send a Flat Stanley. The website includes images of other classes with their Flat Stanleys, including images of a Flat Stanley on a yak in Tibet, at the Taj Mahal, in Russia and Paris, and in Antarctica studying penguins. Thousands of Flat Stanleys have been welcomed at the White House by Secretary of State Condoleezza Rice, President George W. Bush, and former White House Press Secretary Ari Fleischer (www.flatstanleyproject.net/whitehouse/whitehouse.htm). Students make use of the Internet to play games on the Flat Stanley website, look at pictures from the picture gallery, locate addresses from the list of participants, and even view their own writing and pictures of themselves. In addition, they use search engines to locate mailing addresses of celebrities, sports figures, and other people of interest.

The technology used within the Flat Stanley Project encompasses both traditional technology—pencils, paper, and snail mail—and new technology—e-mail, scanners, digital cameras, instant messaging, electronic bulletin boards, and the World Wide Web. I recently digitally recorded one of my students reading her Flat Stanley story and posted it in MP3 audio format to the Flat Stanley website at www.flatstanleyproject.net/new_story.htm. Knowing her final product could be heard by listeners from around the world was certainly an incentive for her to create a quality story and make her best effort to read it aloud as I recorded it.

When we speak of technology, it is important to remember that chalk and pencils are examples of technology, and although they are not hi-tech, in the hands of a da Vinci, they can create more beauty than I can produce with the latest version of Adobe Photoshop. It is easy to become beguiled by the latest technology instead of engaged by the results that technology produces. The Flat Stanley Project uses technology that has become commonplace in the world of business. It is this combination of related technologies that creates the synergy of the Flat Stanley Project. Although the technology I mentioned is no longer considered cutting edge by experts in the field, it is just as powerful as ever and just as exciting to new users as it was to the experts. What makes it special is that it is in the hands of some of our youngest citizens. The Flat Stanley Project inspires primary-grade students to use the available technology, become comfortable with it, and benefit from it. This ease and familiarity will give them many advantages as they grow older and become involved with more sophisticated technology. If students can become competent with this technology at 7 and 8 years of age, imagine what their comfort level will be in later years with more advanced tools.

Motivated to Learn Through the Flat Stanley Project

People spend countless hours doing something they enjoy and not thinking of it as work. Visit any fitness club, and you will see people running on treadmills, lifting weights, and exerting themselves to their limits—it is hard to believe that they pay for the privilege. If their employers required them to do that, no doubt people would object to the working conditions. It is the same in the classroom. Most students usually are able to focus their attention for extended time on activities that they enjoy. This does not mean that the entire classroom experience always has to be nothing but fun and games, but it is worth noting that people do their best work when they are doing something they enjoy. Generally, students enjoy communicating. However, many teachers spend a great deal of time trying to make students stop communicating with one another and focus their attention on the teacher. An activity that involves communication can, therefore, be highly motivating. As Mark Twain observed, "The secret of success is making your vocation your vacation" (About, Inc., 2005).

There are now many entertaining websites for children, but a scarcity of websites that promote intrinsic literacy. By *intrinsic literacy* I mean personal motivation to learn a new skill or improve an existing one. This personal motivation is key to the success of the Flat Stanley Project. Some teachers may try to get students to work harder and spend extra time on their writing by cajoling, encouraging, and offering rewards, but with intrinsic motivation the students seek to independently improve their skills because they want to. Why do they want to? Partly because the recipient of a Flat Stanley is someone they want to impress or at least give a good first impression. Therefore, creating actual letters that students will mail is an authentic opportunity for students to contact a student in another class, a celebrity, an athlete, a politician, a relative, or someone with whom they have a special connection. I remember Ayan, an English as a second language student who was very reluctant to take chances and experiment with English. She rarely wrote at the beginning of the year, but by the year's end, I had a hard time sending her out for recess because she wanted to stay in the classroom to write more Flat Stanley letters to celebrities.

Sometimes students complain that they cannot think of anything interesting to write, so it is a revelation when they discover that things that are ordinary to them are extraordinary to others. For example, I photographed a visiting Flat Stanley from Hawaii playing with my students, who were up to their waists in snow. The snow was a common winter occurrence to my students, but the Hawaiian students—who saw the photograph on the Flat Stanley Project website—were amazed by it. One of our Flat Stanleys visited Australia and spent time in a kangaroo's pouch. My students were amazed by that, although kangaroos are commonplace to Australian students. The Flat Stanley Project provides wonderful opportunities for students worldwide to discover their similarities and celebrate their differences.

Authentic Learning Through the Flat Stanley Project

We can view children as immigrants. They are newcomers to the society in which they are born and have to become accustomed to the tools and rules within their new culture. Students have to learn the language; the clothing styles; the dietary preferences; the proper manners; the songs; the roles of men, women, adults, and children; and everything else that is part of a culture. Technology is one of the defining characteristics of any society. Archaeologists try to determine the tool-making skills of ancient civilizations and from that deduce language, cooperation, and other significant markers. While all components of society evolve and adapt, recent Western technology has been changing at a far faster rate than any other part of our society. For adults to adapt to a new technology it may be necessary for them to unlearn a previously learned skill or approach. Children who are surrounded by new technology simply take part in it without having to unlearn anything. Being naturally less inhibited, children are more willing to engage in the technology. Adults are often much more reluctant, especially when it comes to computers. Most of the students in my third-grade class were more competent with using the mouse and more eager to try new programs than most of the teachers in my school.

In *The Book of Learning and Forgetting*, Frank Smith (1998) explains that learning is effortless, enjoyable, and ongoing and that meaningful experiences stay with learners for a lifetime. He points out that repeating information by rote does improve memory but is only remembered in the short term and soon forgotten. Information learned in authentic, real-life situations will be remembered for much longer, sometimes forever.

The Flat Stanley Project calls on students to actually use some of the skills they have learned. If a student wants to write a letter to a celebrity and make a good impression, then that student is more interested in using the proper formatting than the student who is simply writing a letter because the teacher has assigned it. Students want to be successful and take pride in quality work. First, however, they have to make a commitment to it. Authentic learning is one way to help students make that commitment.

Students usually consider Flat Stanley letter writing as something special. It is a privilege to host the Flat Stanley and a privilege to write in the journal. Consequently, students are inspired to complete high-quality work. With traditional homework, many parents often find it difficult to help their children. Although it is good to be independent, many students reject the help that a parent offers, and the homework that is completed is, many times, below standard. A letter that is going to be read aloud to another class changes this by intrinsically motivating students to produce high-quality work. Therefore, students are more likely to seek parental assistance.

Children and adults, parents and teachers—all of us like to be recognized for our work. Many teachers have a bulletin board in their classrooms where exemplary student work is posted. This public acknowledgment is a good incentive for most students, but now that the Internet is ubiquitous, teachers have a much larger arena in which to post students' work. As the creator and facilitator host of the Flat Stanley Project, I invite teachers to send me letters of interest and high-quality student work for publication on the Flat Stanley website. Grandparents and other relatives from all over the world can access the website and read what the students have written. Many examples of student writing are available on the Flat Stanley website.

The Internet is not limited only to text documents. It is possible to post recordings of students reading their work in MP3 format. I plug a microphone into my laptop and have students read their work aloud, save it, and send it to me as an e-mail attachment to publish on the Flat Stanley website. A great piece of free software for recording students as they read is Audacity (http://audacity.sourceforge.net). Now friends and relatives can visit the website from all over the world and hear the actual voices of the students reading. This is outcome-based learning at its best—

authentic opportunities to produce real-life results. I also use Audacity when I do individual reading assessments with students. As they read, I record the sessions on my laptop computer so I can play them back later to measure improvement or at parent-teacher conferences.

In addition to the list of participants (www.flatstanley.com/list_map.htm) of the Flat Stanley Project, the curriculum suggestions (www.flatstanley. com/curriculum.htm), the pictures of Flat Stanleys in various locations (www.flatstanley.com/picture_gallery.html), and other information for teachers that are posted on the website, the website includes a games section (www.flatstanley.com/game_pointer.htm). Many school boards have policies that prohibit the use of games on computers, but many teachers wisely ignore this policy. After all, one of our goals as teachers is to encourage students to make better use of the technology. What better way to introduce technology than by letting students do something they enjoy? The games on the Flat Stanley website do require some thought and planning and are probably intellectually beneficial, but they certainly are fun.

Recognition of the Flat Stanley Project

As teachers, we often are not aware of the impact that we may have on our students. Pete Seeger, the folk singer and music pioneer, once played the bango and guitar for a second-grade class. One student in that class was the young Don McLean. Had Seeger not visited that class, would McLean still have grown up to become a musician and write songs like "Vincent" and "American Pie"? That is a question we can never answer for sure, but as teachers, we like to believe that we have made a difference. Occasionally, project participants will contact me to let me know how successful the Flat Stanley Project was for them. A few examples of this correspondence follow:

> My special education students in grades K–2 at Plains Elementary School in Timberville, Virginia are HUGE Flat Stanley fans! We have sent our Stanleys and he has had some incredible adventures! It's amazing how "Flat Stanley Fever" can strike so many, and spark so many imaginations. (J. Bridges, personal communication, 2002)

> The Flat Stanley project has allowed my first grade class not only to travel to the mainland United States but also to find so many caring people. They are totally in awe of what different classes have sent us through both the mail and the Internet. They have touched fall leaves, buckeyes, cotton plants and seen snow. Not something usually done here. We have made lifelong friends because of one flat boy. (J. Jacobs, personal communication, 2001)

I think that this was not only a learning experience for my students, but for myself as well. I have made so many friendships with people around the world, too! We share ideas, lesson plans, and those "cute" teacher stories we all have of our students. I recently gave a workshop on cooperative learning, and shared "our" special project with other colleagues in my school board. Thank you so much, Dale! (L. Sklavounos, personal communication, 2000)

Although I refer to this project as *my* Flat Stanley Project, I realize that its success is a result of the creative and innovative teachers who use it. Teachers and others who have hosted Flat Stanleys have contributed many of the images that I posted on the Flat Stanley website. One picture shows a Flat Stanley aboard the space shuttle Discovery and a certificate of authenticity from National Aeronautics and Space Administration stating that he traveled 4.6 million miles and completed 217 orbits of earth. Another picture shows a Flat Stanley on a dog sled in Antarctica.

When new participants join, they have the option of telling me how they heard about the Flat Stanley Project. The one that surprised me the most was when a new member told me he had seen it on the U.S. Department of State webpage. Sure enough, there was a picture of former U.S. Secretary of State Colin Powell with a Flat Stanley. I eventually added it to the Flat Stanley website (see www.flatstanley.com/colin_powell.htm). Not only that, but someone had made a great effort to write about what the former secretary of state and Flat Stanley had done together:

Stanley was very tired by the time they boarded Air Force One to fly back to Andrews Air Force Base on Sunday. When someone told him that by the time they got back to Washington they would have traveled nearly 9,200 miles, he felt even more tired—9,200 miles in four days! He barely kept his eyes open long enough to meet some more of the really great people who travel with the President, and then he settled back into his seat and drifted off to sleep, wondering where his next adventure would take him and how many miles he would travel on that trip. He loved riding on Air Force One, meeting all of the great people who travel with the President, and meeting Presidents and Kings and Prime Ministers, but he kind of hoped the next trip wouldn't be quite so hectic! (Craig Kelly, personal communication, April 2002)

The website included a link to my Flat Stanley website, so I sent a thank you note to the webmaster. Imagine my surprise and delight when, a few days later, I received the following message:

Dear Mr. Hubert
    Your e-mail made it! Thanks for your kind note. We enjoyed traveling with Flat Stanley.
    Colin Powell (personal communication, March 13, 2002)

Since only 13 classes participated in the Flat Stanley Project that first year (the 1994–1995 school year), the numbers have increased beyond my expectations. The Flat Stanley Project gradually became better known and began to achieve some formal recognition. In addition to Colin Powell insisting that his Flat Stanley story be posted on the State Department's website, there have been formal awards. The Flat Stanley Project received a Roy C. Hill Award in 1998, a Childnet International Award in 2001, and in the same year I was honored with the Prime Minister's Award for Teaching Excellence. Not long after receiving these awards, I received a Miss Rumphius Award icon to attach to the Flat Stanley website. At the time, I was neither familiar with the Miss Rumphius Award nor the nomination procedure. I soon discovered that other teachers decided my project was worthy to be recognized for its contribution to education.

Perhaps, for me, even more meaningful than the formal award is the recognition I receive from everyday people—parents, teachers, and children—who enjoy participating in the Flat Stanley Project just because. For example, imagine how touched I was after receiving the following message:

Dear Mr. Hubert:

I have to tell you how sweet my little 10-year-old Douglas is. A couple of years ago, he was given the project of making Flat Stanley and sending him on his journeys.

Well, Douglas chose his great aunt Pam to be Stanley's host although he didn't see her very often. Pam never had grandchildren and was thrilled to do this for Douglas. She was in the process of moving from CT [Connecticut] to KY [Kentucky] and she got numerous pictures of the move with Stanley. She even made an album and sent it back to Douglas to take to school. The funny part of Stanley's adventure was that he was accidentally packed in a crate by the movers. When Pam discovered that Flat Stanley was missing. She made everybody stop and find him. She even took a picture of him being "rescued" from the crate.

Well, when Pam got sick with cancer, Douglas sent her another Flat Stanley via the fax as a get well card. When I went the last time to see her she was in and out of confusion. But, as I sat there and held her hand, she opened up her eyes and smiled and said "Flat Stanley, huh." Her involvement with Flat Stanley really meant a lot to her.

When I got home yesterday, I had to break the news that Pam had died. She was 58. Douglas said, "I know what I'm going to do." "What?" I asked. He said "I'm going to make a Flat Stanley for Pam's grave for her to take with her."

He completed his Flat Stanley last night. He put a couple of little silk flowers in one of his hands and a little Hershey's miniature candy bar in the other (she really loved chocolate). I told him that Pam was really going to love having Flat Stanley go to heaven with her. He smiled.

Prior to receiving Michele's note, there were times when I felt like discontinuing the Flat Stanley Project. As it grew, it became more of a time commitment with some days requiring hours of my time just to keep up with adding new members and responding to e-mail. Michele's note helped me realize the effect of the project and encouraged me to resolve to continue it.

How to Bring Technology in the Classroom and Watch Students Learn

Often, teachers are frustrated because their goals for technology in the classroom surpass the tools they have at their disposal. If a classroom is not adequately outfitted with computers (my class had none when I first started), teachers should not despair—but rather go get them. I had the advantage of looking for computers just prior to the Y2K "crisis," and many businesses were giving away their older computers. Being Y2K compatible is not a concern with many of the activities my students undertake. I was able to collect 18 older computers, although they did require a good deal of maintenance to keep them running.

A year later (in 2001), I was astonished to discover that my school board was discarding computers that were more advanced than the ones I was scrounging under the assumption that no one would want older machines. I do not expect that my school board is any different from others, so I suggest that teachers befriend someone at the board office who is as frustrated as they are at the lack of technology in the classroom. The contact I made provided me with computers in his spare time, and it made him feel better because he did not have to watch as good machines were discarded and stripped for spare parts. He was able to provide me with many computers. If school boards cannot help, businesses probably can. What do businesses do with computers when they upgrade? Often, they discard them. Many businesses would really like to see their older hardware put to good use, but school boards are often reluctant to take on these machines. The school boards might wonder who will maintain these computers if they break, whether they are compatible with the ones the school district already has, and if they are good enough to use in the classroom. This is a wonderful opportunity for teachers to demonstrate leadership and just go out and get them. Over the years my double-sized team-taught classroom of 50 students acquired 26 P-166 computers with 2 gig hard drives, one PII-233 and one PII-450 with a 20 gig hard drive. For those not familiar with computer jargon, I can summarize by saying that these were very limited, very dated computers well past their prime, but still just as able to do word processing, browse the Web, and run programs as when they were new. They certainly met our needs. An additional bonus was that I found many parents of my students had either formal or informal computer training and they were very pleased to volunteer their time setting up computers, troubleshooting network issues, and offering free advice.

One or two computers cannot be considered a computer center for good technology integration. Teachers should aim to get enough computers so that one third of the class can be working on them at the same time. Once they have the computers, they will need to set them up in their classrooms in a way that maximizes space. I found that when the computers were very close together, there was no room for the students to use the mouse without bumping into the keyboard beside them. I made shelves and placed the keyboards on them, leaving a space underneath for the mouse. The shelves were attached to sections of 2-by-4s cut to 6-inch lengths and attached to the table with double-sided tape (Figure 8.1). Notice that the students can reach underneath the keyboards to operate the mice. This setup allowed us to have more computers situated in a confined area.

Figure 8.1 Keyboard Shelf

Once teachers have the necessary hardware, they will need to make some software decisions. Because I had no budget for software, I had to rely on freeware. An excellent open source word processing suite called Open Office (www.openoffice.org) is very similar to Microsoft Word but is available as a free download. In addition to the word processing program, the suite offers a presentation program, a spreadsheet program, and a drawing program. I installed Open Office on every computer and then assigned one computer to be the save location, which allowed students to go to any computer in the classroom and open their documents using the network instead of having to go back to the same machine each time. Open Office also has a webpage editor program.

The third-grade students I worked with were only 8 and 9 years old. The program was basic enough, however, that they were able to do the following:

- Use the word processor to write Flat Stanley letters; spell check, edit, and revise them; and save them for later use.
- Use the spreadsheet to create bar and pie graphs and compare data (e.g., I had the students use the Web browser to go to the Toys-R-Us website, copy and paste names of toys and their prices into the spreadsheet, and then run the program to add up the totals to see what their Christmas lists would cost).
- Use the Web browser to collect information on various themes we were studying (urban and rural, mining, forestry, weather, and magnets) and copy and paste them into their word processing documents.
- Use the presentation program to create page displays with transitions and images to support the themes they were researching.
- Use the webpage editor to create basic webpages with text, animation, and links to several webpages.

In addition to the computers, students engaged in Readers Theatre activities, and when they felt they had perfected their readings, I would record them using Audacity. I then published their readings on the classroom's webpage in MP3 format. Friends and relatives from anywhere in the world could then click and listen to these students read. This outcome-based approach provided incentive for the students to persevere and develop good reading skills.

We also used Read Please (www.readplease.com), a freeware text-to-speech program. Students who had difficulties reading could copy and paste information from the Web into the Read Please document and follow along as the synthetic voice read to them.

Later, in addition to the computers, we were able to borrow a set of 10 iPAQ Pocket PCs. The iPAQ Pocket PC is a handheld device, similar to the better-known Palm Pilot. The Pocket PC, however, runs Microsoft Word and when students write on the touch-sensitive screen using a stylus, the program converts it to typing that can then be printed or saved to a file on a computer. Some students even took notes on the Pocket PC while I was teaching a lesson and then printed them out. Another feature of the Pocket PC is that students are able to e-mail files to each other. Therefore, one student could take some notes and then wirelessly share them with peers. Students also learned how to download and install freeware games. By far, the most impressive part of using the Pocket PCs was how easily these 8-year-old students figured out how to use them and became totally at ease with them. I presented an introductory tutorial to the students, but after that, students discovered on their own the functions of the devices and began teaching each other how to use it.

Conclusion

The Flat Stanley Project has been a wonderful adventure for me and one I did not expect to have. I have had the privilege of interacting through e-mail with hundreds of teachers and knowing that tens of thousands of students have taken part. Numerous books and articles have covered the Flat Stanley phenomenon, and countless newspapers have featured stories about local Flat Stanley visits.

Through the Flat Stanley Project I was able to meet author Jeff Brown and even be a guest at his home. Sadly, Jeff Brown died on December 3, 2003. In an e-mail a few days prior to his sudden passing, Jeff told me he was planning to begin a new Flat Stanley book. He credited the Flat Stanley Project as one of the reasons for the continuing success of his book, and he was always an enthusiastic supporter. The Flat Stanley Project, in accordance with the wishes of Jeff Brown and his family, will continue.

REFERENCES

About, Inc. (2005). Retrieved January 13, 2005, from http://quotations.about.com/cs/inspirationquotes/a/Work12.htm

Smith, F. (1998). *Book of learning and forgetting*. New York: Teachers College Press.

CHILDREN'S LITERATURE

Brown, J., & Bjorkman, S. (1964). *Flat Stanley*. Ill. T. Ungerer. New York: HarperCollins.

CHAPTER 9

Connecting Technology and Literacy: A Journey From "How Do I Turn on This Computer?" to "My Class Is Blogging Their Book Reviews for Literature Circles."

Mary Kreul

In 1990, I moved into a classroom that had a computer and printer. I did not know what to do with either of them, so I pushed both into a corner, kept the plastic on the computer cart, and used the cart as an extra storage unit. It was not until a few years later, as I was completing my master's degree, that I began to read about how teachers were using the Internet and organizing webpages for and with their students. Because I needed a few more credits to fulfill degree requirements, I enrolled in a course on using the Internet in education. As I look back at the first day of class, when I needed to ask the instructor how to turn on the computer, I am amazed at the progress technology—and I—have made! Ten years later, I was fortunate to be recognized for my work with literacy and technology by winning a Miss Rumphius Award.

The Miss Rumphius Award was presented for the literacy-based technology work featured on the Grade 2K webpage (see Figure 9.1). My second-grade students and I created and maintained this website from 1998 to 2002. The webpage has served as a vehicle for sharing student work with the Richards Elementary School community (Whitefish Bay, Wisconsin), my students' families and friends (those in Whitefish Bay and worldwide), our Internet telecollaborative project partners, and the local community. The website also helped to open our classroom door to the wider world, provided an authentic audience for student work, and increased student motivation and effort as they discovered that people other than their teacher would be viewing their efforts.

Figure 9.1　Grade 2K Webpage

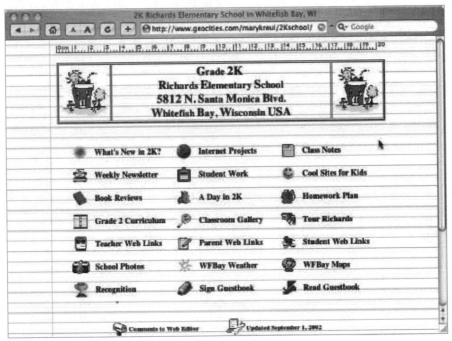

Working With Second Graders

The Beginning of My Internet Telecollaborative Projects

My students and I began our technology journey around the same time I was in graduate school, participating in basic e-mail projects that could be done on the only Internet-connected computer in school, which was in the library. I previously had written and was awarded a minigrant for US$500 through the school district to purchase a modem and Internet dial-up account. My students and I would discuss and plan our writing in the classroom. I acted as a scribe, writing down student ideas on chart paper. Later, when we could schedule time in the library computer lab, we would bring the chart paper, and I would type as my students helped me write and edit our message. Students did not and still do not have e-mail access at my school, so all e-mail was sent and received via my e-mail account.

The students and I participated in several Internet projects that first year. One of our early projects included participating in a survey run by students in a class in England who were wondering how students traveled to school. For this project we used a map of our town to locate the streets where students lived, and we calculated the number of blocks between their homes and school. Several students lived in Milwaukee, so we looked at a city map and made approximations for the number of miles they traveled to school from home. As we read other classes' responses, we learned that many students had similar experiences walking or being driven to school, but we were surprised that some students in other locations took a train or subway. Another project was sending e-mail messages with the months of our birthdays to students in a class in Illinois who were working on a data-collection project. Their teacher sent us a spreadsheet that graphed the final totals for the project. My students learned that we also could use AppleWorks presentation software to create bar or circle graphs of our birthdays.

After participating in several projects designed by other educators, I decided to sponsor a keypal project in which our class would exchange newsletters every month with several other second-grade classes from around the United States and the world—from places such as California, Maryland, Michigan, Missouri, New York, Texas, Canada, Ireland, and Sweden. The monthly keypal news included information about students' schools, towns, or cities; favorite books and authors; collections and hobbies; and summer plans. Depending on the topic, the entire class or small groups of students wrote letters as group writing activities, or each student wrote a letter as an independent writing activity. The keypal project, which was repeated with each new class of second graders for several years, provided an authentic reason for my students to learn to write clearly about specific topics, use correct writing conventions, and use voice to make their writing more personal and interesting.

All of these projects provided a wonderful opportunity for my second graders to communicate with their peers around the United States and the world—an authentic audience for their writing. They also learned geography skills as they located schools by latitude and longitude, math skills as they read graphs tallying favorite books, and science skills as they compared our weather to the weather where our project partners lived. One of my students even visited one of our partner classes while she was on a family vacation.

Connecting to Others Using Telecollaborative Projects

Telecollaborative projects, in which teachers and students connect via the Internet to work together on specific activities, looked like an interesting next step in my class's journey with literacy and technology. Global Schoolhouse (www.gsn.org), Scholastic.com (www.scholastic.com), and Intercultural E-mail Classroom Connections (www.iecc.org) are websites on which teachers may advertise their class projects and ask for classes to join in any number of short- and long-term activities.

A few of my favorite telecollaborative projects are Signs of Autumn, Signs of Spring (www.telecollaborate.net/education/ssf/index.html); Oh, the Places We'll Go (www.mrsmcgowan.com/places.htm); and Fairy Tale/ Folk Tale CyberDictionary (see Figure 9.2).

Signs of Autumn, Signs of Spring, sponsored by NickNacks Telecollaborate! and organized by Nancy Schubert, asks students to sharpen their observation skills as they observe changes in the seasons where they live. Students observe for changes in weather, the sky, temperature, plants, animals, and even people as fall turns to winter and again as winter turns to spring. Students share their observations through writing, drawing, and photography, which are published in an online format called a "zine." Each week, participating students can read about the changes in the season in places around the world and compare those changes with those changes they observed in their own locations. An interesting twist occurs when students learn about the seasonal differences in the northern and southern hemispheres. Children in Wisconsin are quite envious when they read that their project partners in the southern hemisphere are getting out their shorts,

Figure 9.2   Favorite Telecollaborative Projects

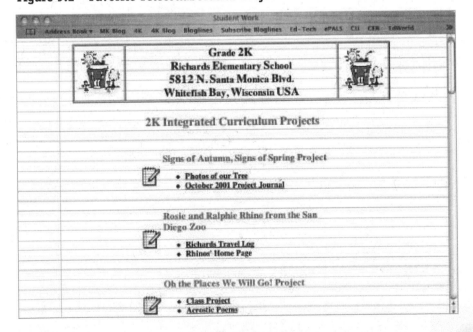

sunglasses, and T-shirts while they are getting out boots, hats, and mittens. Because our second-grade Full Option Science System (FOSS) science curriculum has a weather unit, this telecollaborative project easily fit into our curriculum. Along with science concepts, students also learned reading and writing skills as they read and composed their weekly weather messages.

Oh, the Places We'll Go was designed by Marci McGowan (see chapter 6, this volume) for primary-grade students. Classes were asked to read Margaret Wise Brown's *The Important Book* (1949) and then think about what makes a special place so important. Each class wrote a poem based on the pattern from *The Important Book*. Students shared their descriptive writing along with a matching illustration or photo on the project website. The poems focused on a place, and included interesting details about these places. My second-grade class wrote a group poem about Wisconsin, which was posted on McGowan's website at www.mrsmcgowan.com/placeskruel. htm. We did not stop there, however. Students then chose places that were important to them and each wrote an acrostic poem as well as a poem based on *The Important Book* pattern. Students used Kid Pix to illustrate their important place poems and crayons and markers to illustrate their acrostic poems. As an additional skill, they learned how to use a scanner to scan, crop, and save their paper drawings as Joint Photographic Experts Group (JPEG) images, a format for saving images for use on webpages. I posted the final, illustrated acrostic poems and important places poems on our class webpage (www.geocities.com/marykreul/2Kschool) so everyone's work was available to a wide audience of friends and families.

Janet Barnstable's website, Fairy Tale/Folk Tale CyberDictionary, provided a way for my students to learn about the literary elements of folk tales while they practiced their reading and writing skills. During the 2001–2002 school year, I chose the tall tale of Paul Bunyan, the famous character from the U.S. Midwest, for our folk tale project. The students and I read and compared several versions of Paul Bunyan and decided our favorite was Stephen Kellogg's (1984) retelling. The challenge was to write a retelling of Paul Bunyan's story in the format of an alphabet book. As a class we combined Bunyan's most exciting adventures into one extended tall tale that would be understood by younger as well as older children. It was quite a challenge, but this group of second graders retold the story using each alphabet letter, first in the usual story format and then in the format of an illustrated alphabet story. Our retelling of Paul Bunyan's story was posted on the project website (www.op97.k12.il.us/instruct/ftcyber/bunyan/index.html) for our partner classes to read. My students enjoyed reading the other fairy tale and folk tale retellings on the project website and were especially impressed with those from Australia and Venezuela. As they worked on this project, the students learned about the literary elements and structures of the fairy tale and folk tale genres, both of which are included in Wisconsin's reading and language arts standards. In addition, they read and compared different versions of stories, practiced writing descriptive sentences, became more skilled at story sequence, and decided on how best to illustrate their story.

Each of these projects focuses on literacy skills students acquire and practice as they read a variety of texts as part of a read-aloud, partner-read, or independent reading session. Discussions in my class focused on vocabulary specific to science, poetry, tall tales, story elements, and story sequence. Students learned to brainstorm ideas for writing, to organize those ideas using a graphic organizer and a storyboard, and to peer edit classmates' writing to help improve writing. They also practiced a variety of technology skills, such as word processing and digital photography, within the context of the curriculum, which transferred to many other activities during the school year. The most important consideration was that these students were using a variety of literacy skills for real purposes—sharing their learning with a wide audience of peers, teachers, and families using technology and the Internet.

None of these projects would have been as motivating or meaningful without the power of the Internet. From discovering the projects, to finding data, to viewing our partner class's work, to sharing student learning via project websites, to making the curriculum more engaging and relevant, my students and I were excited to be part of this telecollaborative work.

Software for Creative Students

In addition to projects that solely focused on the Internet, I taught my students to use software programs that supported their creativity. The idea was to teach them an array of skills, with the hope of merging these skills in more sophisticated projects. One of the earliest software projects I taught my students was how to make personal stationery using Broderbund's Print Shop Deluxe (PSD) (see www.broderbund.com), which was available in our computer lab and on our classroom computer. This software also can be used to make cards, posters, and banners. I demonstrated for students how to create a border, add and change fonts, and choose images for stationery. Next, we created a stationery template together step by step, and then students worked on their own unique, personal stationery. This easy activity enabled me to teach students basic computer skills such as opening an application, creating and saving a document on the server, adding text in a specific format, searching for images, revising text and images, and printing a document. We also discussed stationery design in terms of text size, font choice, images that portrayed personality and interests, and overall look of the final product. I provided students with 20 copies of their original designs to use for writing lists, thank you notes, and letters. Later in the year, students designed original stationery for teachers and other staff members as gifts for Teacher Appreciation Day. Recipients of these gifts were very impressed with the design and technology skills of these second-grade students.

Another invaluable software application for students is Kid Pix Deluxe (see www.kidpix.com), which also was available for my students' use in the computer lab as well as on the classroom computers. Several of my second-grade students were more familiar with this application than I was, so they helped teach their classmates how to use its many features. This opportunity to share their expertise was a wonderful experience for those who know how to use the software, especially two students who faced challenges learning in the regular education classroom. Those two second-grade students were able to gain the confidence and respect of their peers as they demonstrated their knowledge and assisted classmates with their projects.

Students were learning about family celebrations as part of the second-grade social studies curriculum, so we used this topic as a theme for a Kid Pix Deluxe slide show. After brainstorming the aspects of a celebration—decorations, special food, gifts, guests, and so on—we created a graphic organizer shaped like a spider web to help organize ideas. Each student then worked on a storyboard that included text and images to describe a special family celebration. A peer editor proofread the storyboard to make sure the student included important parts of the celebration. (Creating a pencil-and-paper storyboard first made our time in the computer lab more efficient and successful.)

This experience was valuable because it not only took students through the writing process but also demonstrated how a variety of technology skills came together in one project. After learning the technology skills necessary to create beautiful work in the form of a slide show, students then were able to use the Internet to share their work with others (www.geocities.com/marykreul/2Kschool/celebrations2001/index.html).

To Web or Not to Web

While thinking about the time and energy needed to create and maintain a class website, I decided there were several important reasons to do so. The Internet could do the following:

- provide my students with an authentic audience for their work,
- motivate them to do their best work because many people—families, friends, classmates, teachers, and project partners—would be viewing it, and
- connect reading and writing to other curriculum areas and teach important technology skills at the same time.

Although I learned how to write hypertext markup language (HTML) code, I did not have the time or interest to create the webpages by hand. I instead used webpage applications such as Claris HomePage and Adobe Page Mill to create my first class website. It was a very exciting and frustrating experience as I began to put together the first pages of a class website. When I ran into difficulties with font sizes, images, broken links, and much more, I found myself scouring the Web for helpful websites, reading technology books in the local bookstore, and sending e-mail to knowledgeable friends for help.

I checked the Web for other school and classroom websites to find out what other teachers were posting on their websites. At the University of Minnesota, I found the website Web66 (http://web66.coled.umn.edu), a treasure trove of school websites from around the world. I was especially impressed with the website of Arbor Heights Elementary School in Seattle, Washington, with its clean and colorful design (see chapter 3, this volume). I decided to design a website with the same friendly interface.

The first webpages I added to the start, or index, page were a calendar page, a student hyperlinks page, a class notes page, and a curriculum page. As my students became familiar with technology skills and telecollaborative projects, I gradually began to add their work to the website, and it has grown from there. Over the years, I have tried several different designs for the website, but I have always decided to keep the original design. The design works well for me—and my students—and it will probably remain as it is now for the foreseeable future.

Changing Grades

Creating Space for Technology

In fall 2002, I went from teaching second graders to teaching fourth graders. Although I was excited about the challenge of working with older students, I was concerned that I would no longer be able to collaborate with my online primary-grade colleagues on the wonderful projects we had worked on through the years. I also was concerned about the increased curriculum expectations for fourth grade and the fact that I would not have my homeroom class the entire day because students switched among teachers for certain subjects at this grade.

On the plus side, several of my fourth-grade students had been in my second-grade class, so I knew they would be able to help their classmates with computers and software. I was confident that I could take technology use to a higher level with these older children. The students had some keyboarding practice in third grade, so I hoped they would be fairly comfortable using computers for a variety of writing projects. Many students had experience using AppleWorks, Kid Pix, and Kidspiration in the primary grades, so I knew we could use those applications with a few quick review and practice sessions.

I wanted to have as much technology available in our fourth-grade classroom as possible, so when I moved classrooms, I brought along five Mac Performas (older Apple desktop computers). I scoured eBay (www.ebay.com) for printers and recycled some of my gently used home technology for school. On carts and tables throughout the classroom, we now have four Performas that share a printer and zip drive (a file storage device attached to a computer); another Performa that has a scanner, a printer, and a zip drive; two PowerBooks (older Apple laptops) that have printers, CD-ROMs, and zip drives; and an iMac (an Apple desktop computer), with a printer and a zip drive, that is connected to the school's network. I have my own personal iBook (an Apple laptop computer) and printer on my desk, which students cannot use, to keep track of grades, write letters, and work on other teacher responsibilities.

Kicking It Up a Notch

My fourth-grade students started off with the same PSD stationery project I had used with second graders. These fourth graders were able to do this project in less than half the time it took the second-grade students. The stationery project allowed fourth graders to be creative while learning and practicing computer and software skills. Students also created stationery for teachers and other staff members for Teacher Appreciation Day and received many positive comments on their computer design skills.

There were other advantages to using technology as a learning tool with 9- and 10-year-olds. I was able to teach two students how to use software applications, as well as the printer, zip disks, and the scanner; then those two students would teach the next set of partners, who would teach the next set of partners—a "train the trainer" model of learning. Students knew they could ask classmates to help them with questions or problems they had using the computers and not have to wait until the teacher was available. For example, while working on a webpage project, I showed two students how to use one of the scanners in our classroom and helped them to train another set of partners. These two students, who eventually became the scanner experts in the room, showed two other classmates how to scan their drawings. Classmates would go to these two students for scanner assistance before they came to me—a timesaver for me and a self-esteem builder for the scanner experts.

The fourth-grade students worked more independently on assigned or free-choice writing than my second-grade students did. Fourth graders also could start word processing their stories, reports, and poems quite early in the school year. The ability to use computers motivated students who were reluctant to write because of a variety of reasons. For example, students who had handwriting challenges were able to produce an attractive written product, which lessened stress and increased pride in their work. Fourth graders worked on peer-editing skills and were happy to help classmates revise their word-processed pieces. Peer editing word-processed pieces seemed much easier for many students without having to deal with issues of their own or their peer's handwriting and overall legibility of the writing.

Students were able to use their literacy and technology skills for several wonderful curriculum projects. The aforementioned Marci McGowan had introduced me to the concept of book reviews with her Junie B. Jones project when I taught second grade. I decided to replace the usual fourth-grade book reports with book reviews as a way to introduce persuasive writing and encourage students to read books recommended by their peers. We looked at models of book reviews on Marci's website and on other school and library websites. The class also helped to create an anchor chart, a reference that listed the features of an exemplary book review, which students used throughout the year.

By the end of the year, students had written and illustrated several book reviews, independently and with partners, which I posted on the class website. These Book Reviews by Kids for Kids (Figure 9.3) were intended for students to share good books with classmates and friends and to provide authentic writing experiences. Several of my students were familiar with the book reviews written by readers on Amazon.com and library websites, so they helped classmates see the advantages of reading published reviews before deciding which books to purchase. I hope to have students add to the book reviews on the class website each year to provide a wide variety of information on books popular with fourth-grade students.

Figure 9.3   Fourth-Grade Students' Book Reviews

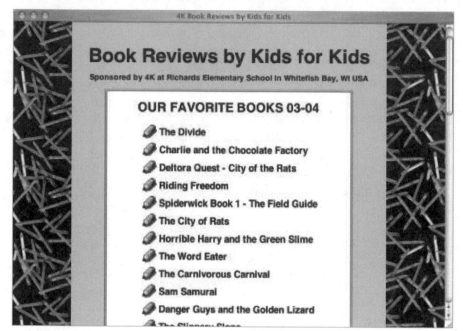

An offshoot of the book review activities was an ongoing classroom chart on which students listed books they wanted to recommend to their classmates. I often noticed students checking the recommendations on the chart, then choosing to read those books. Book reviews and recommendations are powerful ways to motivate students to increase the amount of reading they do—peer pressure in the most positive way.

Each year fourth graders from our school take a field trip to Wade House, which contains a restored stagecoach inn, blacksmith shop, and sawmill built in the 1860s in Greenbush, Wisconsin. A highlight of the trip is learning the stories of the children and adults who visited or lived at Wade House in the early days of Wisconsin statehood. As a follow-up activity, students imagine that they are living in the 1860s and write descriptive essays from the viewpoint of a person who visited or lived at Wade House. After creating story webs to organize their ideas, students typed first drafts, worked with peer editors to polish their writing, and checked with me for a final edit before producing final copies of their essays. Students also drew portraits of their characters, which they scanned for the class webpage. These descriptive essays and illustrations, which I posted to the class website (Figure 9.4), helped students

Figure 9.4 Wade House—Life in Wisconsin in the 1860s

connect their lives to the lives of people from the past. The class received several e-mails from parents, grandparents, and district staff members complimenting them on their knowledge of history and their writing and illustrating skills.

Later in the year, fourth graders studied Wisconsin history as part of the social studies curriculum. Lisa Roberts, our library media specialist, helped students research famous Wisconsinites using a variety of online and school library sources. In the classroom, students continued their research using Grolier compact disks, World Book Online, encyclopedias, biographies, and other materials, and they created graphic organizers to plan their writing. As students worked on their essays, wonderful side conversations took place. Students worked together discussing their ideas and verifying dates and facts. This assignment went far beyond a basic written piece to a literacy experience in which students brought personal interests and background information to experiences in reading, writing, listening, speaking, thinking, and researching. At the end of the school year, students often mentioned the Famous Wisconsinites project, in which they used a variety of technologies to create a published Web product (see Figure 9.5), as one of their favorite activities of the year.

Figure 9.5 Famous Wisconsinites Webpage

Smile and Click

Visual literacy is the ability to use images to create and convey meaning. Annette Lamb (2001) writes, "Just as we learn how to read text, we need to learn how to read pictures. Students need skills and strategies for reading, interpreting, using, applying, designing, composing, and creating visuals from line drawings to color photographs." A digital camera is one of the best tools teachers and students can use to share teaching and learning with one another and a wider audience in a visual format. My second graders had participated in a "Day in the Life of..." project, but digital camera technology was not available at that time. I decided that my fourth graders would learn how to use a digital camera and work on descriptive writing skills by creating a similar project—A Day in 4K (www.mskreul.com/dayin4K/dayin4k.htm)—which I could post on the class website.

As a class, we set up a timeline of the most important events that occur during the school day. Students worked in small groups to create event storyboards as they planned their part of the project. Several students had digital camera experience, either in second grade or at home, so those students became the photo experts. Planning the photos was a challenge because school district policy does not allow teachers to post student photographs online. These students had to draw from their creativity and originality to portray the busy day of a fourth grader—without using any fourth graders in the photos. The resulting project was very successful as students learned about telling a story using images as the centerpiece and text as an added feature. As they worked on these exciting technology projects, my students were learning how to use new technology and literacy skills to help them comprehend and convey meaning.

Telecollaboration Connections

Telecollaborative Internet projects are a wonderful way to integrate different areas of the curriculum and develop students' interpersonal skills. These projects help students become skilled in "new literacies" (Leu, 2001). As previously stated, telecollaborative Internet projects help students connect with peers from around the United States and the world and provide authentic purposes for reading and writing. Teachers also can integrate telecollaborative Internet projects with other curriculum areas such as science, social studies, and technology, not just reading and writing.

I was very happy to be able to continue several of my favorite telecollaborative Internet projects with fourth graders. Postcard Geography, a wonderful social studies project organized by Leni Dolan, asks classes to send snail mail or e-mail postcards to partner classes around the United States and world (http://pcg.cyberbee.com). Postcards include textual and pictorial information about each class's geographic location, which helps students learn about the social and physical geography of various communities.

My students worked in teams to gather data for Signs of Autumn, Signs of Spring, which was different from the whole-class data collection done by second graders in previous years (www.mskreul.com/signsspr03.html). Fourth graders practiced collaboration skills in small groups and decided how to represent their data using a combination of text, numbers, and drawings. They were able to compare and contrast their autumn and spring data collections and the collections of project partners in a much deeper way than second graders could.

There were exciting new telecollaboration projects for fourth graders to join, including You Are My Hero: A 9/11 Remembrance Project (www.angelfire.com/ny/ProjectKAVE/index1.html). This project, sponsored by Harriet Stolzenberg, helped students remember the heroes of September 11, 2001, by honoring the heroes in their own lives. We read and talked about heroes and compiled a list of qualities a hero might have.

Students then had the difficult decision of choosing a person they had read about or a person in their lives who has the qualities of a hero. Fourth graders demonstrated their knowledge of using voice in their writing as they composed these heartfelt tributes to their heroes.

Technology, literacy, and social studies were the focus of the Student Created Document Based Questions project (http://comsewogue.k12. ny.us/~ssilverman/dbq2003/index.htm), organized by Susan Silverman and Melissa McCullan. In this project, students interpreted primary source documents using their schema, the words and images in the documents, and research skills. Because fourth graders study Wisconsin as part of the social studies curriculum, we used primary source documents about the history of Wisconsin, which we found at the Library of Congress website (www.loc.gov). A favorite image of ours from that website was the sheet music for the University of Wisconsin school song, "On Wisconsin," from the early 1900s, which shows the image of a Badger football player. An interesting part of this project was working with my fourth graders to review the editorial comments about their document-based questions made by other students via e-mail. As students read the comments, they discussed the need to write clearly and use correct spelling and punctuation when writing for an Internet audience. Knowing that their writing would be read by a wide audience motivated students to work harder on the characteristics of their written work, including what they had learned about using ideas, voice, word choice, fluency, and conventions.

One of my fourth-grade classes worked with Rachel Karchmer's preservice teachers and Marci McGowan's first graders on telecollaborative literature circles based on two popular children's books—Judy Blume's *Tales of a Fourth Grade Nothing* (1972) and Astrid Lindgren's *Pippi Longstocking* (1950). (Go to www.mskreul.com/Tales/index.htm and www.mskreul. com/Pippi/pippi.html for more information on each project.) Each group read and discussed the books with its classmates in a literature circle format that fit the age of the readers. After they had finished the book, first graders, fourth graders, and college students created a variety of wonderfully written and illustrated projects based on ideas shared by the college preservice teachers. All student work was posted on their respective classroom websites and linked together so all participants could view it.

If I Had Three Wishes...

There are certainly frustrations in the teaching profession today—the lack of time to plan integrated lessons and teach those lessons; the focus on standardized tests, which narrows the choices teachers have for teaching and students have for learning; the lack of access to current technologies caused by financial concerns and school priorities; and the lack of vision for the many ways technology can inspire learning.

If I had the proverbial three wishes, I would wish for a wide range of technology in my classroom that students could use throughout the day whenever it fit into the fourth-grade curriculum, regardless of the subject or time of day. We would have a wired laptop cart containing 15 iBooks, which students could use in and outside our classroom. We also would have several digital cameras, a digital video camera, a scanner, a photo printer, and age-appropriate software, so students could work on classroom and telecollaborative projects at any time rather than wait for a scheduled time slot in the computer lab or share equipment.

I also would wish for the vision, funding, and support needed to provide the technology and curriculum materials to best prepare my students for the future. Vision is imperative—for the possibilities of technology to enhance learning for students of all abilities and ages; for the new literacies that technology requires of our students; and for technology that challenges teachers and students to create new ideas, tasks, and meanings. Sufficient funding is very important, even in these days of tight school budgets. Students and teachers need hardware and software that enable them to strengthen and expand the curricula, thus leading to increased curiosity, knowledge, and comprehension of the world around them. Support ranges from administrators who model and encourage technology use, to parents who encourage school board support of technology funding, to colleagues who collaborate to create lessons and activities using technology, to technology staff who promote and ensure technology access for student use.

My final and most important wish would be for more time—time to plan creative and motivating projects with colleagues (both online and in my district); time to work on integrating literacy skills and the use of technology into my entire grade-level curriculum; and time to work with my students on projects that help them to be creative, solve problems, learn skills, and work with peers as collaborative partners.

The Next Steps in My Journey to Connect Technology and Literacy

One of the next steps I plan to take is to experiment with using blogs, or weblogs, with my students. In summer 2004, I attended a motivating session at the National Educational Computing Conference (NECC) on educational blogging presented by Tim Lauer, Marion Holland, and others (Richardson, Laver, Holland, & Schlick-Noe, 2003), and decided that this would be an exciting way to promote new literacies with my fourth graders. Blogs allow teachers—and students—to post their ideas and comments on the Web quickly and easily, without having to create a webpage. We simply can type the text into a text box, proofread, and immediately post the writing to a blog page. My students have started to "blog" their book reviews as well as descriptions of what happens in curriculum units; activities in art, music, and library; special assemblies; and classroom guests, just to list a few. I will gradually move information and student work I previously posted on the class website to Ms. Kreul's Class Blog (see Figure 9.6) to give students a more active role in the blogging process.

In the future, I would like to have students record daily classroom news, report on field trips, create timelines for classroom activities, and add photos to a class blog. I also would like to create a teacher blog, similar to the one Tim Lauer of Lewis Elementary School, Portland, Oregon, uses to communicate with parents and students (www.lewiselementary.org).

Figure 9.6   Weblog of Life in a Fourth-Grade Classroom

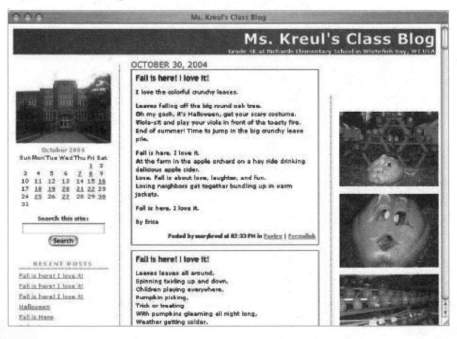

Conclusion

Technology and the Internet have become important tools to help me integrate language arts skills and informational literacy skills within the context of my school's second- and fourth-grade curricula. The use of technology has changed my teaching style, which is now more project-based and student-centered with an emphasis on process over product. My students develop important literacy skills—communication, collaboration, problem solving, and purposeful reading and writing—as they send e-mail to keypal friends and read their replies, help build class webpages to share their poems and science logs with a worldwide audience, and use digital cameras and scanners to record the visit of a stuffed-animal platypus from Australia. My website illustrates the various activities my students engage in as I use the Internet to support their learning.

As I begin my second year as a fourth-grade teacher, I feel more confident in my knowledge of the grade-level curriculum and standards and the abilities and interests of students this age. Another important step will be to better integrate the curriculum to include literacy skills across the content areas and to make better use of our classroom time.

Technology and the Internet have changed the way my students learn through the use of real-time communication with peers and experts, student-created webpages, and curriculum-based collaborative projects. My students now have the opportunity to communicate using multimedia resources, acquire information from a variety of sources, and share their learning with a worldwide audience. Plus, all our activities focus on literacy skills that are aligned with district standards and curriculum goals.

The Internet also has provided me with a wonderful network of colleagues and friends who have helped me grow as a teacher and a technology user. One of the reasons for the success of the Famous Wisconsinites project previously mentioned was the library media specialist and I worked together to plan and organize student learning. I strongly encourage teachers to collaborate with their library media specialists, technology teachers, art teachers, and other colleagues to bring the fullest range of expertise to integrated curriculum projects. Collaborators can brainstorm ideas, share resources, and provide support and encouragement for one another as they integrate technology into the curriculum. Those friends and colleagues have motivated me to try new technologies, encouraged me when I became discouraged, and created wonderful collaborative projects that I could use with my students to enhance our classroom activities. Together, we have created a true community of learners, which has allowed me to open my classroom door and venture into an exciting new world of teaching and learning.

REFERENCES

Lamb, A. (2001). Digital glyphs: Imaging ideas in a visual world. *Eduscapes*. Retrieved January 2, 2004, from http://eduscapes.com/sessions/digital/digital1.htm

Leu, D.J., Jr. (2001, March). Internet project: Preparing students for new literacies in a global village. *The Reading Teacher, 54*, 568–572. Retrieved February 24, 2005, from http://www.readingonline.org/electronic/elec_index.asp?HREF=rt/3-01_column/index.html

Richardson, W., Lauer, T., Holland, M., & Schlick-Noe, K. (2003, July). *Bringing literature circles to the Web: Blogging about books.* Presented at the National Educational Computing Conference, Seattle, WA.

CHILDREN'S LITERATURE

Blume, J. (1972). *Tales of a fourth grade nothing.* Ill. R. Doty. New York: Dutton.

Brown, M.W. (1949). *The important book.* Ill. L. Weisgard. New York: HarperCollins.

Kellogg, S. (1984). *Paul Bunyan.* New York: HarperTrophy.

Lindgren, A. (1950). *Pippi Longstocking.* New York: Viking.

CHAPTER 10

Bee Stings, Wooden Blocks, and Web Browsers

Tim C. Lauer

It was the second day of the school year, a warm September day. Just after lunch, students were working at various learning centers around the classroom, when Ted, a first-grade student in my mixed-age K–2 classroom, was working on a project at the Lego table. Ted came up to me and informed me that a bee had stung him. I checked the sting area and called the nurse to make sure Ted was okay. He was, so we went over to the Lego table and found the offending bee on the carpet. The students were very excited and concerned about the bee. Malia, a second-grade student, suggested we look at the image under our video microscope. This technology allowed us to view things under the microscope on a classroom television. We set up the microscope area as a classroom learning center, and students examined the bee. As the students and I looked at its wings and legs, we decided that Ted should write about this incident and post the story on our classroom website. After using the digital camera to capture images of the bee, we uploaded them and Ted's story onto our classroom website.

After a few days, we started to receive e-mail from people who had read of Ted's bee-sting adventure on our website. Most people expressed appreciation for the images and the story. One particular e-mail was from Dr. Stephen Buchman, an entomologist at the University of Arizona. He wrote to send good wishes to the students and explained that he was an expert on bees and wasps. He wanted to let us know that the culprit was not a bee. From looking at the images on our webpage, he determined that the insect was a yellow jacket wasp. He explained the differences between these insects and referred us to several Internet resources where we could learn more about bees and wasps. I shared this information with the students. From our discussion we decided that we needed to fix what we had posted on the Web because it was wrong. The students and I made trips to our school library and found books about bees and wasps. Using a data projector to display the computer on a screen, we visited the website shared by Dr. Buchman and began to learn about the differences between bees and wasps. After this research, we edited our website to reflect our learning. In addition, we sent Dr. Buchman an e-mail to thank him for correcting our mistake, for sharing his knowledge and expertise, and for starting us down a road that improved our knowledge and research skills.

This particular example brought home to me the promise of the Web as a publishing and communication tool in my classroom. By putting classroom projects on the Web, we are working to develop an awareness of an audience for the students' work. When my students learned that we published incorrect information, their first inclination was to fix it. Without the ability to share our work with others, we might never have had this opportunity.

The Buckman School Room 100 Classroom Webpage

My Miss Rumphius Award–winning project, the Buckman School Room 100 Classroom Webpage (Figure 10.1), involved the publication of a website devoted to sharing my experiences as a teacher and the experiences of the students in my mixed-age early-childhood classroom.

The website slowly grew, at first just containing general information about our classroom and our school. Gradually, I began to add content related to classroom experiences that took place in Room 100. Our school staff added newsletters, daily announcements, and homework assignments, and by the time I left Buckman, the website had become not only a vehicle for sharing our classroom experiences but also a communication device that informed parents of upcoming events and daily classroom news, and it also served as a platform to let anyone connected to the Internet learn about our class.

My Learning Journey of the Internet

During the 1993–1994 school year, I had the opportunity to work at the Oregon Museum of Science and Industry in Portland, Oregon, as a Teacher in Residence. This experience allowed me to work at the museum on a project of my own choosing. My major focus was on the Internet. At that time, Mosaic, the first graphical Web browser, had just been introduced by the National Center for Supercomputing Applications and the University of Illi-

Figure 10.1   The Buckman School Room 100 Classroom Webpage

Room 100, Buckman Elementary School

Welcome to Room 100
Buckman Elementary School

320 SE 16th Ave • Portland, Oregon, USA • 503-916-6230

Digital Photograph by Rose

Welcome to the **Buckman School, Room 100** World Wide Web Server. We are a mixed age K, 1, 2 elementary school classroom located in Buckman Elementary School in Portland, Oregon, USA.

We have two teachers in our classroom. **Tim Lauer** teaches in the morning and **Beth Rohloff** teaches in the afternoon.

Beth's Links: Links to Internet resources related to subjects we are currently studying.

Class Projects and Student Work

Buckman School Auction
The Buckman School Auction was held Friday, February 28. See what students in Room 100 did to help support the Buckman School Auction.

Bus Safety Rules:
How to be safe when riding on the school bus.

Space Alphabet Book:
A is for...

Happy Mother's Day:
A tribute to our moms.

The Hovercraft:
Take a spin on our Hovercraft.

Done

---

nois. The public perception of the Internet was just forming. During my time at the museum, I had the opportunity to learn about the technology behind webpages. It seemed like every day someone was posting another interesting resource on the Web. My initial focus was to bring this technology to classrooms so students and teachers could have access to learning resources such as maps or images not readily available in schools. Over time, I began to get excited about the *two-way* Web. Not only could you bring resources to your classroom, but you also could present your students' work to a larger audience.

In fall 1994, when I returned to my school from my yearlong residence at Orgeon Museum of Science and Technology, I set up the Buckman Web server. I published our first webpages, running our server out of the office of Mark Gillingham at Washington State University—Vancouver. We used a program called MacHTTPD, a very barebones Web server. Initially, we posted only general information about the school, but we slowly started to add work my students already were doing, including images of student artwork, images of insects we viewed under our digital microscope, and classroom information such as fieldtrip notices. Basically, we would share any classroom-oriented material on the website.

For example, in my mixed-age K–2 classroom, students had many opportunities to create books based on popular stories. One such book was *My Dream of Dr. Martin Luther King, Jr.,* by Faith Ringgold (1995). The book tells the story of a young girl's dream about the life of Dr. Martin Luther King, Jr. In the back of the book is a timeline of the major events in Dr. King's life. I used this timeline as the basis for a class book. Each student was assigned an event to illustrate.

After we made the classroom book, we decided to share it by posting it on our website. Under the guidance of a parent volunteer, students took turns scanning the images and saving them on the computer. Once all the images were scanned and the pages were written, we posted them on our website. This particular website has became very popular; the website was moved to the main school district Web server, which was able to handle the Internet traffic. The website is still the most popular material on the district Web server, receiving over 40,000 visits each year.

The website became a catalog of the work taking place in Room 100. Wooden block structures, stories of classroom pets, science experiments, summer postcards from students, and even a gerbil webcam became content for our classroom website. The feedback and kind words from others who visited our website was something that always impressed my students.

Weblogs

My work at Buckman Elementary School led to a curriculum development position with my school district. I worked with other teachers to develop programs to help integrate technology across the curriculum. One area where I concentrated my efforts was on learning about tools that would make Web publishing easier and more accessible to teachers. The most effective use of technology I had seen was when teachers used it as a communication tool. Although many teachers could see the value in this, the process of actually creating and posting content on a website was beyond most teachers' knowledge base, and they needed tools to more easily share their information.

I investigated a number of Web-based publishing tools that lowered the technical skills teachers need to publish on the Web. Among these tools is a class of applications called weblogs. Weblog-publishing software allows an author to publish easily images, short stories, or classroom notices using a very simple webpage interface. By filling out a Web form and clicking a few buttons, a teacher easily can do these tasks. I found these tools to be very appealing to teachers.

In addition, weblogs have a feature, Real Simple Syndication (RSS), which is a two-way method of publishing and notifying and writing and receiving feedback, which I believe has great promise in education. On a very basic level, this means that when a student writes and posts something online using Weblog software, a teacher running an application called an aggregator is notified of the writing and then reads and responds to it using a commenting feature.

RSS is very popular and is used by blog authors and major publishers to push their content out to readers. RRS is transforming how people interact with the Web. Instead of visiting favorite websites to check for new posts and information, by using an aggregation tool such as Bloglines (websites that allow for the organization of favorite website feeds; see Figure 10.2), a reader can subscribe to RSS feeds and automatically be informed when an update takes place. At its most basic level, the use of RSS and an aggregator allows the information to find the user, rather than the user having to find new information. At Lewis Elementary School in Portland, Oregon, where I currently am the principal, we use the weblog technology Moveable Type, in which the user enters text in the editing page, saves it, and it is published automatically to the school webpage. No special Web-editing skills are needed to publish material (Figure 10.3). Teachers and staff use Moveable Type to publish our school website, staff bulletin, classroom updates, parent resources, and several classroom websites.

I developed the staff bulletin, for example, to publish information of interest to our teaching staff. This information includes school district notices, school announcements, professional development opportunities, birthday wishes—basically, the everyday things that are associated with a school. The ease of publication allows me to publish the bulletin in a timely manner. Each item is time and date stamped and archived. This allows our staff

Figure 10.2   An Example of Bloglines

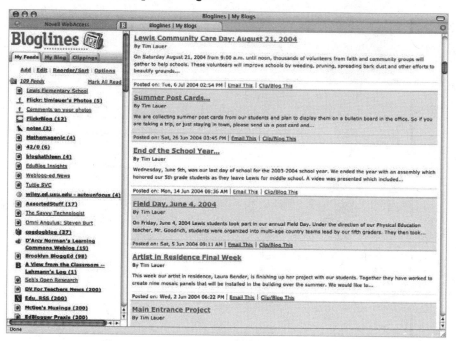

members to review easily and revisit information. In addition, I enabled a feature called *comments* (which allows readers to leave a comment regarding a specific post) on this website for staff members to add information, post questions, and clarify comments. This allows my staff to use the technology as an extension of face-to-face meetings and keep staff informed of school news in a timely manner. Teachers also contribute weekly to a Classroom Notes website (Figure 10.4, http://lewiselementary.org/notes). The idea behind this website is to allow teachers to share timely information about their classrooms with the students' families and the larger school community. Each week during our regular staff meeting, teachers compose and post their weekly update.

The ease of weblog publication allows our school reading specialist to share resources and materials on our school website with students' families. In addition to a newsletter for parents, the website shares resources such as our interactive leveled-books database, a resource of common trade book titles leveled to Reading Recovery levels. Parents can use the leveled-books database to choose books that are appropriate to their children's reading level and to guide them when checking out books for

Figure 10.3 The Moveable Type Weblog Tool

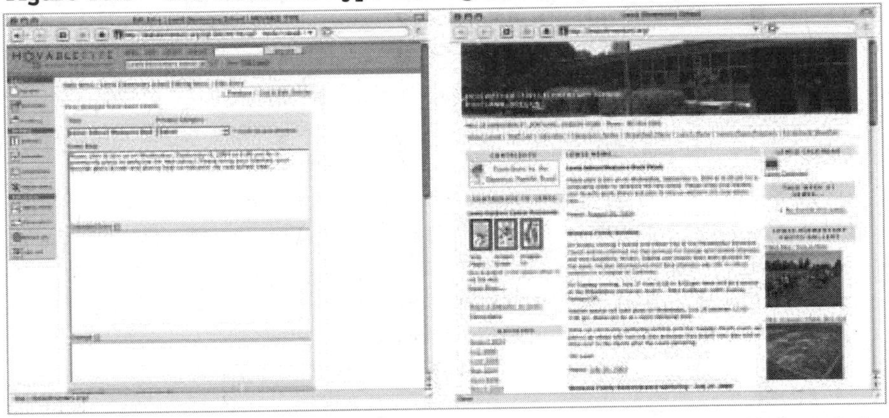

Screenshots of Moveable Type are licensed courtesy of Six Apart, Ltd.

Figure 10.4 Lewis Elementary School Classroom Notes

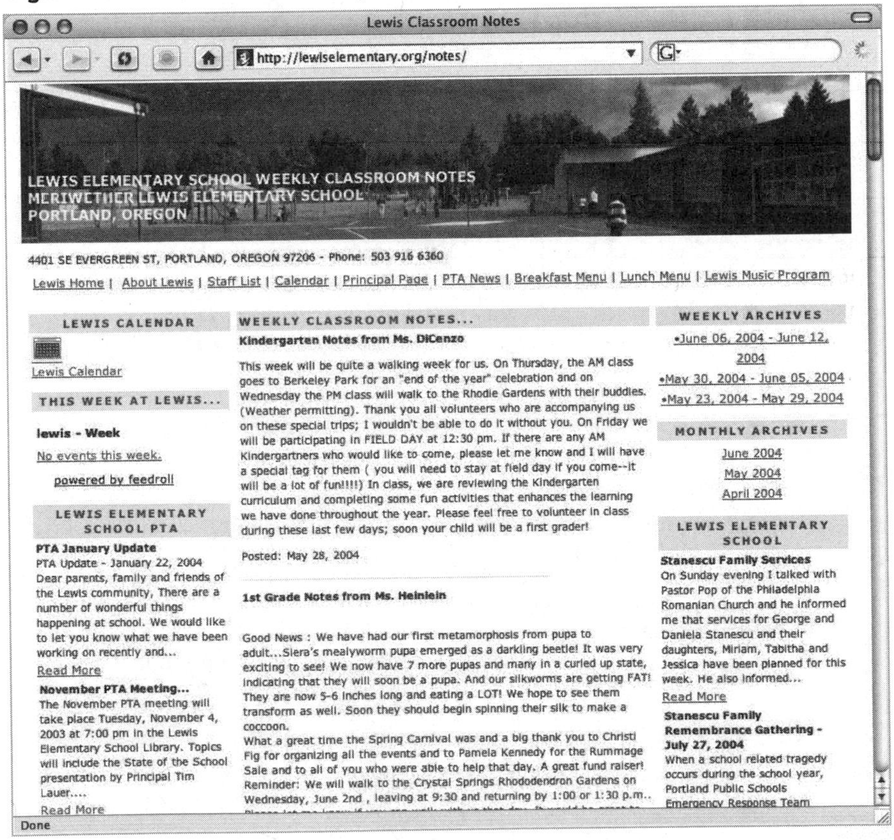

their children from the school or local library. By making the resource available on the Web, we offer this not only to our local school families but to anyone who may find it useful.

Several classroom teachers are embracing this weblog technology and are using it to share information with the families of their students. For example, our music teacher, Tony Jamesbarry, posts schedules of band events and practices for his band students and publishes recordings of their work on his website. Megan Revell-Lovell, our media specialist, uses her weblog to share book and author recommendations with students and parents.

Our goal is to use this technology with our fourth- and fifth-grade students. Students can use a weblog to post assignments to teachers, who in turn use the aggregate software to be notified of turned-in assignments and respond to students using the comments feature. This could be expanded to allow parents to view student work. Teachers can develop a digital portfolio to organize and share student work with parents, teachers, and other students.

Conclusion

For the past 10 years, I have been exploring the use of the Internet and Web publishing in schools. In my various positions as classroom teacher, curriculum developer, and now as an elementary school principal, I have focused on using the Internet to give teachers, educators, and parents a better understanding of the teaching and learning taking place in classrooms. The debate about the use of new technology, such as the Internet, in early childhood classrooms often involves an either/or argument. On one hand, technology is seen as a replacement for some other aspect of the curriculum. On the other hand, it is disdained completely as a waste of time, which takes away from more developmentally appropriate activities. I propose that teachers and educators seek a middle ground where technology is seen as a communication tool. In reality it can be an enhanced telephone that allows students and teachers to see and hear things of value and substance that they would not have experienced otherwise. It allows teachers to bring into their classrooms images and sounds that can enrich an already-rich classroom environment.

CHILDREN'S LITERATURE
Ringgold, F. (1995). *My dream of Martin Luther King, Jr.* New York: Crown.

CHAPTER 11

Fundamental Qualities of Effective Internet Literacy Instruction: An Exploration of Worthwhile Classroom Practices

Linda D. Labbo

One of the things I enjoy most about being a university researcher is the opportunity to go into classrooms and learn how teachers make effective use of the Internet for literacy instruction. After visiting a classroom one warm day in April 2004, I interviewed Ms. Phillips, a first-grade teacher, about the wonderful computer activities I had observed. I asked her to reflect on the effectiveness of the learning environment she had created by viewing and discussing three videotaped segments of the class activities:

- *Video Segment 1*: Students working in the computer lab exchange e-mail messages with keypals in another city. Teacher Comments: "Notice how carefully students are composing their messages because they're communicating with a real audience."

- *Video Segment 2*: Small groups of students gather information about dinosaurs from a website (www.alfy.com/teachers/teach/thematic_units/Dinosaurs/Dinosaurs_1.asp). Teacher Comments: "By preloading the webpage I saved a great deal of downloading time and kept the kids on task. I picked up that tip from another teacher on a listserv" (RTEACHER listserv: www.reading.org/resources/community/discussions_rt_instruct.html).

- *Video Segment 3*: A group of three students play an interactive matching game on the Internet at the National Wildlife Federation website (www.nwf.org/kidzone/kzPage.cfm?siteId=2&departmentId=150). Teacher Comments: "It's amazing to watch the children work together to problem-solve. They develop oral language and visual literacy skills."

Even though Ms. Phillips had taught for 13 years, she had been using computers in her classroom for only 2 years. Thus, she considered herself a computer novice who had much to learn. She expressed concern about her ability to gain more expertise because she was the only teacher in her school that was using the Internet. In addition, her school district had announced that because of budget reallocations, they would not be offering any technology-related staff development until the following year.

Ms. Phillips and other educators who are interested in applying effective Internet-literacy instruction to classroom practices are fortunate because recent groundbreaking work provides much-needed direction in this area. New information arises daily from a growing body of classroom-based research (Labbo & Reinking, 2003) and thoughtful statements and standards posted by professional organizations (IRA, 2001). Large-scale research projects, such as the Case Technologies to Enhance Literacy Learning (Teale, Leu, Labbo, & Kinzer, 2002), draw key insights from effective teachers who are willing to share their wisdom with us (Labbo, et al., 2003).

We also are fortunate that a grassroots movement is occurring that recognizes teachers as qualified and proficient guides in this area. In this chapter I draw on these resources to discuss *fundamental qualities and characteristics of effective teachers* of effective Internet literacy instruction. More specifically, after a brief review of key issues, I focus on four characteristics of effective teachers and three qualities of successful student–Internet collaboration. Insights into fundamental qualities arise from observations that take place in real time in real locations, such as Ms. Phillips's first-grade classroom, and from visits to the websites of Miss Rumphius Award winners (www.reading.org/resources/community/links_rumphius_links.html). These individuals generously share their experiences with us in the pages of this book.

What Are the Key Issues Related to Effective Internet-Literacy Instruction?

To successfully traverse the Internet, teachers and students routinely use skills and strategies related to traditional language arts, namely, reading, writing, speaking, and listening. For example, students read text on screen pages, write letters or messages online, speak as they record their voices for PowerPoint presentations, and listen to music or audio messages on websites. However, to fully realize the potential of the Internet as a powerful instructional tool, teachers and students also must continually acquire new literacies that are essential for ensuring our children's successful literacy futures in an increasingly global, electronic economy (Leu, 2000).

New literacies include (1) assembling knowledge from multimedia resources, (2) strategically navigating through hyperlinks, (3) critically comprehending various forms of information, (4) engaging in electronic forms of communication, (5) expressing ideas in multimedia formats, and (6) socially mediating problem solving through online and real-time collaborations. Thus, the Internet can be a tricky landscape for novices to negotiate, but we can learn a great deal by identifying the fundamental qualities of effective Internet-literacy instruction that expert teachers exhibit.

What Are the Characteristics of Teachers Who Effectively Integrate the Internet With Literacy Instruction?

The stories of the Miss Rumphius Award winners provide an eloquent testament to the fact that any teacher who has access to a classroom computer and an Internet connection can integrate successfully the Internet into effective literacy instruction. However, consider these four essential characteristics that play key roles in the success of each teacher's journey from computer novice to Internet expert: (1) making the cutting edge a comfortable place to be, (2) having and sharing good ideas, (3) not allowing a digital divide (the socioeconomic gap between communities that have access to computers and the Internet and those who do not), and (4) making a good print-based literacy curriculum even better.

Making the Cutting Edge a Comfortable Place to Be

First and foremost, what teachers know makes a difference in the quality of students' computer-related learning experiences (Clairana, 1990; Labbo & Teale, 2001). The International Reading Association position statement (IRA, 2002) on technology and literacy instruction clearly expresses the expectation that teachers will be skilled in the effective use of the Internet and other information and communication technologies (ICTs). Teachers who successfully integrate the Internet into the literacy curriculum are technologically literate. According to the U.S. Department of Education (1997), technological literacy consists of the ability to use computer technologies to increase productivity, learning, performance, and the knowledge for using technology tools to improve students' academic achievement in subject areas.

What the Department of Education does not address is that teachers who successfully integrate the Internet into the literacy curriculum are not only technologically literate, but they are constantly in a state of becoming technologically literate. This is an important clarification that reflects the commitment that dedicated teachers make toward keeping up with technological innovations (Leu, 2000). What the Department of Education also does not state is the fact that teachers take various paths, as the following examples show, in their personal and professional quests to become technologically literate:

- *Enroll in educational technology courses at a local university.* For example, Mary Kruel, Richards Elementary School, Whitefish Bay, Wisconsin (see chapter 9), enrolled in a one-credit course on using the Internet in education. By taking that course, she received the motivation to take more courses and purchase a home computer so she could access the Internet anytime.

- *Attend staff development workshops in real time or online.* For example, as the Instructional Technology Integration specialist for the Comsewogue School District, Port Jefferson Station, New York, Susan Silverman offers staff development training and locates Internet resources for teachers. Ms. Phillips, who expressed a concern in the opening classroom scenario about the lack of timely staff development, could go to the Mariposa County Unified School District website, which offers online staff development tutorials, www.sps3000.net/mariposa. Educators also may view other tutorials online, for example, a tutorial on how to review a website at Education World's www.educationworld.com/a_tech/techtorial/techtoria1002.html.

- *Go to professional conferences* (www.reading.org/association/meetings/index.html, International Reading Association, and http://proflearn.classroom.com/ProfDev/conferences). For example, Susan Silverman (see chapter 7) notes that her entry into the world of Internet projects began on her way home from attending presentations at the 1997 Classroom Connect Conference. Her reflections on the lectures she heard provided her with a vision for effective Internet-literacy instruction that transformed her teaching practices.

- *Read professional articles* (Reading Online, www.readingonline.org/articles/art_index.asp), *position statements published by professional organizations* (www.naeyc.org/resources/eyly/1996/09a.htm), *and National Education Technology Standards for Teachers* (http://cnets.iste.org/teachers/t_stands.html; ISTE, 2000) *published online*. Through the Internet, teachers can have 24-hour access to online professional resources. Internet access allows for on-demand learning, which helps teachers overcome the barrier of researching print-based journals that may be located in a distant library or teacher resource room on a school campus.

Internet access to these and other resources for professional development can help make the cutting edge of technology innovation and classroom application a comfortable place to be.

The Having and Sharing of Good Ideas

It also is worth noting that each teacher builds a knowledge base about computer technologies from various resources that involve collaborating with mentors (see Labbo, Sprague, Montero, & Font, 2000) and colleagues. Unfortunately, many pioneering teachers, such as first-grade teacher Ms. Phillips, discover that they are the only teacher in their grade level, school campus, or district who are delving into Internet literacy instruction. Thus, it is understandable that many teachers report that online networking with other teachers helps them overcome feelings of isolation and provides them with a plethora of practical ideas that have been field-tested by their colleagues in classrooms.

Furthermore, teachers who effectively use the Internet for literacy instruction share one characteristic in common—the having and sharing of good ideas, which results in the best type of borrowing, because borrowed ideas are eventually transformed to reflect each teacher's instructional style and the local context. As the following tenets show, various forms of effective Internet teacher collaboration occur in supportive social environments that continue to thrive as a result of teachers' shared interests, mutual respect, and trust.

Participate in listservs and chat rooms (The Reading Teacher Listserv, www.readingonline.org/communities/comm_index.asp) *that provide a forum for expanding teachers' I.Q.—Internet Quotient*. When teachers share ideas or pose questions on a listserv, they amplify their knowledge base and technology-related insights. When many minds work to resolve a problem, teachers find solutions and expand their options. For example, Ms. Phillips told members of a listserv that her students frequently became distracted and restless when waiting for a webpage to open. Several respondents suggested that Ms. Phillips download the webpage beforehand to save time and offset students' frustration.

Visit websites of other teachers that provide educators and teachers with a vision of instructional possibilities, examples of students' work, and countless ideas for practical classroom applications. For example, a visit to fourth-grade teacher Mary Kreul's website (www.mskreul.com/index.html) is bound to inspire countless activities that have been tested in a real classroom.

Participate in Internet projects. For example, Susan Silverman learned about being a project coordinator for an Internet project through her participation in the Flat Stanley Project (http://flatstanley.enoreo.on.ca) (see chapter 8, by Dale Hubert). Mary Kreul arranged for her class to participate in a telecollaborative project with Susan Silverman's class (http://comsewogue.k12.ny.us/~ssilverman/applebytes).

Obtain copies of lesson plans online. Go to http://school.discovery.com/lessonplans/k-5.html, Kathy Schrock's Guide for Educators (http://school.discovery.com/schrockguide), or to CyberGuides (www.sdcoe.k12.ca.us/score/cyberguide.html). Social studies lesson plans from www.csun.edu/~hcedu013/index.html provide teachers with resources that outline in detail computer-related lesson materials, objectives, procedures, and assessment. In other words, there is no reason for a teacher to have to reinvent the wheel for every computer-related lesson plan when so many excellent plans are readily available on the Internet.

Exchange e-mail messages with mentors and colleagues to honor the voices of other educational professionals and creates relationships that are long lasting. For example, when exchanging e-mails with a trusted colleague, there is no such thing as a bad question. Additionally, teachers seek online mentors with particular areas of expertise for their contributions. Mentors become valuable resources for other teachers in the electronic literacy community.

Not Allowing a Digital Divide

Recent statistics indicate that the digital divide, the difference in computer access between high and low socioeconomic status schools that was so prevalent in the early 1990s, recently has diminished in classrooms across the United States (National Center for Education Statistics, 1999). However, a digital divide can still exist within the walls of a classroom unless all children have equal access to a computer. Indeed, effective teachers arrange daily schedules, lessons, and curricular activities in ways that ensure that all students have access to computers. Doing so provides students with numerous occasions to acquire traditional and new literacies (IRA, 2002; Labbo, Reinking, & McKenna, 1995).

Computers cannot be relegated to a corner of the classroom or to a few minutes at the end of class as a reward for completing paper-and-pencil assignments for computers to affect students' learning. Computer usage needs to be interwoven throughout the instructional day and integrated into the curriculum for students to receive adequate access. The National Association for the Education of Young Children has a position statement (www.naeyc.org/resources/eyly/1996/09a.htm) (NAEYC, 1996) that highlights the important role teachers play in providing all students with computer access. Sutton (1991) has found that girls use computers in and out of school less often than boys do; African American students have less access to computers than white students; and schools with more resources buy more equipment and more expensive equipment than schools with fewer resources. If educators do not work to provide access to technology for all students, the gaps in students' ability and familiarity with technology will widen. Technology has many potential benefits for children with special needs and may be essential for successful inclusion in the regular classroom.

Teachers also provide computer access when they creatively exploit unique multimedia features of computer applications and Internet sites to meet the learning needs of students of varying literacy abilities (Eisenwine & Hunt, 2000; Labbo et al., 2000). For example, a CD-ROM talking book or stories posted on an Internet site may make text accessible to nonreaders through an interactive interface that reads the text aloud. Beginning readers who are in the process of building sight words and mastering the ability to decode text independently may read the same story by clicking on words they do not know how to pronounce. Fluent readers may read the same text aloud first, and then listen to a narration of the story to hear models of more expressive reading (Labbo, 2000). Additionally, many CD-ROM talking books or stories online (e.g., *Story Book: Folktales from around the World,* http://story.lg.co.kr:3000/english/story/index.jsp) include an option for listening to the story in another language, a feature that enables students for whom English is a second language to comprehend the story by hearing it first in their indigenous languages (e.g., Spanish, Japanese, French, Korean, Chinese).

Making a Good Print-Based Literacy Curriculum Even Better

Teachers who routinely address units and topics are grounded in effective print-based literacy practices that may be improved or enhanced by Internet project activities. For example, children's literature extension activities involving old favorites, such as *Stellaluna* (Cannon, 1993), *Thomas' Snowsuit* (Munsch, 1985), *Flat Stanley* (Brown, Bjorkman, 1964), and *The Important Book* (Brown, 1990), come to life with Internet projects. Imagine the delight of thousands of students across the United States who, after reading the story of a little bat who was forced to live like a bird after getting lost from her mother, were able to conduct and share research on the real-life behavior and habitats of bats (http://kids-learn.org/stellaluna), an activity that continues to dispel bat myths for many youngsters. Well-designed Internet projects align with traditional-literacy standards and objectives as defined by the school district, the state, and professional organizations. For example, Susan Silverman's Internet project, Winter Wonderland, required students to meet traditional-literacy objectives, such as students writing book reviews and new story endings. However, by working on the Internet, students accomplished new literacy standards and objectives—such as using multimedia features of sound and interactivity to play wintry mood music and following on-screen directions to play interactive games that involve manipulating the mouse, clicking on links, and dragging objects across the screen (www.northcanton.sparcc.org/~ptk1nc/frosty2005/index.html).

What Are the Fundamental Qualities of Successful Student Internet Collaboration?

The Internet lends itself to student exploration and collaboration. When ICT tools, such as search engines, hyperlinks, e-mail, chat rooms, and interactive multimedia, combine with well-designed Internet projects, opportunities for socially mediated learning and collaboration abound. Thus, effective teachers design Internet activities that build learning communities within the walls of the classroom and extend the learning community beyond the walls of the classroom. The descriptions of the Miss Rumphius Award–winning Internet projects included in this book point to essential qualities and various conditions necessary for successful collaborations: (1) collaborating via the Internet means *really* writing to *real* people; (2) *connectivity* and cross-cultural student collaborations; and (3) students as critical friends, e-problem solvers, and cyber navigators.

Collaborating Via the Internet Means "Really" Writing to "Real" People

A few weeks ago I was visiting a prekindergarten classroom during a time of day when the teacher was working with a little girl to dictate a draft of a letter to a "Dear Friend" at the writing center. About halfway through the dictation the teacher stopped the child, read the draft aloud, and asked her if the letter made any sense. She reminded the child that the letter was going to be e-mailed to a new friend in another pre-K classroom in another city. The child replied sagely, "Oh, you mean we're *really* writing to real people, not pretend people? Can I start over?" (Labbo, unpublished field notes, 2004).

Keypal projects, such as those explained by Mary Kreul (see chapter 9), invite young students to compose and exchange messages about topics of interest. As noted by Ms. Phillips in the scenario at the beginning of this chapter, students take more care when writing messages by attending to content, composition, and form when they are writing to an audience other than the teacher. Young children who are fortunate enough to engage in authentic communicating via the Internet are able to grasp fundamental concepts about language and literacy through these exchanges. Of course, one of the most motivating aspects of e-mail collaborations is the exciting moment when messages are answered from people in distant locations. Over time, children learn to use the conventions of e-mailing, such as contextualizing comments, referring to previous messages, and considering the point of view of their responsive audience. These and other Internet activities fulfill a key tenet of the IRA position statement (2002) for crafting a literacy curriculum that integrates the new literacies of the Internet and other ICTs into instructional programs.

When the World Wide Web is used to showcase activities such as stories, webquest results, artwork, and the like for a general Internet audience, students are motivated to produce their best work. Parents, grandparents, and aunts and uncles who live in distant cities are more likely to feel closely connected to the school and to their young family members when viewing a student's work is as easy as clicking on an Internet link to a teacher's website. Students are more likely to produce higher quality work and put more effort into their work when family members are a likely audience. Additionally, there are frequent occasions for communicating and collaborating with experts, for example, Tim Lauer's (see chapter 10) class posting a photograph of a bee that had stung a child, and an expert e-mailing the class with information clarifying the insect's identity as a wasp.

Connectivity and Cross-Cultural Student Collaborations

Exchanging information via the Internet has encouraged thoughtful information exchanges between students around the world (Garner & Gillingham, 1998; Tao & Reinking, 2000). Zhao and colleagues (1999) note that the Internet is especially useful for literacy instruction because it offers a high level of connectivity: "Connectivity relates to the capacity for communication among peers and between students and experts as students access information beyond the classroom walls, but also enables seamless data sharing across activities" (p. 5).

Early telecommunicative projects highlight the notion of connectivity. For example, almost two decades ago, Riel (1985) invited students from various geographic regions to work collaboratively to produce a newspaper on an electronic newswire. He found that communication between students in California and Alaska was difficult initially because their cultural backgrounds were vastly different. Shortly thereafter, Cohen and Riel (1989) asked middle school students from different geographic regions in Israel to create an electronic newspaper. They found that articles written for culturally different, far-away peers were of better quality than those that were written by students solely for their teachers. In other words, students included more details and more succinct writing when trying to communicate culturally relevant information to an authentic audience from a different cultural region. More recently, Garner and Gillingham (1998) noted that students who exchange cross-cultural messages acquire new literacy skills, such as learning to embed topics in ongoing exchanges to create a meaningful context for their geographically and socially different correspondents, delete irrelevant details in messages that may be confusing, and craft appropriately responsive messages.

It is clear that when students gather and share cultural information for a cross-cultural Internet project, students engage in reading that is inherently meaningful, insightful, and motivating. The Internet opens up the world to students and helps them develop a respect for diversity. Students also may enjoy gathering different cultural perspectives on a topic. For example, Mary Kreul (see chapter 9) reports that one of her first projects involved an exchange of information with students in a class in England who wanted to know more about forms of travel to and from school. Sharing their findings allows students to better understand cross-cultural similarities. One of Susan Silverman's first experiences as an Internet Poetry Project Director attracted responses from students in Australia—"this simple little poetry unit had become a genuine multicultural experience..." (p. 106)—while one of Susan's later projects involved students' communication with a class in Russia. Perhaps one of the most popular and widely recognized Internet projects, created by Hubert (see chapter 8) in the realm of international communication, is a fairly simple activity that uses a storybook character, Flat Stanley (http://flatstanley.enoreo.on.ca)). Explanations of the activity on the Internet make the project easily accessible to children around the world. Project designer Hubert also provides an online forum that fosters cross-cultural understanding in the form of a multilanguage chat room that allows students to communicate online. The chat page can instantly translate nine languages! In addition, a brief look at the success stories link on the homepage reveals the broad cross-cultural travels children experience vicariously through the travels of Flat Stanleys.

Students as Critical Friends, E-Problem Solvers, and Cyber Navigators

Collaborating through Internet projects equips students to become experts in new literacy skills and strategies. One of the most important skills required for our children's future in the workforce is the ability to critically comprehend and evaluate information. A case in point is provided by Susan Silverman whose students learn how to evaluate the Web publications of other students by designing a rubric. Small groups of students try out sample rubrics. The resulting class discussions reveal the high levels of complexity of the students' critical thinking.

Children who learn how to critically read information are prepared to provide scaffolding and support for less-capable peers. These and other Internet activities fulfill a key tenet of the IRA position statement (2001) for crafting instruction that helps children develop the critical literacies essential to information use on the Internet. Students in effectively designed ICT learning environments also learn how to work collaboratively to solve problems such as interacting with multimedia interfaces, locating online information, publishing research findings, or exchanging data with other classrooms. At the beginning of this chapter, Ms. Phillips notes that her students were able to solve collaboratively problems related to playing an online game. In addition, children who participate consistently in relevant Internet projects quickly become experts in various ICT skills and strategies. For example, in classrooms I have visited, it is not uncommon for children who have different areas of expertise to be called by another small group of children to serve as a consultant on a project. Ryan, a second grader who knew how to conduct an advanced Internet search on Yahooligans (http://yahooligans.yahoo.com), frequently acts as a consultant for groups at the beginning of projects. In fact, he earns such great respect and recognition from his peers that they gave him the superhero nickname "Cyber-Navigator."

In another instance, Marisa, who is an expert on importing digital photographs into electronic slide shows for publication on her class website, is frequently called on by small groups who are trying to storyboard or put into sequence a series of photographs as a culmination of research projects. She serves as an electronic-problem solver for her peers. Collaboration and cooperative-learning classroom practices, which have been widely adopted after the 1970s, result in classrooms where students are encouraged to "discuss, debate, disagree, and ultimately to teach one another" (Slavin, 1999, p. 193). Children who have opportunities to collaborate during ICT activities frequently scaffold Internet learning for their less-capable peers and teach one another.

Conclusion

This chapter is about pausing to celebrate and analyze the work of effective teachers of Internet literacy instruction in order to identify worthwhile classroom practices. As we reflect on the experiences of Miss Rumphius Award winners, it becomes clear that successful teachers are effective because they are continually in the process of becoming technologically literate. This is an important, positive mindset if teachers are going to remain on the cutting edge of technology innovation and application. Thus, effective teachers use ICT as a vehicle for professional development and networking.

Effective teachers use ICT to make a good, traditional literacy curriculum even better. However, they also skillfully provide occasions for students to acquire new literacy skills within the context of accomplishing communicative goals and completing assignments with ICT tools and applications. For example, students may learn about strategic Internet navigation when assembling knowledge about a topic from several Internet sites as part of an Internet project. They may learn about file saving, graphics creation, scanning images, or creating slides for a multimedia presentation as they prepare a final report on a research project that uses computer applications. As a result, embedded instruction is interwoven throughout the day as an important form of on-the-job training that occurs during teachable moments.

This chapter also is about reflecting on how technologically literate teachers create social learning environments that foster constructive student collaborations and shared construction of meaning. Socially mediated learning environments have stable routines and processes that enable students to enjoy the full benefits of collaborative endeavors. Positive learning climates foster relationships among classroom peers, online keypals, and content-area experts. Collaborations allow students to acquire habits of mind that are important for their literacy futures: contributing key ideas to a team effort, exchanging ideas with an authentic audience, developing positive relationships with others, and portioning project tasks.

It is worth noting that the guidelines I provide in this chapter are but a snapshot of teachers' and students' ongoing adventures. I report the notion that there is no one type of experience that all teachers have with technology in the classroom (Labbo & Reinking, 1999). Indeed, there is a wide range of experience with ICT and classroom technologies that continue to expand as new technologies come into play. Teachers who are hesitant to enter the wonderland of Internet-related instruction are going to take first steps on their ICT journeys. Indeed, as we move forward, every educator has an awesome opportunity and responsibility to play a key role in thoughtfully exploring and sharing effective ICT practices.

This material is based on work supported by the National Science Foundation under Grant No. 0089221. Any opinions, findings, and conclusions or recommendations expressed in this material are those of the author(s) and do not necessarily reflect the views of the National Science Foundation.

REFERENCES

Clairana, R.B. (1990). *The teacher is a variable in reading computer-based instruction.* East Lansing, MI: National Center for Research on Teacher Learning. (ERIC Document Reproduction Service No. ED 317966 CS 010014)

Cohen, M., & Riel, M.M. (1989, Summer). The effect of distant audiences on students' writing. *American Educational Research Journal, 26,* 143–159.

Eisenwine, M.J., & Hunt, D.A. (2000). Using a computer in literacy groups with emergent readers. *The Reading Teacher, 53,* 456–458.

Garner, R., & Gillingham, M.G. (1998). The Internet in the classroom: Is it the end of transmission-oriented pedagogy? In D. Reinking, M.C. McKenna, L.D. Labbo, & R.D. Kieffer (Eds.), *Handbook of literacy and technology: Transformations in a post-typographic world* (pp. 221–231). Mahwah, NJ: Erlbaum.

International Reading Association (IRA). (2002). *Integrating literacy and technology in the curriculum.* Retrieved November 18, 2004, from http://www.reading.org/downloads/positions/ps1048_technology.pdf

International Society for Technology in Education (ISTE). (2000). *Educational technology standards and performance indicators for all teachers.* Retrieved January 6, 2004, from http://cnets.iste.org/teachers/t_stands.html

Labbo, L.D. (2000). Twelve things young children can do with a talking book in a classroom computer center. *The Reading Teacher, 53,* 542–546.

Labbo, L.D., Leu, D.J., Jr., Kinzer, C.K., Teale, W.H., Cammack, D., Kara-Soteriou, J., et al. (2003). Teacher wisdom stories: Cautions and recommendations for using computer-related technologies for literacy instruction. *The Reading Teacher, 53,* 300–304.

Labbo, L.D., & Reinking, D. (1999). Negotiating the multiple realities of technology in literacy research and instruction. *Reading Research Quarterly, 34,* 478–492.

Labbo, L.D., & Reinking, D. (2003). Computers and early literacy education. In N. Hall, J. Larson, & J. Marsh (Eds.), *Handbook of early childhood literacy research* (pp. 338–354). London: Sage.

Labbo, L.D., Reinking D., & McKenna, M.C. (1995). Incorporating the computer into kindergarten: A case study. In A. Hinchman, D.J. Leu, Jr., & C.K. Kinzer (Eds.), *Perspectives on literacy research and practice* (44th yearbook of the National Reading Conference, pp. 459–465). Chicago: National Reading Conference.

Labbo, L.D., Sprague, L., Montero, M.K., & Font, G. (2000, July). Connecting a computer center to themes, literature, and kindergartners' literacy needs. *Reading Online.* Retrieved November 18, 2004, from http://www.readingonline.org/electronic/elec_index.asp?HREF=labbo/index.html

Labbo, L.D., & Teale, W.H. (2001, April). *Figuring out how computers fit in: Practical classroom applications for K–3 computer-related literacy instruction.* Paper presented at the International Reading Association Annual Convention, New Orleans, LA.

Leu, D.J., Jr. (2000). Literacy and technology: Deictic consequences for literacy education in an information age. In M.L. Kamil, P.B. Mosenthal, P.D. Pearson, & R. Barr (Eds.), *Handbook of reading research* (Vol. 3, pp. 743–770). Mahwah, NJ: Erlbaum.

National Association for the Education of Young Children (NAEYC). (1996). Early years are learning years: Technology in early childhood programs. Retrieved September 20, 2003, from http://www.naeyc.org/resources/eyly/1996/09a.htm

National Center for Education Statistics (NCES). (1999). *Internet access in public schools and classrooms: 1994–1998.* Retrieved January 18, 2005, from http://nces.ed.gov/pubs99/1999017.html#table1

Riel, M.M. (1985). The computer chronicles newswire: A functional learning environment for acquiring literacy skills. *Journal of Educational Computing Research, 1*(3), 317–337.

Slavin, R.E. (1999). Synthesis of research on cooperative learning. In A.C. Ornstein & L.S. Behar-Horenstein (Eds.), *Contemporary issues in curriculum* (2nd ed.). Boston: Allyn & Bacon.

Sutton, R.E. (1991). Equity and computers in the schools: A decade of research. *Review of Educational Research, 61*(4), 475–503.

Tao, L., & Reinking, D. (2000). E-mail and literacy education. *Reading & Writing Quarterly, 16*(2), 169–174.

Teale, W.H., Leu, D.J., Jr., Labbo, L.D., & Kinzer, C. (2002). The CTELL project: New ways technology can help educate tomorrow's reading teachers. *The Reading Teacher, 55,* 654–659.

U.S. Department of Education. (1997). *President Clinton's call to action for American education in the 21st century: Technological literacy.* Retrieved May 23, 2001, from http://www.ed.gov/updates/PresEDPlan/part11.html

Zhao, Y., Englert, C.S., Chen, J., Jones, S.C., & Ferdig, R. (1999). *TELE-Web: Developing a Web-based literacy learning environment.* (CIERA Report No. 1–006). Ann Arbor: University of Michigan.

CHILDREN'S LITERATURE

Brown, J., & Bjorkman, S. (1964). *Flat Stanley.* Ill. T. Ungerer. New York: HarperCollins.

Brown, M.W. (1990). *The important book.* New York: HarperTrophy. (Originally published 1949)

Cannon, J. (1993). *Stellaluna.* New York: Harcourt.

Munsch, R.M. (1985). *Thomas' snowsuit.* Toronto, ON: Annick Press.

A Commitment to Teacher Education and Professional Development

T he first two sections of this book illustrate why it was necessary for the Miss Rumphius Award winners to seek their own opportunities to learn how to use technology to enhance their teaching. Fortunately, in recent years there has been more interest in integrating technology training into teacher education and professional development programs. To emphasize the importance of providing teachers with valuable, effective training, we conclude this book with a section designated to the topic.

In chapter 12, Denise Johnson examines the relationship between literacy and technology. Johnson frames her chapter around the idea of using Miss Rumphius as a role model for preservice teacher educators. Johnson gives an overview of preservice education with respect to technology proficiency, and then reports on the findings from a survey she conducted with Miss Rumphius Award winners. Johnson analyzes how preservice teachers can become educated about the integration of technology in their classrooms by learning about the Miss Rumphius character and the work of the award recipients.

In chapter 13, Julie Coiro focuses on how the work by the Miss Rumphius Award winners can contribute toward effective professional development for practicing teachers. Coiro thoroughly discusses the nature of effective professional development in the integration of literacy and technology based on research and her own firsthand experiences in offering professional development to teachers. The chapter concludes with lessons she believes we can learn by studying the journeys of the Miss Rumphius Award winners.

CHAPTER 12

Miss Rumphius as a Role Model for Preservice Teachers

Denise Johnson

In the evening Alice sat on her grandfather's knee and listened to his stories of faraway places. When he had finished, Alice would say, "When I grow up, I too will go to faraway places, and when I grow old, I too will live beside the sea."

"That is all very well, little Alice," said her grandfather, "but there is a third thing you must do."

"What is that?" asked Alice.

"You must do something to make the world more beautiful," said her grandfather. "All right," said Alice. But she did not know what that could be. (Cooney, 1982, n.p.)

This excerpt is from the book *Miss Rumphius* by Barbara Cooney (1982). The story of Miss Rumphius is an appropriate backdrop for the award given to outstanding teachers of literacy and Internet technologies. In a different way, the story of Miss Rumphius also parallels the journey of preservice teachers as they go through their teacher preparation programs. They listen as their methods professors tell them that they must integrate the Internet into the literacy curriculum if they are to prepare students for the future. Preservice teachers experience limited aspects of teaching through field placements with practicing teachers who many times do not integrate the Internet into their classrooms. Therefore, as in the excerpt from *Miss Rumphius* that opens this chapter, for many preservice teachers, the story of their preparation for the integration of the Internet into the literacy curriculum ends with their uncertainty of what it will be. In this chapter I explore how the Miss Rumphius Award winners can assist preservice teachers on their journey to understanding effective literacy instruction, which necessarily includes the Internet, so that the Miss Rumphius Award winners' seeds of success spread to beginning teachers everywhere.

The Story of Preservice Teacher Education

An important dimension of high-quality teacher preparation that will help prevent the attrition of first-year teachers, according to the National Commission on Teaching and America's Future (2003), is the use of modern learning technologies information and communication technologies.

> Teachers in the 21st century schools must become technology-proficient educators, well-prepared to meet the learning needs of students in a digital age. During their preparation and clinical practice experiences, teachers should become fluent in the use of these powerful tools.... Teachers also should be prepared to use technologies to support their own professional growth, participating in networked professional learning communities during their induction years, and sharing and expanding their expertise through regular interactions with colleagues and other educators throughout their careers. (p. 20)

To meet this challenge, a common practice in teacher education programs is to require an introductory course in technology for some or all preservice teachers. Many educational technology courses emphasize the mechanics of computer use rather than the essential connection of technology and curriculum. A National Survey on Information Technology in Teacher Education (Milken Exchange on Education Technology and International Society for Technology in Education, 1999) finds no significant correlation between introductory technology courses and the ability to integrate technology into classroom teaching. A high correlation occurs when teachers deliver technology as part of other courses.

If teacher education programs are to provide preservice teachers with information about computer applications of interest to them and with real application to future teaching assignments, teacher educators must integrate and model the use of technology in all methods courses. This especially is true in reading and language arts methods courses because preservice teachers must be prepared for the challenge of meeting new and changing literacy demands as the form, context, and space for reading and writing changes. As we prepare preservice teachers today to teach (potentially) until the year 2050, teacher educators must know about these new forms of digital literacy (i.e., reading websites) as well as effective methods (i.e., Internet workshops and projects) of incorporating technology into the curriculum. Yet, according to the CEO Forum on Education and Technology (1999), "Despite the fact that the information technology skills of faculty members at teacher colleges are today comparable to their students' skills, most faculty members do not model the use of information technology skills in their teaching" (p. 9). According to Sugrue and Hansen

(1997), "The most successful techniques for changing values involve introducing a respected role model who values the currently undervalued event or task" (p. 37).

Although some university instructors incorporate technology as an integral part of their methods courses for preservice teachers, there is still much progress to be made (Web-Based Education Commission, 2000). Further, the structured fragmentation of traditional programs tends to interfere with or even nullify the positive effects of other programs (Gore & Zeichner, 1991)—fragmentation being the way subject content and pedagogy are broken up into isolated courses in traditional teacher training programs (i.e., social studies methods, math methods, classroom management, etc.). For example, the social studies professor does a wonderful job of integrating technology into his or her courses, but the effects are not felt in the other methods courses because those professors are not integrating technology. This fragmentation of the program limits the preservice teachers' ability to see how the integration of technology can cross the curriculum.

To change the understanding of how technology should be integrated into teacher preparation programs, Hoadley, Engelking, and Bright (1995) state,

> [I]t will require faculty and students to rethink some of the fundamental ideas about what it means to teach and learn. Faculty need to realize that technology, especially multimedia, provides a medium for promoting effective use of teaching strategies, styles, and reflective practice in the classroom and in the field. (p. 4)

Many times, what the preservice teacher learns in the college classroom takes a back seat to what they perceive as reality. Although teacher educators may integrate computer technology into the course curriculum, the vital connection between what preservice teachers learn in the college classroom and the school classroom may not take place. Most preservice teachers enrolled in education programs in the United States neither routinely use information technology during field experiences nor work under master teachers and supervisors who can advise them on the use of information technology (CEO Forum on Education and Technology, 2000; Johnson, 2002; Leu, 2002; Milken Exchange on Education Technology and International Society for Technology in Education, 1999). Therefore, teacher educators must be explicit about how computer technology will benefit preservice teachers and the students they will teach in the future.

A Survey of the Miss Rumphius Recipients

A survey of the Miss Rumphius winners conducted by Johnson (2004) reveals that the Miss Rumphius Award–winning teachers have an average of 19 years of teaching experience. Therefore, it is no surprise that 74% of the respondents report that they did not take a preservice course specifically in technology. Although 19% indicate that they did take a course in technology, it did not prepare them to integrate technology into their classroom because most technology courses offered by universities at that time primarily involved programming. Only 7% of the respondents indicate that they did take a course in technology that did prepare them to integrate technology in the classroom.

The survey also ascertains whether the Miss Rumphius Award winners' reading or language arts method coursework included technology integration for literacy instruction. Again, their responses are much the same as for the technology course, with 89% indicating that their reading or language arts methods course did not include technology integration primarily as a result of the fact that it was nonexistent or not an area of emphasis at the time the majority of the Miss Rumphius Award–winning teachers received their teacher preparation.

In response to both questions about teacher preparation in the area of technology, several respondents indicate that they had participated in several school- or district-sponsored workshops on technology integration. When asked about the quality of their school or district's professional development, 22% indicate that it is excellent; 22%, good; 30%, adequate; and 26%, poor. This finding is quite interesting. Considering that 56% of the respondents indicate that the quality of their school or district's professional development is either adequate or poor, how do these Miss Rumphius Award–winning teachers achieve the level of sophistication in the use and integration of technology apparent from their websites? The following excerpt gives us some insight:

> In the book, *The Sun, the Genome, and the Internet,* Freeman Dyson discusses how scientists in various disciplines display different attitudes toward their tools, affecting dynamics of professional collaboration and innovation in their fields. Although Dyson was reflecting on the field of gravitational tomography, his observations aptly describe the manner in which some educators are proactively finding new instructional uses for technology, "The style of the work...is opportunistic, unorganized, spontaneous. Nobody planned it and nobody administered it from the top. A new tool became available...and a number of bright people grabbed hold of it for a variety of purposes.... The style of the work is dominated by two factors, local enthusiasm and the Internet." (Johnson, 2000, n.p.)

The preceding description of some teachers' and educators' style of working with the Internet aptly portrays the surveyed Miss Rumphius Award winners. Eighty-nine percent of the respondents state that it was their own enjoyment of technology and desire to learn that influenced their ability to integrate technology into the literacy curriculum, and 92% state that enhanced and expanded opportunities for student learning is the greatest influence on their desire. However, this should be no surprise. Anyone perusing the websites created and designed by the Miss Rumphius teachers and their students can see the award winner's vision of literacy and literacy instruction.

The survey also reveals that a large majority (81%) of the Miss Rumphius teachers share their ideas with other teachers and educators through authored books and articles; local, state, and national conference presentations; inservices and workshops; classroom demonstrations; and e-mail. A majority also indicate that they created their website, at least in part, to serve as an instructional resource for other teachers. Obviously, these Miss Rumphius Award winners view their relationship to other teachers and educators within and beyond the school as an important determinant of quality student learning. According to a study conducted by Riel and Becker (2000), "professionally engaged teachers are more expert using computers to facilitate complex academic work by students and may be more accomplished at integrating computer technology into their own lives" (n.p.). The survey also identifies the Miss Rumphius teachers as holding a constructivist teaching philosophy. Constructivism is the belief that knowledge is temporary, developmental, and relies heavily on social and cultural factors. Teachers holding a constructivist philosophy attempt to incorporate as much hands-on experience, real-life application, group discussion, and individual reflection as possible. Those surveyed cite minilessons, modeling, demonstrating, hands-on experience, and peer teaching as their main methods for preparing students for using technology. The Miss Rumphius Award–winning teachers also cite problem solving, critical thinking, synthesizing, questioning, reflecting, inquiry, planning, collaboration, and experimentation as the predominant strategies students learn from the integration of technology into the literacy curriculum. This also is supported by Riel and Becker's (2000) study, which finds that professionally engaged teachers are more likely than other teachers "to see good teaching in terms of facilitating student inquiry rather than directly transmitting knowledge" (n.p.).

The Miss Rumphius Award winners incorporate their knowledge of learning tools, authenticity and motivation, the literacy curriculum, and the literacy development of students into the development of each website. They hold a multiple-literacies perspective with other teachers and alongside their students. This perspective requires us to consider new ways of defining literacy and reading instruction with respect to emerging information and communication technologies such as the Internet.

Evidence garnered from the survey of Miss Rumphius Award winners indicate that they incorporated their knowledge of learning tools, authenticity and movitation, the literacy curriculum, and the literacy development of students into the development of each website. If universities are to prepare future teachers to promote creative problem solving and constructive, independent thinking, the most effective way to achieve this may be to design a system whereby preservice teachers are encouraged to be thoughtful, creative problem solvers in the design of learning environments for students.

Miss Rumphius as a Role Model for Preservice Teachers

As stated previously, to a large extent reading and language arts methods faculty do not model effective integration of the Internet in their courses, which is compounded by the fact that many times it is difficult to find field placements for preservice teachers to observe and engage in effective practice with teachers who are integrating the Internet into the literacy curriculum. Yet acquiring sophisticated, in-depth knowledge, resulting in reflective and analytic practice, is an ongoing process that takes time, support, and a variety of experiences that are more powerful than simply reading and talking about research-based best practices (Hiebert & Stigler, 2000; Johnson & Altland, 2004). Teachers learn best by studying, observing, analyzing, doing, and reflecting; by collaborating with other teachers; by looking closely at students and their work; and by sharing their perspectives (Commeyras & DeGroff, 1998; Darling-Hammond & Falk, 1997; Lyons & Pinnell, 2001; Reil & Becker, 2000). Through collaborative conversation, teachers become active in the knowledge-building process. Teachers discuss, elaborate on concepts, and mediate relationships between themselves. Teachers view multiple perspectives on concepts or issues and generate understanding based on prior knowledge and current understandings (Cunningham, Duffy, & Knuth, 1993). This kind of learning cannot occur in university teacher preparation programs removed from practice in school classrooms. "Preparing teachers for more potent yet realistic teaching roles, without considering changes in schools' need to enable contemporary conceptions of learning and teaching, is folly" (Howey & Zimpher, 1994, p. 159).

Yet the Internet affords teacher educators and preservice teachers the opportunity to take advantage of resources that would otherwise not be available and would allow this kind of learning to take place. According to Leu, Karchmer, and Leu (1999), "The Internet breaks down traditional classroom walls, making each envisionment immediately accessible to other classrooms. This access allows each of us to benefit from other classrooms' environments and to include them in our curriculum" (p. 638). Each of the Miss Rumphius Award winners, their students, and their websites have much to offer preservice teachers. Cochran-Smith and Lytle (1999) use the term "local knowledge" (p. 291) to describe both a way of knowing about teaching and what teachers and communities come to know when they build knowledge collaboratively. In this way, preservice teachers join practicing teachers and teacher educators on a joint academic adventure to discover the "limits of expert knowledge." The Internet can facilitate the essential connection and community building between preservice teachers and Miss Rumphius winners, who can serve as the role models they so vitally need, through online projects. Leu (2002) reports on a study in which

> [s]tudents engaged in an online project over the Internet reported increased confidence in carrying out and presenting a research project with this even newer technology. Teachers in the same study, many of whom were using the Internet for the first time, reported greater use of the Internet technologies after the project was completed. (p. 320)

When using online projects, the role of the teacher educator becomes that of facilitator, guiding preservice teachers to appropriate online resources, such as the Miss Rumphius sites, while taking advantage of the scaffolded electronic learning environment (Coiro, 2003). One such learning environment is the webquest.

WebQuest: Teachers Helping Teachers Integrate Technology Into the Classroom

A WebQuest facilitates the acquisition, integration, and extension of a vast amount of information through tasks specifically designed to engage the learner in analysis and demonstration of understanding. According to Dodge (1998) and March, creators of the WebQuest,

> A WebQuest is an inquiry-oriented activity in which most or all of the information used by learners is drawn from the Web. WebQuests are designed to use learners' time well, to focus on using information rather than looking for it, and to support learners' thinking at the levels of analysis, synthesis and evaluation. (n.p.)

WebQuests are built on a constructivist philosophy, and therefore, cooperative learning and scaffolding are important components. Cooperative work on a WebQuest creates an exchange of ideas, insights, and opinions. During these exchanges, the participants' understanding increases based on the information presented through the WebQuest resources. Scaffolds are provided to support participants through the structure and resource links that are built into the WebQuest. Participants—in this case, preservice teachers—do not have to search the Internet to find relevant, valid websites, because the teacher educator has already selected the websites, and ensured that preserice teachers spend high-quality time interacting with information rather than surfing the Web.

Currently, teachers develop most WebQuests for elementary and secondary students. But the principles that support an effective, well-designed WebQuest for students also hold true for educators (Johnson & Zufall, 2004). The following sections explain the five essential components of a WebQuest: (1) introduction, (2) task, (3), resources, (4) process, and (5) evaluation. I use the Miss Rumphius Site: Teachers Helping Teachers Integrate Literacy and the Internet (see Figure 12.1, www.wm.edu/education/research/cdjohn/webquest.php) to show how the WebQuest design is critical to being an effective instructional resource.

Component 1: Introduction

The purpose of the introduction is both to prepare and hook the reader by relating to the reader's interests or goals or engagingly describing a compelling question or problem. The introduction builds on the reader's prior knowledge by mentioning explicitly important concepts or principles, and it effectively prepares the reader for the lesson by foreshadowing new concepts and principles. The introduction to the Miss Rumphius Site: Teachers Helping Teachers Integrate Literacy and the Internet WebQuest is meant to draw preservice teachers into the topic of technology and literacy by asking a series of questions: Do you want to use technology in your classroom as part of your literacy program but don't know how to get started? Are you apprehensive or ambivalent about using the Internet yourself or with students? Do you wish there were other educators who could serve as role models for using technology in the classroom? The introduction then explains that in order for teachers to prepare their students for the future, teachers must integrate technology into the literacy curriculum.

Figure 12.1   The Miss Rumphius Site: Teachers Helping Teachers Integrate Literacy and the Internet

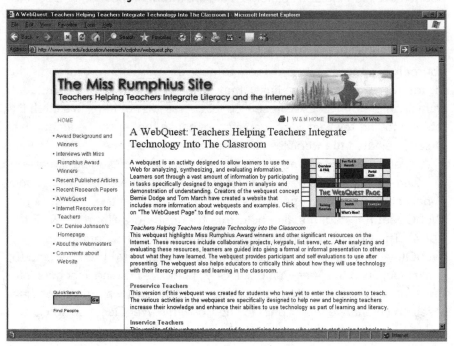

Component 2: Task

The WebQuest task focuses learners on the culminating performance or product that drives all the learning activities. The task requires the synthesis of multiple sources of information, taking a position, or going beyond the data given and making a generalization or product. For the Teachers Helping Teachers Integrate Literacy and the Internet WebQuest, the preservice teachers are directed to go to the resources webpage and explore the many websites listed there. While exploring these websites, the preservice teachers are encouraged to join a listserv, e-mail a Miss Rumphius Award winner, peruse the winners' webpages, join a collaborative project, and read winners' interviews. Preservice teachers also are encouraged to keep a journal to document ideas, materials, activities, or connections they make. These notes will be helpful with activities preservice teachers will do which are explained in the process component of the WebQuest.

Component 3: Resources

Resources are a critical component of a WebQuest because they provide links to various websites that are linked to technology and literacy. On the Teachers Helping Teachers Integrate Literacy and the Internet WebQuest, these links are separated into five categories: (1) Miss Rumphius Award winners, (2) mailing lists or listservs, (3) collaborative partnering or projects, (4) keypals, and (5) other significant websites. Next to each link is a brief description of what can be found at that website. There also are a few links to specific articles by the Miss Rumphius Award winners and about effectively using technology in the classroom. Exploring these websites is the basis for what preservice teachers will do next during the process component.

Component 4: Process

A WebQuest is a long-term activity that will take preservice teachers several weeks to complete but will cultivate new learning. The process provides specific steps broken down into three parts for preservice teachers to follow: (1) making the connections, (2) recognizing the connections, and (3) implementing activities in the classroom.

PART ONE: MAKING THE CONNECTIONS. Using the resources, the preservice teachers follow specific tasks to investigate most of the websites. For example, before using the Teachers Helping Teachers Integrate Technology into the Classroom WebQuest site, the first step is for the preservice teachers to go to the Miss Rumphius Award winners' websites and carefully view the projects the award-winning teachers created with their students. The preservice teachers also should browse several of the mailing lists or listservs, choose one to join, and enter into a discussion with other educators about topics related to integrating literacy and technology into the classroom. Other resources include looking at and evaluating collaborative partnering sites, keypal sites, and other significant teacher resource sites. The preservice teachers should write down in their journals anything they find interesting.

PART TWO: RECOGNIZING THE CONNECTIONS. Preservice teachers are to evaluate critically each one of the resources they have explored. Using a website evaluation tool protocol to assist in critically evaluating the various aspects of a website and their journal notes, the preservice teachers fill out a resources guide of the best resources they found on the Internet and list the strengths and weaknesses of each resource.

PART THREE: IMPLEMENTING ACTIVITIES IN THE CLASSROOM. The Teachers Helping Teachers Integrate Literacy and the Internet WebQuest site concludes with a brief summary of the significant connections to various resources that the WebQuest provides. This WebQuest serves only as a beginning for the use of technology in the classroom. Preservice teachers use the classroom connections guide to delve deeper into specific activities and strategies they can use in their future classrooms. The preservice teacher must think about the resources they are comfortable using, the feasibility of using technology in their potential classroom or school, and how using technology to enhance literacy instruction and learning ties in with the literacy curriculum. By engaging in this type of analysis, the preservice teachers should be able to take the appropriate first steps to integrate technology in their future classrooms.

Component 5: Evaluation

The evaluation section provides a way for the preservice teachers to extend their new-found knowledge and collaborate with one another about technology and literacy. Preservice teachers design a small presentation that includes the connections made through the WebQuest, including people, resources, and websites for their peer class of other preservice teachers, which they have carefully planned and organized to provide maximum benefits for the participants. Ultimately, the idea behind sharing this new information is the ongoing process of teachers helping other teachers. A presentation guide is provided to assist the preservice teachers in planning and organizing and to help guide their thinking. This guide addresses topics before, during, and after the presentation. Space is provided for the preservice teachers to write down their thoughts as the preservice teachers construct an effective presentation. The preservice teachers evaluate themselves as presenters by filling out a self-evaluation form that is clearly linked to the before, during, and after format of the presentation guide. The class peers of the presentation also will complete an evaluation.

In addition to face-to-face presentations, an online option is available also for preservice teachers to present their findings. Teacher educators who teach distance education courses or who have limited access to equipment for face-to-face presentations may want to use this option. The online presentation guide will assist preservice teachers in creating a PowerPoint presentation that can be posted on the Internet for all class peers to view. It is very important that a method of feedback is provided, either in class or online. Several examples of preservice teachers' Power-

Point presentations are available to view on the WebQuest evaluation page (www.wm.edu/education/research/cdjohn/preservicequest/evaluation.php).

Preservice Teachers' Responses to the WebQuest

During the fall 2003 semester, 25 preservice teachers who enrolled in a reading methods course also participated in the Miss Rumphius Site: Teachers Helping Teachers Integrate Literacy and the Internet WebQuest, as part of the course requirements. The WebQuest was assigned early in the semester. The instructor of the course introduced the purpose and framework of the WebQuest and then provided a demonstration of how to access the website and complete the different requirements of the five components. The preservice teachers approximately had two months to work through the five components. Throughout the semester, the instructor made connections to the Miss Rumphius websites and resources as they related to relevant course content.

At the end of the semester, the preservice teachers were asked to anonymously complete an open-ended questionnaire about the Miss Rumphius Site: Teachers Helping Teachers Integrate Literacy and the Internet WebQuest. Specifically, they were asked to relate the connections they made from the WebQuest to their field experiences, the effective instruction and learning of literacy, and the effective use of technology. Preservice teachers were asked to indicate on a scale of 1 to 4 how often they had observed their practicum teachers use the Internet in their practicum classrooms over the course of the semester (1 = never, 2 = one or two times, 3 = three to five times, 4 = six or more times). All 25 preservice teachers indicated that they had never seen their cooperating teachers use the Internet with their students.

Though none of the preservice teachers are able to observe their cooperating teachers using the Internet, 96% made connections from their participation with the WebQuest to their practicum experiences, and 56% indicated that they tell their cooperating teachers about one or more activities the preservice teachers see on the Miss Rumphius websites that are relevant to the literacy instruction in the classroom. One preservice teacher states, "My cooperating teacher [is] doing a unit on poetry, and I [tell] her about the fall poetry project I [see] on one of the Miss Rumphius sites." In addition, 28% of the preservice teachers state that they think about specific student's needs in relationship to the activities on the Miss Rumphius websites. For example, one preservice teacher reveals, "There is this one student that I spend a lot of time with whenever I go to my classroom and the teacher gives a writing assignment, because he really needs help with his writing. I wonder if he would be more motivated to write if he could participate in some of the online writing projects I [see] on the Web quest [sic]." A smaller number (12%) of the preservice teachers indicate that they use ideas from the WebQuest to develop lesson plans and conduct lessons in their practicum classrooms.

Of course, the preservice teachers also are making connections to effective literacy instruction and learning within the context of their field placement. When specifically asked about these connections, all the preservice teachers write one or more comments that convey their understanding of the link between effective literacy instruction and learning and the Internet. Comments include authentic learning, inquiry, higher-order and critical-thinking skills, motivation and engagement, building background knowledge, supporting the curriculum, and meeting individual student needs.

The question about connections to the effective use of technology and the Internet reveals a broad range of responses that fall into several categories. One category that emerges is the preservice teachers' confidence or lack of confidence in creating their own Internet projects once they begin teaching. Although a small percentage (12%) of preservice teachers indicate they are intimidated by the Miss Rumphius websites and do not think they could develop such websites themselves, these same preservice teachers state that they feel comfortable involving their future students in existing online projects. However, a majority (64%) indicate that they feel confident in developing their own online projects; in fact, several of these preservice teachers state that they already had planned these activities with other preservice teachers in the class. For example, one preservice teacher states, "I think the use of the Internet to create an authentic audience for students' writing is something I really want to try when I start teaching. Jamie, Cindy (pseudonyms), and I have decided to keep in touch so that we can have our students write to each other."

A few (12%) preservice teachers comment on the lack of connection between the educational technology course they had taken the previous semester and the information in the WebQuest. One preservice teacher comments, "Even though we looked at lots of teachers' websites and created our own website in the Ed. Tech. course last year, I didn't really see how I could use it until now." Other preservice teachers generally comment that they thought technology is important and that teachers should use it in the literacy curriculum. They cited the preparation of their future students for the future in the job market as the impetus.

The preservice teachers also were given the opportunity to make comments about the Miss Rumphius websites, teachers, or other resources on the WebQuest that they did not have the chance to state elsewhere in the survey. The following comments stood out as especially significant:

- I wrote to one of the Miss Rumphius teachers, and she e-mailed me right back. She was so nice and encouraged me to try creating my own online project.
- I was very surprised by the listserv I joined. The teachers were very supportive of each other and spent a lot of time sharing ideas.
- I felt like I was getting a peek inside the Miss Rumphius teachers' classrooms when I visited some of the sites.
- I got a lot of great ideas that I want to try when I start teaching.

The results of this survey indicate that the WebQuest project not only raises the awareness level of how the preservice teachers can integrate the Internet into the literacy curriculum but also provides a scaffold for making important connections among the reading-methods-course content, the educational-technology-course content, and their practicum classroom over time. There also is some indication that a sense of collegiality had developed among the preservice teachers, their cooperating teachers, and the Miss Rumphius Award–winning teachers. Many of the preservice teachers indicate that they felt confident in their own ability to create Internet resources or involve their students in existing Internet activities as a means of enhancing the literacy curriculum, meeting individual student needs, providing students with motivation and engagement, and promoting inquiry and higher-order thinking among students. This especially is encouraging given the fact that none of the preservice teachers observed their cooperating teachers using the Internet with their students. It seems more than likely that many of these preservice teachers will put into practice much of what they have learned through their participation in the Miss Rumphius Site: Teachers Helping Teachers Integrate Literacy and the Internet WebQuest.

Concluding Thoughts

According to a report by the Web-Based Education Commission (2000),

> not enough is being done to assure that today's educators have the skills and knowledge needed for effective Web-based teaching. And if teacher education programs do not address this issue at once, we will soon have

lost the opportunity to enhance the performance of a whole generation of new teachers, and the students they teach. (p. 2)

At the same time, the CEO Forum on Education and Technology (2000) suggests that teacher preparation institutions should offer a "technology warranty" (p. 7), certifying that their graduates are technologically prepared educators. A technology warranty may be a step too far, but teacher educators must continue to experiment with effective approaches to provide meaningful experiences with computer technology for preservice teachers. Leu et al. (1999) state, "teachers who develop highly effective and widely recognized envisionments for literacy may serve as central informants for effective instructional practice" (p. 642). Online projects such as the Miss Rumphius Site: Teachers Helping Teachers Integrate Literacy and the Internet WebQuest, brings the local knowledge and expertise of outstanding classroom teachers like the Miss Rumphius Award winners into the literacy methods classroom to serve as role models for future teachers. Yet, the inclusion of a WebQuest does not diminish the importance of the university instructor's role as a model, facilitator, and guide in the use of technology, and the importance of providing explicit instruction about how computer technology will benefit preservice teachers and their future students.

The online learning environment created by the structure of the WebQuest provides a context for preservice teachers to engage in studying, observing, analyzing, doing, reflecting, collaborating with other teachers, and looking closely at children and their work. Solomon (2002) states, "When students create and share reports, Web pages, or digital presentations that require higher-order skills, they are empowered as learners and thinkers" (p. 19). Teachers who are empowered as learners and thinkers become thoughtful and creative problem solvers in the design of learning environments for students.

REFERENCES

CEO Forum on Education and Technology. (1999). *Professional development: A link to better learning.* Retrieved October 2, 2000, from http://www.ceoforum.org/downloads/99report

CEO Forum on Education and Technology. (2000). *Teacher preparation STaR chart: A self-assessment tool for colleges of education.* Retrieved October 2, 2003, from http://www.ceoforum.org/downloads/tpreport.pdf

Cochran-Smith, M., & Lytle, S. (1999). Relationships of knowledge and practice: Teacher learning in communities. In A. Iran-Nejad & P.D. Pearson (Eds.), *Review of research in education* (pp. 249–305). Washington, DC: American Educational Research Association.

Coiro, J.L. (2003). Reading comprehension on the Internet: Expanding our understanding of reading comprehension to encompass new literacies. *The Reading Teacher, 56,* 458–464.

Commeyras, M., & DeGroff, L. (1998). Literacy professionals' perspectives on professional development and pedagogy: A United States survey. *Reading Research Quarterly, 33,* 434–472.

Cunningham, D., Duffy, T., & Knuth, R. (1993). The textbook of the future. In C. McKnight, A. Dillon, & J. Richardson (Eds.), *Hypertext: A psychological perspective* (pp. 19–49). New York: Ellis Horwood.

Darling-Hammond, L., & Falk, B. (1997). Using standards and assessments to support student learning. *Phi Delta Kappan, 79*(3), 190–199.

Dodge, B. (1998). *The WebQuest page.* Retrieved November 18, 2004, from http://webquest.sdsu.edu/webquest.html

Gore, J.M., & Zeichner, K.M. (1991). Action research and reflective teaching in preservice teacher education: A case study from the United States. *Teaching and Teacher Education, 7*(2), 119–136.

Hiebert, J., & Stigler, J.W. (2000). A proposal for improving classroom teaching: Lessons from the TIMSS video study. *The Elementary School Journal, 101*(1), 3–20.

Hoadley, M., Engelking, J., & Bright, L. (1995). A model for technology infusion in higher education. In D.A. Willis, B. Robin, & J. Willis (Eds.). *Technology Education Annual, 1995: Proceedings of SITE '95—Sixth International Conference of the Society for Information Technology and Teacher Education.* Charlottesville, VA: Association for the Advancement of Computing in Education (AACE).

Howey, K.R., & Zimpher, N.L. (1994). Nontraditional contexts for learning to teach. *Educational Forum, 58*(2), 155–161.

Johnson, C.D. (2002). Electronic dialoguing in a preservice reading methods course: A yearlong study. *Reading Online.* Retrieved January 19, 2005, from http://www.readingonline.org/articles/art_index.asp?HREF=johnson/index.html

Johnson, C.D. (2004). *A survey of the Miss Rumphius Award winners: Designers of the new literacies of the Internet* (Manuscript submitted for publication).

Johnson, C.D., & Altland, V. (2004). No teacher left behind: The development of a professional collaboration. *Literacy Teaching and Learning, 8*(2), 63–82.

Johnson, C.D, & Zufall, L. (2004, March). Not just for kids anymore: WebQuests for professional development. *Reading Online.* Retrieved January 19, 2005, from http://www.readingonline.org/electronic/elec_index.asp?HREF=webwatch/webquests/index.html

Johnson, M. (2000). *New roles for educators: Milken Family Foundation.* Retrieved November 15, 2003, from http://www.mff.org/edtech/article.taf?_function=detail&Content_uid1=290

Leu, D.J., Jr. (2002). The new literacies: Research on reading instruction with the Internet. In A.E. Farstrup & S.J. Samuels (Eds.), *What research has to say about reading instruction* (3rd ed., pp. 310–336). Newark, DE: International Reading Association.

Leu, D.J., Jr., Karchmer, R.A., & Leu, D.D. (1999). The Miss Rumphius effect: Envisionments for literacy and learning that transform the Internet. *The Reading Teacher, 52,* 636–642.

Lyons, C.A., & Pinnell, G.S. (2001). *Systems for change in literacy education: A guide to professional development.* Portsmouth, NH: Heinemann.

Milken Exchange on Education and International Society for Technology in Education. (1999). *Will new teachers be prepared to teach in the digital age? A national survey on information technology in teacher education.* Retrieved October 2, 2000, from http://www.mff.org/publications/publications.taf?page=154

National Commission on Teaching and America's Future. (2003). *No dream denied: A pledge to America's children.* Retrieved November 18, 2004, from http://www.ecs.org/html/Document.asp?chouseid=4269

Riel, M.M. & Becker, H. (2000). *Teacher professional engagement and constructivist-compatible computer use.* Retrieved September 29, 2003, from http://www.crito.uci.edu/tlc/findings/report_7

Solomon, G. (2002). Digital equity: It's not just about access anymore. *Technology & Learning, 22*(9), 18–26.

Sugrue, B., & Hansen, S. (1997). It's in the mind of the performer. *Performance Improvement, 36*(8), 36–37.

Web-Based Education Commission. (2000). *The power of the Internet for learning: Moving from promise to practice.* Retrieved November 18, 2004, from http://www.ed.gov/offices/AC/WBEC/FinalReport/WBECReport.pdf

CHILDREN'S LITERATURE

Cooney, B. (1982). *Miss Rumphius.* New York: Viking.

CHAPTER 13

Every Teacher a Miss Rumphius: Empowering Teachers With Effective Professional Development

Julie Coiro

In my travels as an educator, researcher, and provider of professional development, I often meet inspirational teachers, like the Miss Rumphius Award winners featured in this book, who are taking risks, exploring new paths, and providing new learning opportunities for their students. Similarly, I have conversations with other educators prompted by easy Internet access to publish research in scholarly journals and online discussion boards that help bridge the gap between research and practice. I have spent quite a few years observing the process that occurs among school administrators and teachers as they learn more about linking models of effective professional development with elements of a new literacies perspective (Leu, Kinzer, Coiro, & Cammack, 2004) and other effective practices for integrating literacy and Internet technologies.

The purpose of this chapter is to summarize findings from current research, my work with educators, and the journeys of the Miss Rumphius Award winners to answer two questions: First, *What is known about the nature of effective professional development in the area of technology use and integration with literacy instruction?* Second, *What characterizes Miss Rumphius Award winners, and what do their stories reveal about how teachers learn to successfully integrate technology into the curriculum?* To address the first question, I begin by sharing two scenarios from my own experience as a staff developer. Then I review research into the current state of professional development, briefly examine studies of more effective models, and outline four lessons learned while working closely with teachers in a range of school settings. To answer the second question, I explore commonalties among the Miss Rumphius Award winners featured in this book and provide insight into how their stories can motivate other educators to bravely face the challenges associated with learning on the Internet. Although each teacher's journey is uniquely different, I conclude the chapter by highlighting seven lessons we, as educators, can learn from these award-winning stories about teaching and learning with information and communication technologies (ICTs).

As I begin, I invite you to join me in a journey back to my own teaching about four years ago that was a turning point in my development as a literacy and technology integration specialist. I share this with you as an introduction to the lessons we can learn as each of us seeks to develop effective ways of learning and teaching with technology in our classrooms. As you read, imagine yourself as one of the teachers in the audience.

It is the day before the school year begins at Smith Elementary School, and the faculty of 35 teachers and 5 teaching assistants are gathered in the auditorium for a day of inservice.

"Good morning teachers," the principal announces from the microphone, breaking up the small clusters of conversation spread around the room. "Let's everyone find a seat so we can begin today's program."

As the invited presenter, I offer a friendly smile and wait as teachers begin to find their seats. A small group of excited teachers take their seats in the front row and return my smile. The majority of the teachers meander to the middle rows, and I hear three teachers whispering to see if anyone knows the topic of the presentation. And in the back row, I spot two teachers setting up shop with folders, scissors, and a basket of some sort. Shortly after, I realize they have brought along two long strips of laminated bulletin board shapes that need to be cut out before school begins the next day. Every teacher knows the feeling of preparing your classroom for the new year each fall, so I am not really that surprised that they already have begun cutting as I make my way up to the microphone to begin my presentation.

The principal announces, "The topic of our two-hour session this morning will be about best practices in integrating the Internet into your literacy curriculum." Low mumbles and groans of surprise rise from the audience, as the principal continues. "Now, I know originally the primary teachers were scheduled for a session about guided reading, and grades 4 and 5 were going to meet in their grade-level teams, but we've moved the grade-specific sessions to the afternoon, after deciding technology integration is an important issue for all of us. Besides, this way, you'll all be prepared when we finally are able to get all your classrooms wired, probably sometime this spring." The principal nods a bit apologetically to me, realizing that not all of the teachers seem quite as receptive to my presentation as he was hoping. He turns back to his staff and proudly announces, "So without further ado, please welcome Mrs. Coiro."

With that, I take the stage, making a mental note of the sense of disengagement permeating the auditorium and the fact that the principal, their leader, is leaving the room for more important places. I cannot help but think that this will be yet another traditional stand-up presentation doomed to inspire little more than frustration, defensiveness, and a sense of being overwhelmed by a large group presentation that moves too quickly for some teachers, too slowly for others, and often, too far from reality for most. I find myself wondering why some schools offer no alternatives to this format of professional development when research shows that fewer than 10% of teachers implement new ideas learned in traditional workshop settings (Joyce & Showers, 1988).

Despite signs of interest from a few teachers, I ponder how things might be different if teachers were asked to voice their own agendas for professional development ideas around technology integration. I wonder what would happen if I had more time in small groups to listen to teachers' concerns, validate their attempts to learn more, and remind them that effective change with new technologies is a slow and thoughtful process requiring long-term commitment and support from the entire school community. As my presentation comes to a close, I decide to learn more about the elements of effective professional development models and how to employ these in ways that empower teachers as literacy leaders, improve instructional practices, and increase student academic achievement.

Now, four years later, things have changed quite a bit in terms of my own understanding about professional development and in terms of the changes that have taken place in schools, with teachers, and with technology. Ironically, I find myself back at Smith Elementary School, this time virtually meeting over the Internet with a group of four first-grade teachers who have volunteered to be literacy leaders in their school. These teachers meet every two weeks for half-hour study group sessions to discuss an agenda that they determine. This week, they have completed the first stage of a collaborative Internet project entitled That's What Happens When It's Spring (see www.mrsmcgowan.com/spring/index.html), which Marci McGowan is coordinating. She is one of the Miss Rumphius Award winners featured in this book (see chapter 6). For her project, she first invites classes of primary school students to read a book of their choice about spring. Then, she invites all participating classes to draw and write about the unique signs of spring that occur in their different school communities and publish their work online at her website. As the teachers gather for their study group meeting, they are eager to reflect on the successes and challenges of implementing McGowan's spring project so far. They have invited the principal to share their progress, the library media specialist to help develop an action plan of next steps, and me to support their work virtually using iSight video technology (see more at www.apple.com/isight). As a result, I can see and hear their entire meeting, and they can see and hear me via the Internet on the computer screen.

In contrast to my presentation experience four years earlier, the teachers now are actively engaged in their own learning, are in full control of their study group's agenda, and are excited about sharing their teaching progress. The principal's presence provides an important layer of support and vision beyond the collegiality the teachers share with one another. The library media specialist is excited to be developing lessons collaboratively in a way that ties her library media curriculum to the first-grade literacy curriculum. And I, now an ongoing, equal participant rather than an outsider presenting unrelated information, am able to hear the teacher's immediate needs. After hearing their discussion, I point them to an article entitled "Internet Project: Preparing Students for New Literacies in a Global Village" (Leu, 2001) appearing in the Web-based journal *Reading Online* (www.readingonline.org), which validates their Internet lessons as effective literacy instructional practices. Clearly, the nature of literacy, instruction, and professional development is transformed by new ICTs.

What Does Research Reveal About the Nature of Effective Professional Development in the Area of Technology Use and Integration With Literacy Instruction?

Scenarios like the one I just described prompts the need to change how we think about literacy, learning, and professional development. Research also reminds teachers and educators that they presently stand at an important crossroads in education. The nature of literacy rapidly is changing as new technologies emerge (DiSessa, 2000; Dresang & McClelland, 1999; Leu et al., 2004; Reinking, McKenna, Labbo, & Kieffer, 1998), and recent literature addresses the need for changes in the way educators think about literacy as influenced by technology. For example, in their literacy and technology position statement, the International Reading Association (2001) suggests "traditional definitions of reading, writing, and viewing, and traditional definitions of best practice instruction—derived from a long tradition of book and other print media—will be insufficient"(n.p.). Similarly, the recent report of the RAND Reading Study Group (2002) argues that "accessing the Internet makes large demands on individuals' literacy skills; in some cases, this new technology requires readers to have novel literacy skills, and little is known about how to analyze or teach those skills" (p. 4).

These rapid changes in literacy demand new ways of thinking about the nature of classroom instruction and professional development (Coiro, 2003a; Leu et al., 2004). Federal legislation (U.S. Department of Education, 2001) currently mandates that teachers ground their instruction in current research-based practices for literacy and technology integration. However, evidence suggests that teachers receive very little support in the way of research-based instructional strategies or opportunities for quality professional development (President's Committee of Advisors on Science and Technology, 1997; Trotter, 1999). Pianfetti (2001) describes a "lack of digital literacy among educators...[that signals]...a change in the professional development of preservice and in-service teachers" (p. 255). Studies show that teachers continue to use technology to emphasize game playing and drill-and-practice activities as opposed to using technology as part of a more meaningful and engaging learning opportunities (Carey & Worthington, 1997; Solomon, 2002). In addition, several documents outline the lack of quality professional development programs for teachers exploring ways of integrating technology into their instruction (Lemke & Coughlin, 1998; National Center for Education Statistics, 1999; Task Force on Technology and Teacher Education, 1997). If educators are to keep up with the advances in technology and the resulting changes in literacy, it is imperative that schools adopt new practices for professional development.

Recent research suggests that the most successful professional development models engage and empower teachers to have a stronger voice in directing their own learning (Educational Research Service, 1998; Lyon & Pinnell, 2001; Robb, 2000). Effective models of professional development in the area of literacy and technology integration follow three premises. They (1) recognize a developmental process through which teachers use technology, (2) validate the different dispositions that teachers bring to their use of technology, (3) and employ job-embedded study groups as a means of empowering teachers to take a more active role in their own learning. Below, I briefly explore each of these three elements in more detail.

First, Apple Classrooms of Tomorrow (1995), after studying the impact of technology on student learning, suggests that as teachers integrate technology into their curriculum, they tend to progress through a developmental continuum of abilities consisting of four stages: (1) *adoption*, or using technology to support traditional instruction; (2) *adaptation*, or integrating technology into existing classroom activities; (3) *appropriation*, or developing new approaches to teaching that take advantage of technology; and (4) *innovation*, or discovering entirely new uses for technology tools. A teacher's thoughtful movement through these four stages, which more recently is recognized as an "evolution of thought and practice" (Apple Education, 2004), occurs over the course of several years rather than after a few workshop sessions. More importantly, "this evolution refers not to teachers' progression through a set of technology skills, but rather describes their way of thinking and acting when it comes to integrating technology into their teaching" (n.p.). The most effective designers of professional development recognize these developmental stages of thinking in their programs. They guide each teacher's realistic assessment of where he or she currently sits on the developmental continuum and where he or she should be headed next in her thinking about technology use for teaching and learning.

Other researchers describe similar developmental continuums through which teachers move as they explore new literacies with technology in their classroom. Gilbert Valdez and his colleagues (2000) at the North Central Regional Educational Laboratories (NCREL) highlight three distinct phases in the evolution of the use and expectations for technology integration: (1) print automation, wherein students and teachers use technology that automates print-based practices with some increase in active hands-on learning; (2) expansion of learning opportunities, wherein students use technology in small groups to produce and share work products; and (3) data-driven virtual learning, wherein a shift in classroom dynamics results from a well-designed systemic integration of learner-centered approaches to education.

The Texas Center for Educational Technology (1999) has collected and adapted several instruments designed to help characterize the phases of teachers' technology use and adoption into the curriculum. This online collection includes instruments that measure levels of proficiency with various digital technologies, the degree of technology integration into their classroom curriculum, and the attitudinal changes of teachers as they use technology over time.

The notion of developmental continuums such as these validates the reality that no teacher becomes an innovative technology user overnight, and in fact, the process often takes up to five years or more. Moreover, individual teachers may enter into the continuum at different stages and most often move through these stages at different paces, depending on their prior experience with technology and personal beliefs about technology's role in the classroom. Thus, these continuums provide a context for staff developers as they first assess the needs of individual teachers within a school faculty and then design programs that more appropriately address each teacher's unique learning needs.

A second finding of research in this area shows that the most effective facilitators recognize the important role a teacher's belief system plays on how he or she receives recommendations about how technology should be used in the classroom. Work in this area suggests the presence of distinct groups of teachers with different purposes and different beliefs about the use of technology in their classrooms (e.g., Balajthy, 2000; Honey & Moeller, 1990; Labbo & Reinking, 1999). Labbo and Reinking (1999), for example, argue that educators perceive the potentials of technology use through at least five different lenses, or goals, that influence a teacher's interpretations of a certain technology's value and worth in his or her curriculum. Their framework for integrating technology with literacy moves from goals that are more traditional (e.g., new, digital technologies used to enhance the goals of conventional literacy instruction) to goals that "place technology in a more active, transforming role" (e.g., new technologies used to empower students) (p. 481). Different teachers possess different goals, and in turn, these goals influence how certain digital technologies may or may not be used in their classrooms.

Christenson and Knezak (2001) have developed a technology and reading inventory to assess how differences in teaching style, reading instruction preference, and technology beliefs affect the overall effectiveness of using technology to develop reading, writing, and thinking skills. Thus, the presence of different beliefs or multiple lenses within any group of educators is a reminder that teachers bring to their professional-development opportunities diverse beliefs about classroom pedagogy and the value of technology for learning. Consequently, the "one-size-fits-all [professional development] experience seldom addresses teachers' specific needs or skill levels, resulting in uneven or infrequent implementation that rarely leads to instructional change" (Gora & Hinson, 2003, p. 36).

A third area of research of effective models of professional development evaluates the utility and success of various alternative formats to large-group training presentations. Several examples in the literature illustrate the potential of job-embedded focused study groups, otherwise known as peer mentors or communities of learners, for empowering teachers and facilitating change in the quality of professional development (e.g., Lyon & Pinnell, 2001; McKenzie, 2001). Generally, faculty study groups serve many functions or purposes most often that occur simultaneously. Murphy and Lick (2001) outline the following purposes:

1. developing a deeper understanding of academic content,
2. supporting the implementation of curricular and instructional initiatives,
3. integrating and giving coherence to a school's instructional programs and practice,
4. targeting a school-wide instructional need,
5. studying the research on teaching and learning,
6. monitoring the impact or effects of instructional initiatives on students, and
7. providing a time when teachers can examine student work together. (p. 18)

Similarly, in her book *Redefining Staff Development,* Laura Robb (2000) constructs a workshop model for job-embedded professional study in which facilitators "invite teachers to learn" (p. 25) rather than forcing teachers to change. Facilitators build topics and timelines directly from teachers' own questions, needs, and concerns, rather than dictating to teachers a particular agenda. This more engaging process serves to build internal capacity, peer mentoring, self-reflection, teacher decision making, and collaborative networking.

Customized variations of the study-group model have proven successful in professional development environments, focusing on both literacy and technology integration. The Center for Improvement of Early Reading Achievement, for example, reports the opportunity for teachers to engage in ongoing inquiry and action research, regarding how to help students meet standards in study groups or professional learning communities. This is one of several effective school practices associated with high student performance in reading (Taylor, Pearson, Clark, & Walpole, 1999). Lyon and Pinell (2001) outline a version of study groups for literacy education that is grounded in principles of constructivist-based teaching and "system thinking." They provide explicit procedures and strategies for improving instruction as well as student literacy achievement. In their model, study-group facilitators guide faculty through a professional development program framed in 10 components. Facilitators

1. assess the context for teaching and learning,
2. provide the basics of a new approach with concrete examples of organization and routines,

3. demonstrate the procedures with explicit examples,

4. establish a clear understanding of the rationales of the new approach,

5. engage the teachers in active learning and exploration of new techniques,

6. invite teachers to try out new techniques and share their analyses of process and results,

7. establish routines and procedures for pursuing a plan of action,

8. coach for shifts in teacher and student behavior,

9. coach to support teacher reflection, analysis and continual refinement of their teaching, and

10. extend learning through small group conversations that connect theory with practice and build networks among teachers. (p. 14)

Throughout this process, teachers begin to take ownership "because it includes them and gives them a chance to grow, change, and contribute... in ways that are intimately related to their own professional goals, visions and needs" (p. 183).

The study group has proven particularly effective in supporting technology integration among teachers. Garry and Graham's (2004) study-group model, for example, is built around a support system that progresses naturally through four phases. As study groups evolve, "they provide an avenue for addressing multiple classroom and school issues in a context of collegiality...[while]...emphasizing the incremental and collaborative nature of effective professional growth that is vitally important in learning new approaches towards teaching with technology" (pp. 2–3).

The study-group model is used effectively for professional development in many programs around the United States. Administrators and technology facilitators in Louisiana successfully use the Technology Study Group Professional Development Model to increase teachers' comfort levels for using technology and to promote positive change in instructional practice (Gora & Hinson, 2003). In New Mexico, 419 teachers involved in weekend workshops with tech-savvy classroom teachers serving as "peer technology experts" demonstrate significant increases in confidence, technology use, collegial behavior and a willingness to lead others in the change process (Martin, Hupert, Gonzales, & Admon, 2003). In Missouri, Branigan's study (2002) demonstrates the impact of an inquiry-based peer coaching professional development program called Enhancing Missouri's Instructional Networked Teaching Strategies (eMINTS) on student learning outcomes.

Results show that a larger percentage of students in eMINTS programs scored higher on standardized achievement tests as compared with students who took the tests without using the eMINTS program. Indeed, effective models of professional development for integrating technology directly can lead to increases in effective teacher practices as well as increases in student academic achievement.

What Have I Learned From Teachers About Effective Professional Development for Technology Integration?

In the next section, I share four important lessons I have learned from teachers that continue to influence my current beliefs about effective professional development for technology integration. In doing so, I hope to validate the concerns of other teachers who may be reading this book. At the same time, I invite administrators, researchers, and public policymakers to consider these four issues when framing a vision for change.

First, my experience confirms that *professional development opportunities are most effective when teachers are empowered to determine their own needs for professional study with regard to literacy and technology integration.* A recent review of the research in this area reports that "involving teachers in planning the goals of the technology program will help to decrease teacher resistance, and increase the staff's sense of ownership and commitment" (Educational Research Service, 1998, p. 2). My experience confirms that when given an opportunity, most teachers rise to the challenge of clarifying their needs and learning agendas within the broader context of whole-faculty development offerings. Likewise, teachers are motivated by the opportunity to pose questions, voice their concerns, and see the connection that learning to use technology may impact student achievement.

This is not to say, however, that administrators do not play a vital role in fostering the vision and leadership that prompts teachers to use technology effectively in their classrooms. Part of my role as a facilitator of professional development provides me opportunities to work with administrators around the state of Connecticut (see more at Coiro & Leu, 2003). In these sessions, my colleagues and I work to support administrators as they develop and articulate a school-based educational vision for the future. Engaged in large- and small-group activities, these administrators reflect on the challenges associated with a broader vision of education that includes the new literacies of the Internet. They brainstorm alternative formats for professional development. They struggle to balance issues of access, accountability, student safety, classroom instruction, and new ways of measuring learning with and from the Internet. Most importantly, they seek to clarify the changes that are taking place in their own roles as well as in the roles of teachers and students as a result of emerging technologies in schools. Administrators are to be commended for their close attention to issues that will affect children's literacy futures in a global information economy. Administrative leadership in developing a common school vision that empowers teachers while addressing district concerns is the first step toward promoting effective instructional change with technology in classrooms.

The second lesson I learned is to *listen carefully to a teacher's needs and provide resources that address those needs from a realistic classroom perspective*. One area in which teachers feel especially ill prepared, particularly amid the current pressures from U.S. federal mandates such as the No Child Left Behind Act of 2001 (U.S. Department of Education, 2001), is in the quest for strategies for selecting and using educational software and Internet technologies for classroom instruction. Teachers are frustrated with software programs that are packaged and described in ways that look impressive and are marketed to the educational community "regardless of its real educational value in improving students' reading performance" (Snow, Burns, & Griffin, 1998, p. 265). Teachers are frustrated with the lack of common standards for evaluating software that meets students' diverse literacy learning needs and confused by the changing and repackaging of old titles to look like new ones. Teachers crave more support in the form of guided exploration of children's software. They welcome facilitators who listen to their needs and then preview relevant literacy software titles according to their instructional purpose. Teachers invite ideas on how to link each program to authentic literacy practices and invite time to explore these programs with their students. Teachers also are disappointed in the shortage of unbiased research in scholarly journals that deals specifically with the educational benefits of using particular software programs or the Internet in their classroom.

Similarly, classroom teachers feel overwhelmed and unprepared to develop lessons and strategies for teaching the new critical literacies that reading for information on the Internet demands (see Coiro, 2003b). They appreciate guided overviews of informative websites such as the Media Awareness Network (www.media-awareness.ca), the Cybersmart Curriculum (www.cybersmartcurriculum.org), and Evaluating Web Information from Virginia Tech (www.lib.vt.edu/help/instruct/evaluate/evaluating.html).

The third lesson I learned is that *classroom teachers are desperately seeking research-based effective practices that support integrating technology into instruction and assessment*. Many teachers are interested in the trend toward more learner-centered approaches to using technology (e.g., involving authentic inquiry-based questions for meaning generated by student interest), as some have long recommended (e.g., Lemke & Coughlin, 1998; Marzano, 1992). Unfortunately, there is little research that investigates the effectiveness of learner-centered Internet inquiry projects or suggests alternative ways to measure learning with Internet technologies. As a result, teachers are on their own to explore these new approaches with a diverse range of students while still being held accountable by more traditional curricula and standardized assessments.

The National Institute of Child Health and Human Development (NICHD, 2000) reviewed experimental research from 1980 to 1996 to investigate which types of technologies, if any, increased student reading achievement among students in grades K–12. They concluded that there were too few studies to make any specific instructional recommendations. In light of U.S. federal mandates, I found these disappointing conclusions had a significant impact on a school's willingness to support teachers' use of technology in the classroom. Teachers wondered why they should bother if there is no evidence that using technology makes a difference. Teachers wondered about the dearth of studies focusing on Internet instruction and reading achievement. Finally, they wondered how they should be using technology with diverse student populations not included in the panel's findings, such as students with learning disabilities or those that speak English as a second language (ESL).

This led me to take a closer look at the research in this area. I worked with several colleagues to extend the results of the NRPs Technology Subcommittee Report (see Coiro et al., 2003) and found more optimistic results to share with teachers. We located more than twice as many studies that met the original NRP criteria, and nearly 10 times as many studies when we extended the criteria to include studies from diverse populations. In contrast to the NRP Subcommittee, we found that there *is* sufficient research to draw conclusions about the use of technology to support literacy instruction in school classrooms.

An analysis of 80 studies that investigated reading comprehension issues, for example, allowed my colleagues and I to identify two important principles of effective practice. First, many different computer technologies, such as Integrated Learning Systems, Computer Assisted Instruction, word prediction software, speech-supported texts, multiple mediated texts, and Internet technologies, appear to contain the potential for supporting the development of reading comprehension. However, the potential of any technology to support the development of reading comprehension may be realized only when teachers make appropriate decisions about its use. Second, educators using technology to support reading comprehension development must consider (a) the design of the technology that is used, (b) the ways in which teachers and students collaborate and interact with one another while using technology, (c) the nature of individual differences among learners, and (d) the nature of how comprehension outcomes are defined and assessed. These findings clearly suggest effective professional development around each of these issues is crucial to the successful use of technology for literacy and learning in the classroom.

Teachers also are concerned about the lack of research-based practices that include newly emerging technologies embedded within the Internet. As other educators, such as those featured in this book, explore Internet projects in their classrooms, I urge more literacy researchers to pursue new collaborative partnerships with teachers (e.g., see Eagleton, Guinnee, & Langlais, 2003) and to provide leadership in documenting teachers' use of Web-based learning projects and their impact on student learning. Only then can teachers regularly and confidently integrate the Internet into their classroom literacy curriculum while still being held accountable for more traditional gains in student achievement.

The fourth lesson that classroom teachers taught me is that *teachers learn best when they are provided with models for linking technology with purposeful reading and writing activities*. With the pressures to meet local and national curriculum standards, teachers welcome appropriate models of guided Internet explorations (e.g., online treasure hunts and WebQuests) and more open-ended inquiry projects during which students pursue answers to their own questions individually or in small groups.

Teachers who share examples of what students can create with electronic tools inspire other educators to network with colleagues and exchange ideas about how their students use computers for literacy learning. The Miss Rumphius Award winners featured in this book provide exemplary models of learner-centered classrooms, inquiry projects, and performance-based assessments of learning with technology in practical terms. These award winners' journeys reveal important skills that teachers need, the processes within which learning with technology takes place, and the power of networking among teachers and educators as they venture into new ways of learning with the Internet.

What Characterizes These Miss Rumphius Award Winners, and What Do Their Stories Reveal About How Teachers Learn to Successfully Integrate Technology Into the Curriculum?

Although the Miss Rumphius Award–winning teachers featured in this book each began their journeys in different places and for different reasons, similarities among their stories reveal seven lessons about how innovative teachers skillfully integrate technology into their curriculum:

1. Start out small and move through stages.
2. Take a few risks along the way.
3. Take a proactive approach to learning.
4. Encourage your students to share their expertise.
5. Never underestimate the power of collaboration.
6. Seek authentic learning opportunities.
7. Be prepared for change.

Start Out Small and Move Through Stages

Miss Rumphius Award winners began their journeys with a mere inkling of an idea, never quite imagining that their projects would grow to have such an impact on others. The natural cycle of the seasons, for example, inspired McGowan's That's What Happens When It's Spring project or Susan Silverman's Kidspired Frosty Readers, while a desire to involve students in community service motivated Mark Ahlness's Earth Day Groceries Project and Gino Sangiuliano's Books on Tape for Kids. Still others, such as Dale Hubert's Flat Stanley Project and Mary Kreul's *Tales of a Fourth Grade Nothing* (Blume, 1972) project, simply sought to build on students' excitement about favorite characters in a book. In turn, students eagerly responded to authentic tasks that connected to their own world, and teachers experienced the power of networking with colleagues outside the four walls of their classrooms. It was then that the Miss Rumphius Award–winning teachers' collaborative journeys with technology integration truly began.

It also is important to note that, in most cases, these award winners began their adventures with little or no prior experience with technology in the classroom. Initially, Sangiuliano struggled to fit computers into his curriculum, Hubert admitted to taking a rather low-tech approach to integration, and McGowan tentatively ventured onto the Internet to locate a resource or two to enrich her traditional reading curriculum. Each of their journeys began at the earlier, albeit different, phases of the developmental continuum of technology integration discussed previously in this chapter. For many, it was only after a year or more that these teachers began to see changes in the way technology was transforming their teaching and their students' learning. Only now, after several years, these Miss Rumphius Award winners have reached the level of *innovation* with technology use, the last phase in Apple's (2004) "Evolution of Thought and Practice." In this phase, teachers view technology as a different way to teach and learn, with more emphasis on project-based learning and student-constructed work that becomes the center of entirely new Web-based learning environments. The evolution of classroom websites, weblogs, digital video, and online professional development opportunities as a result of the Miss Rumphius Award winners' projects clearly illustrates how the Internet enhances teaching and learning. But none of these seemingly grandiose endeavors would have sprouted had it not been for the initial seed of one small idea.

Take a Few Risks Along the Way

These award winners were willing to take risks and venture into unknown places. Cathy Chamberlain took a leap of faith by bravely showcasing her first attempts to create a website for her colleagues that appropriately suited their needs, and Silverman initiated her early Web publishing projects without even knowing how to upload an image. Hubert, despite his initial impatience with computers, enrolled in his first computer class after his principal challenged him to do so. McGowan overcame her inexperience of navigating through websites by inviting her students to learn alongside her, not really worrying if she and her students made some mistakes along the way. Yet, in all these cases, these teachers openly acknowledged their lack of experience and were comfortable letting their students or other teachers see that they did not know all the answers. Taking risks typically is a part of any new learning experience, and technology integration is no exception.

Take a Proactive Approach to Learning

All of the Miss Rumphius Award winners expressed a deep passion for learning. They actively sought out opportunities to explore new ways of teaching and learning with technology and often resorted to teaching themselves new skills and strategies. Several of these teachers taught themselves hypertext markup language (HTML) coding to make their own classroom webpages, and they continue to develop their expertise in Web design with new literacies such as photo editing and graphic design. Ahlness, initially motivated by the unusually high reading levels of informational text on the Internet, began designing more age-appropriate webpages while also devising useful strategies to help his elementary students understand the importance of navigational efficiency on the Internet. Similarly, Tim Lauer noticed the powerful publishing opportunities inspired by classroom webpages and dedicated much of his time keeping up with new technologies that helped to catalog student work. These teachers reminded teachers and educators that there always will be new things to learn and that we often learn best by jumping in and trying things out. For these Miss Rumphius Award winners, professional development opportunities were most effective when grounded in the curriculum-specific needs of teachers on a need-to-know basis.

Encourage Your Students to Share Their Expertise

Teachers should not be intimidated by what students know about new literacies. Many young students understand more about computers and the Internet than most adults, and students are eager to share their knowledge with others. In this book, for example, Kreul learns to take advantage of her students' knowledge by first teaching two students a certain strategy and then having them teach others in her class. In this way, she provides authentic opportunities for her students to join her as literacy leaders and technology experts while creating time for her to work with other students in her classroom. Silverman recognizes the value of student contributions as well. She regularly invites her students into the process of creating rubrics for evaluating webpages as part of their Internet learning experience together. Similarly, Chamberlain respects the contributions that teachers bring to each of her workshops and she reassures her colleagues that each knows something unique and useful to others. Because technology changes so quickly, no one can know everything. The stories in this book taught me that students bring important new literacies from their experiences out of school and are very willing to share with others when given a little space to shine during the school day.

Never Underestimate the Power of Collaboration

These award-winning teachers are willing to collaborate and share ideas. They freely share their time, resources, and expertise without expecting any money in return. Many are quick to mention how the nature of the Internet creates opportunities for less-experienced teachers initially to build their lessons from models shared by other colleagues they have met online. Over time, these newer teachers become more confident and venture in new directions, spreading new transformations of literacy learning opportunities. On the Internet, what initially seems like an overwhelming task to accomplish with just one person becomes much more manageable as teachers work together to compile thematic resources or manage the online publishing of student projects.

Silverman's Webfolio is an impressive model of the multiplicative effects of such collaboration. Silverman first works with another teacher in her school to design an Internet project. Then she invites other teachers from different schools to join her project. Word quickly travels through the online communities, and soon more than 25 teachers have signed up. Each of these 25 teachers has at least 20 students, who each begin to respond creatively to a task, and before you know it, more than 300 individuals are working together to build a showcase of their work as teachers and learners. After the project is completed, teachers from all over the world visit the project archive. These teachers inspire teachers in another school to design a similar project—and the cycle goes on and on. These award winners teach us that the Internet provides a huge network of support, inspiration, and validation for those teachers who may be just beginning to develop Internet projects with students. For teachers who are more experienced with the process, the Internet provides teachers and students new communities of learning to explore, share, and construct creative uses of technology.

Seek Authentic Learning Opportunities

Gone are the days of students writing letters only for a teacher's eyes, and in its place are opportunities for students to write for authentic purposes and audiences from all over the world. Many teachers recognize the advantages of making available authentic Internet communication tasks for students. Students of these Miss Rumphius Award winners have opportunities to share their work and communicate with family members who live far away. They also learn to consider new ways of writing for a more diverse audience. Sangiuliano values the genuine ways in which technology integrates curricular topics with real-world applications. Lauer teaches his students how impromptu e-mail exchanges with science experts can improve their own knowledge and research skills. Ahlness used the Internet with his ESL students to practice informal correspondence via e-mail with peers from their native country, while his other English-speaking students used similar Internet experiences to discover new tidbits of information from another culture. These award-winning teachers work authentic communication opportunities into student Internet projects as a way to motivate high-quality student work and students' connection to the real world. These teachers remind us that the most successful projects enable students to interact with other students and adults in meaningful ways that prepare them for real-life interactions outside of school.

Be Prepared for Change

The Miss Rumphius Award winners are willing to accept the rapid and inevitable change that accompanies technology use in the classroom for literacy learning. New technologies are transforming constantly the nature of literacy and classroom instruction in ways that we cannot even imagine. Many of the Miss Rumphius Award winners willingly redesign their literacy curriculum as they encounter new types of Internet technologies such as digital photography, weblogs, automated Internet forms, and video microscopes. Each of the Miss Rumphius Award winners welcomes change as an opportunity to model for students and their colleagues how to adapt flexibly to the new literacies that continue to emerge in our daily lives. These teachers are eager to break new ground and share their expertise with others educators who explore Internet-based learning with students.

Where Do We Go From Here?

This chapter is about grounding our understanding of effective professional development in perspectives gleaned from research, practice, and the stories the authors feature in this book. Research suggests that effective professional development for technology integration is ongoing, job-embedded, interactive, and reflective. Moreover, teachers learn best when provided with inspiring models for linking technology with purposeful reading and writing. Experience shows that more and more schools are moving toward using small study-group sessions (like the one described at the beginning of this chapter to discuss practical instructional models) and research-based strategies for evaluating the quality and utility of software and Internet technologies.

As teachers and educators seek to keep up with the new literacies and new technologies that continue to emerge, all of the Miss Rumphius Award winners inspire them to start small, take a few risks, establish a network of support, and eagerly welcome change as a part of the learning process. Their journeys make clear that it is not a certain technology or that the Internet by itself makes a difference. Instead, it is the passion and insight of educators like you that ultimately will have the biggest impact on students' lives. Take hold of the challenges that new technologies present, and be confident in your thinking. Regardless of your role as classroom teacher, technology specialist, administrator, or provider of professional development, one small idea can bloom quickly, and *you* may someday be a Miss Rumphius Award winner—transforming literacy and learning and spreading the seeds of exemplary instruction for students.

REFERENCES

Apple Classrooms of Tomorrow. (1995). *Changing the conversation about teaching, learning & technology: A report on 10 years of ACOT research.* Cupertino, CA: Apple Computer. Available: http://images.apple.com/education/k12/leadership/acot/pdf/10yr.pdf

Apple Education. (2004). The evolution of thought and practice. *Technology planning guide: Professional development.* Retrieved February 8, 2004, from http://www.apple.com/education/planning/profdev/index4.html

Balajthy, E. (2000). The effects of teacher purpose on achievement gains. *Reading and Writing Quarterly, 16*(3), 289–294.

Branigan, C. (2002). *Study: Missouri's ed-tech program is raising student achievement.* Retrieved November 18, 2004, from http://www.eschoolnews.com/news/showStory.cfm?ArticleID=3588&CFID=542241&CFTOKEN=84785092

Carey, A.R., & Worthington, K. (1997, November 6). Elementary computing. *USA Today,* p. 4D.

Christenson, R., & Knezak, G. (2001). *Equity and diversity in K–12 applications of information technology: KIDS Project Findings for 2000–2001.* Retrieved November 2, 2003, from http://www.iittl.unt.edu/KIDS2001

Coiro, J.L. (2003a). Reading comprehension on the Internet: Expanding our understanding of reading comprehension to encompass new literacies. *The Reading Teacher, 56,* 458–464.

Coiro, J.L. (2003b). Rethinking comprehension strategies to better prepare students for critically evaluating content on the Internet. *New England Reading Association Journal, 39,* 29–34.

Coiro, J.L., & Leu, D.J., Jr. (2003). *Understanding information technology as a new literacy: School leadership in the instructional use of Internet technologies.* Paper presented at the meeting of the Technology and Leadership & Learning (TL2C), Hartford, Connecticut. Available: http://ctell1.soe.uconn.edu/CTAdminTech

Coiro, J.L., Leu, D.J., Jr., Kinzer, C.K., Labbo, L., Teale, W.H., Bergman, L., et al. (2003, December). *A review of research on literacy and technology: Replicating and extending the NRP subcommittee report on computer technology and reading instruction.* Paper presented at the 53rd Annual Meeting of the National Reading Conference, Scottsdale, AZ.

DiSessa, A.A. (2000). *Changing minds: Computers, learning and literacy.* Cambridge, MA: MIT Press.

Dresang, E.T., & McClelland, K. (1999). Radical change: Digital age literature and learning. *Theory Into Practice, 38*(3), 160–167.

Eagleton, M., Guinnee, K., & Langlais, K. (2003). Teaching Internet literacy strategies: The hero inquiry project. *Voices From the Middle, 10*(3), 28–35.

Educational Research Service. (1998). Professional development and support: An essential ingredient of instructional technology planning. *The Informed Educator Series.* Arlington, VA: Author.

Garry, A., & Graham, P. (2004). Using study groups to disseminate technology best practices. *tech Learning* [Online Serial]. Retrieved January 18, 2004, from http://www.techlearning.com/story/showArticle.jhtml?articleID=17301678

Gora, K., & Hinson, J. (2003). Teacher-to-teacher mentoring. *Learning & Leading with Technology, 31,* 36–40.

Honey, M., & Moeller, B. (1990). *Teacher's beliefs and technology integration: Different values, different understandings.* CTE Technical Report, Issue No. 6. Retrieved November 18, 2004, from http://www.edc.org/CCT/ccthome/reports/tr6.html

International Reading Association. (2001). *Integrating literacy and technology in the curriculum: A position statement.* Retrieved November 18, 2004, from http://www.reading.org/resources/issues/positions_technology.html

Joyce, B., & Showers, B. (1988). *Student achievement through staff development.* White Plains, NY: Longman.

Labbo, L.D., & Reinking, D. (1999). Negotiating the multiple realities of technology in literacy research and instruction. *Reading Research Quarterly, 34,* 478–492.

Lemke, C., & Coughlin, E. (1998). *Technology in American Schools: Seven dimensions for gauging progress.* Retrieved November 18, 2004, from http://www.mff.org/edtech

Leu, D.J., Jr. (2001). Internet project: Preparing students for new literacies in a global village. *The Reading Teacher, 54,* 568–572.

Leu., D.J., Jr., Kinzer, C.K., Coiro, J.L., & Cammack, D.W. (2004). Towards a theory of new literacies emerging from the Internet and other information and communication technologies. In R.B. Ruddell & N. Unrau (Eds.), *Theoretical models and processes of reading* (5th ed., pp. 1570–1613). Newark, DE: International Reading Association.

Lyon, C.A., & Pinnell, G.S. (2001). *Systems for change in literacy education: A guide to professional development.* Portsmouth, NH: Heinemann.

Martin, W., Hupert, N., Gonzales, C., & Admon, N. (2003). Real teachers making real changes: The RETA model for professional development. *Journal of Computer in Teacher Education, 20*(2), 53–62.

Marzano, R.J. (1992). *A different kind of classroom: Teaching with dimensions of learning.* Alexandria, VA: Association for Supervision and Curriculum Development.

McKenzie, J.A. (2001). *Planning good change with technology and literacy.* Bellingham, WA: FNO Press.

Murphy, C.U., & Lick, D.W. (2001). *Whole-faculty study groups: Creating student-based professional development* (2nd ed.). Thousand Oaks, CA: Corwin Press.

National Center for Education Statistics. (1999). *Teacher quality: A report on the preparation and quality of public school teachers.* Washington, DC: United States Department of Education Office of Educational Research.

National Institute of Child Health and Human Development. (2000). *Report of the National Reading Panel. Teaching children to read: An evidence-based assessment of the scientific research literature on reading and its implications for reading instruction: Reports of the subgroups* (NIH Publication No. 00-4754). Washington, DC: U.S. Government Printing Office.

Pianfetti, E.S. (2001). Teachers and technology: Digital literacy through professional development. *Language Arts, 78*(3), 255–262.

President's Committee of Advisors on Science and Technology: Panel on Educational Technology. (1997, March). *Report to the President on the use of technology to strengthen K–12 education in the United States.* Washington, DC: Executive Office of the President of the United States. Retrieved May 19, 2002, from http://www.whitehouse.gov/WH/EOP/OSTP/NSTC/PCAST/k-12ed.html

RAND Reading Study Group. (2002). *Reading for understanding: Towards an R&D program in reading comprehension.* Retrieved February 8, 2004 from http://www.rand.org/multi/achievementforall/reading/readreport.html

Reinking, D., McKenna, M.C., Labbo, L.D., & Kieffer, R.D. (Eds.). (1998). *Handbook of literacy and technology: Transformations in a post-typographic world.* Mahwah, NJ: Erlbaum.

Robb, L. (2000). *Redefining staff development: A collaborative model for teachers and administrators.* Portsmouth, NH: Heinemann.

Snow, C.E., Burns, M.S., & Griffin, P. (Eds.). (1998). *Preventing reading difficulties in young children.* Washington, DC: National Academy Press.

Solomon, G. (2002). Digital equity: It's not just about access anymore. *Technology & Learning, 22*(9), 18–26.

Task Force on Technology and Teacher Education. (1997). *Technology and the new professional teacher: Preparing for the 21st century classroom.* Washington, DC: National Council for Accreditation of Teacher Education.

Taylor, B.M., Pearson, P.D., Clark, K.F., & Walpole, S. (1999). *Beating the odds in teaching all children to read.* CIERA Report No. 2–006. Retrieved January 20, 2003, from http://www.ciera.org/library/reports/inquiry-2/2–006/2–006.pdf

Texas Center for Educational Technology. (1999). *Research instruments.* Retrieved January 8, 2005, from http://www.tcet.unt.edu/research/instrumt.htm

Trotter, A. (1999, September 23). Preparing teachers for the digital age. *Education Week, XIX*(4), 37–42.

U.S. Department of Education. (2001). *The No Child Left Behind Act of 2001: Enhancing education through technology.* Retrieved January 12, 2004, from http://www.ed.gov/policy/elsec/leg/esea02/pg34.html

Valdez, G., McNabb, M., Foertsch, M., Anderson, M., Hawkes, M., & Raack, L. (2000). *Computer-based technology and learning: Evolving uses and expectations.* Naperville, IL: Northeast Central Regional Educational Laboratory.

CHILDREN'S LITERATURE

Blume, J. (1972). *Tales of a fourth grade nothing.* Ill. R. Doty. New York: Dutton.

APPENDIX

We have organized this appendix to help educators to easily locate the URLs of the collaborative Internet projects discussed throughout the book. Each website is listed by chapter and page number of its first mention.

Collaborative Internet Project	URL	Page Number
Chapter 2		
Books on Tape for Kids	www.booksontapeforkids.org	13
Chapter 3		
Earth Day Groceries Project	www.earthdaybags.org	28
Chapter 4		
Elementary Test Prep	www.oswego.org/testprep/ela2.cfm	53
Literacy and Technology	www.oswego.org/staff/cchamber/literacy/index.cfm	46
Mrs. Chamberlain's Second-Grade Authors	www.electricteacher.com/bookpublishing/index.htm	53
NYLearns	www.nylearn.org	53
Online Portfolios	www.electricteacher.com/onlineportfolio/index.htm	53
Study Zone	www.studyzone.org	55
Working With Words	www.oswego.org/testprep/ela4/wwwords1.html	53
	www.oswego.org/testprep/ela4/wwwords2.html	53
Chapter 6		
The Fall Poetry Project	www.myschoolonline.com/folder/0,1872,34898-119831-38-35031,00.html	86
Junie B. Jones Favorites (2002–2004)	www.mrsmcgowan.com/junie/index.html	98
My Town Is Important	www.mrsmcgowan.com/town/index.html	86
My Town Is Important (2001)	www.mrsmcgowan.com/mytown.html	86
Oh, the Places We'll Go!	www.mrsmcgowan.com/places.htm	98
A Patchwork of Places and Poetry (2002)	www.mrsmcgowan.com/quilts/index.html	98
Read a Book—Write a Poem	www.mrsmcgowan.com/winterpoems/index.html.	98
Read a Winter Book... Write a Winter Poem (2003)	www.mrsmcgowan.com/winter2003/index.html	85

(continued)

Page numbers followed by *f* indicate figures.

Texas Center for Educational
Technology, 204, 219
Thompson, V., 107, 120
Trotter, A., 203, 219
Twain, M., 127

U–V

U.S. Department of Commerce, 6, 10
U.S. Department of Education, 1, 5, 10,
52, 64, 167, 178, 203, 209, 219
Valdez, G., 204, 219
Van Allsburg, C., 35, 43

W

Walpole, S., 206, 219

Web-Based Education Commission,
184, 195, 198
White, E.B., 35, 43
Worthington, K., 203, 217

Z

Zeichner, K.M., 184, 197
Zhao, Y., 173, 178
Zheng, D., 217
Zimpher, N.L., 187, 197
Zufall, L., 189, 197

SUBJECT INDEX

Page numbers followed by *f* indicate figures.

C

HYPERTEXT MARKUP LANGUAGE (HTML)
    CODE, 145

I

I HAVE A DREAM PROJECT, 105, 222
IBOOKS, 146
ICTS. *See* information and
    communication technologies
ILS. *See* Integrated Learning Systems
IMACS, 146
INDEPENDENT READING, 80
INFORMATION AND COMMUNICATION
    TECHNOLOGIES (ICTS), 3, 4; examples,
    3; pervasive and rapidly escalating
    nature of, 6; in preservice teacher
    education, 183
INFORMATION SHARING, 38–39
INNOVATION, 204, 213
INSPIRATION, 18–20
INSPIRATION (SOFTWARE), 57
INSTRUCTION: comprehensive, 80;
    decoding, 80; early intervention,
    80–81; fluency, 80; Internet literacy,
    165–179; literacy, 99–100,
    118–119, 210; phonemic
    awareness, 80; principles of effective
    practices related to reading, 80
INSTRUCTIONAL MODELS, 7–8
INTEGRATED LEARNING SYSTEMS (ILS),
    210–211
INTELLIGENCE(S), 107
INTERACTIVE GAMES, 60*f*, 60–61, 107,
    165, 222
INTERACTIVE WEBSITES, 45*f*, 60
INTERCULTURAL E-MAIL CLASSROOM
    CONNECTIONS, 140–141
INTERNATIONAL READING ASSOCIATION
    (IRA): position statement on
    technology and literacy instruction,
    167, 173; professional conferences,
    168; recommendations for student
    preparation, 27; technology and
    Internet resources for teachers, 118;
    website, 103
INTERNATIONAL SOCIETY FOR TECHNOLOGY
    IN EDUCATION (ISTE) STANDARDS, 90,
    118
INTERNET, 3, 4; birth of, 123; children's
    literature and, 13–15; gift economy
    of, 38; integration with literacy
    instruction, 167–172; learning and
    teaching, 49–53, 158–160;

pervasive and rapidly escalating
    nature of, 6; to share knowledge and
    create partnerships, 38–39; use by
    Miss Rumphius Award–winning
    teachers, 184–187
INTERNET INQUIRY, 7
INTERNET LITERACY: classroom practices,
    165–179; fundamental qualities of
    instruction, 165–179; key issues,
    166–167
INTERNET PROJECT, 7
INTERNET PROJECTS, 45*f*, 56–58,
    85–102, 97; beginnings of,
    139–140; collaborative, 86, 98*f*,
    101*f*, 103–120, 139–143,
    172–176; coordination of,
    103–120; cross-cultural
    collaboration, 173–175; current
    projects, 53–63, 117–118;
    fundamental qualities of, 172–176;
    lessons learned, 97–99, 116–117;
    that link students and classrooms
    worldwide, 66; participating in, 170;
    student writing from, 101*f*;
    telecollaborative, 151–152;
    websites, 221–222. *See also*
    specific projects by name
INTERNET PROJECTS (WEBSITE), 39, 53,
    57–58
INTERNET PROJECTS REGISTRY, 66
INTERNET RESEARCH, 75–76, 165
INTERNET RESOURCES, 85–102, 118;
    expanding, 53–63; that link to
    education standards, 53; literacy-
    related, 44–45, 45*f*
INTERNET WORKSHOP, 7
INTRINSIC LITERACY, 127
IPAQ POCKET PCS, 136
IRA. *See* International Reading
    Association
ISIGHT VIDEO TECHNOLOGY, 202

J

JAMESBARRY, TONY, 164
JANE GOODALL INSTITUTE WEBSITE, 36
JOBE, HAZEL, 8, 94
JOINT PHOTOGRAPHIC EXPERTS GROUP
    (JPEG) IMAGES, 142
JUNIE B. JONES FAVORITES (WEBSITE
    PROJECT), 98*f*, 147, 221

K

Karchmer, Rachel, 152
Kathy Schrock's Guide for Educators, 170
keyboard shelves, 134, 134*f*
keypal activities, 66, 140, 165, 173
keywords, 48
Kid Pix, 57, 94, 109, 142, 146; Frosty Readers illustrations, 112, 112*f*
Kid Pix Deluxe, 144
Kidsphere, 29
Kidspiration, 111, 111*f*, 146
Kidspired Frosty, 111, 111*f*; beginnings, 212; website, 222
King Falcon Cam, 36, 39–41, 40*f*
knowledge sharing, 38–39
Knox, Pattie, 110–111, 112
Kreul, Mary, 168, 170, 212, 214; Ms. Kreul's Class Blog, 154, 154*f*, 222

L

Lambchop, Stanley. *See* Flat Stanley Project
language: core curriculum standards for, 90; principles of effective practices related to reading, 80
Language Arts and Technology (course), 117–118
laptops, 70, 146
Lauer, Tim, 154, 214, 215
learner-centered approaches, 210
learning: authentic, 128–130, 215–216; about computers, 122–124; construction of, 4; expansion of opportunities, 204; Internet, 49–53; literacy, 99–100; motivation to learn through Flat Stanley, 127–128; outcome-based, 129–130; proactive approach to, 213–214; train the trainer model, 146; virtual, 204
lesson plans: development of, 209; online, 170
Lewis Elementary School (Portland, Oregon, USA): Classroom Notes website, 162, 163*f*; teacher blogs, 154; weblog, 162
library media specialists, 164, 202
Library of Congress: American Memory, 8; website, 152
listservs, 38, 45*f*, 52, 169. *See also* specific lists by name

literacy: Books on Tape for Kids project, 15–16; changes in learning, 99–100; classroom changes, 35–37; connecting with technology, 138–156, 153–154; contextualizing new literacies, 1–10; core curriculum standards for, 90; critical literacies, 4; definition of, 18; digital, 203; early, 80; emergent, 80; grade-level resources, 55–56; how children think about, 70; Internet resources, 44–45, 45*f*, 53; intrinsic, 127; multiple literacies, 2; new literacies, 167; online resources, 85–102; technological, 167, 168–169; and technology, 4, 44–64; technology integration with, 203; visual, 150. *See also* new literacies
Literacy and Technology (website), 46, 47*f*, 52, 60; website, 221
literacy curriculum: improving or enhancing, 171–172; print-based, 171–172
literacy instruction: changes in, 99–100, 118–119; integrating technology into, 65; integration of Internet with, 167–172; Internet literacy instruction, 165–179; principles of effective practices related to reading, 80; technology to support, 210; technology use and integration with, 202–208
literature-based instruction, 37
literature circles, 152
Literature Circles Extension Projects, 117, 222
literature guides, 45*f*
local knowledge, 188

M

Mac Performas, 146
MacHTTPD, 160
Mae (peregrine falcon), 40, 41, 42
mail rings, 95
Major Missouri Cities Webquest, 93
MarcoPolo Education Foundation, 118
Mariposa County Unified School District (Fresno, California, USA), 168
Mars Pathfinder, 36
McCullan, Melissa, 152

SMOKE (PEREGRINE FALCON), 40, 40f, 41, 42

SMOKE'S FIRST FLIGHT STORIES, 41

SOCIAL CHANGE, 11–12

SOCIAL STUDIES: core curriculum standards for, 90; lesson plans online, 170

SOFTWARE, 135; for creative students, 143–144; evaluating, 209. *See also specific software*

SOWA, MICHELE, 115

STAFF DEVELOPMENT: online tutorials, 168; webpage development, 49–50; workshops, 168. *See also* professional development

STANDARDS RESOURCES, 53–55

STATIONERY: PSD project, 143–144, 146

STELLALUNA'S FRIENDS (WEBSITE PROJECT), 112–114; excerpt, 113, 113f

STOLZENBERG, HARRIET, 151

STORY BOOK: FOLKTALES FROM AROUND THE WORLD WEBSITE, 171

STORY RETELLING ACROSTIC POEM (WEBSITE PROJECT), 101f

STRANGER IN THE WOODS: POEMS AND ACTIVITIES 2002 (WEBSITE PROJECT), 101f, 222

STUDENT COLLABORATION: cross-cultural, 173–175; fundamental qualities of, 172–176. *See also* Internet projects; *specific projects by name*

STUDENT CREATED DOCUMENT BASED QUESTIONS PROJECT, 152

STUDENT-DIRECTED JOURNEYS, 112–114

STUDENT EXPERTS, 175–176, 207, 214

STUDENT PUBLISHING, 173; types of, 101f; Winter Wonderland project, 108

STUDENT WEBPAGES: Books on Tape for Kids project, 16, 17f. *See also* class websites

STUDENT WRITING: authentic, 172–173; from collaborative projects, 101f; Frosty Readers (website project), 109, 110f; published types, 101f; traditional assignments, 101f; Winter Wonderland project, 108

STUDENTS: creative, 143–144; as critical friends, e-problem solvers, and cyber navigators, 175–176; software for, 143–144

STUDY GROUPS: facilitators, 206–207; faculty, 206–207

STUDY ZONE, 55–56; sample practice webpage, 58f; sample resource link, 59f; sample webpage, 57f

SURFING FOR ABC'S PROJECT, 94

SYSTEM THINKING, 206

T

TALES OF A FOURTH GRADE NOTHING PROJECT, 212

TALKING BOOKS, 171

TASK CARDS (WEB ASSIGNMENTS), 36–37

TEACHER APPRECIATION DAY, 144, 146

TEACHER BLOGS, 154

TEACHER EDUCATION, 181; preservice, 183–184; technology integration into, 184

TEACHER WEBSITES, 169–170

TEACHERS, 8; effective, 166, 167–172; effective practices related to reading, 80; empowering, 199–219, 208–209; essential characteristics, 167–172; ICT use, 167; Internet resources, 118; Internet use, 167; making connections, 51–53; Miss Rumphius as a role model for, 182, 187–188; Miss Rumphius Award winners, 184–187, 188, 212–216; preservice, 182–198; professional development for, 199–219, 208–211; project development, 51; Random Thoughts (Schmier) on, 38–39; resources for, 118, 209; role of, 20–21; technological literacy paths, 168–169; technology resources, 118; weblogs, 164

TEACHERS HELPING TEACHERS INTEGRATE TECHNOLOGY INTO THE CLASSROOM (WEBQUEST), 189, 189f, 195–196; essential components, 190–192; preservice teachers' responses to, 193–195; website, 222

TEACHING: Internet, 49–53; resources for, 8

TECHNOLOGICAL LITERACY, 167; teacher paths, 168–169

TECHNOLOGY: adoption of, 204; appropriation of, 204; children's new literacy abilities, 70–77; creating space for, 145–146; to do things differently–to do things better, 23–24; and early literacy development, 80; influences on how children think about communication and literacy, 70; to inspire others, 18–20; resources, 118; role of, 20–21; to support literacy instruction, 210; to support reading comprehension development, 211; video, 202; wishes for, 152–153

TECHNOLOGY INTEGRATION, 118, 200–201; adaptation, 204; authentic applications, 121–137; Books on Tape for Kids project, 16; in the classroom, 94–97, 133–136, 189, 189f; into the curriculum, 212–216; Flat Stanley Project, 126–127; future directions, 216–217; into instruction and assessment, 210; Language Arts and Technology (course), 117–118; to link schools and communities, 66–70; with literacy, 4, 44–64, 138–156, 153–154, 203; in literacy curriculum, 65; with literacy instruction, 202–208; Miss Rumphius Site: Teachers Helping Teachers Integrate Technology into the Classroom, 189, 189f; models for, 211; phases of, 204; in primary grades, 65–66; professional development, 203; professional development for, 208–211; research-based effective practices for, 210; in schools and communities, 65–82, 66–68, 67f; stages of, 204; in teacher education, 184

TECHNOLOGY STUDY GROUP PROFESSIONAL DEVELOPMENT MODEL, 207

TECHNOLOGY WARRANTIES, 196

TELECOLLABORATIVE PROJECTS, 151–152; beginnings of, 139–140; connecting to others with, 140–143; favorite projects, 141, 141f; participating in, 170. See also specific projects by name

TERMINOLOGY, 37

THAT'S WHAT HAPPENS WHEN IT'S SPRING (WEBSITE PROJECT), 98f, 201; beginnings, 212; website, 222

THEORY, 3–5

TICTECH (LISTSERV), 38

TIMBERLEA ELEMENTARY SCHOOL (TIMBERLEA, NOVA SCOTIA, CANADA), 88f

TRAIN THE TRAINER MODEL OF LEARNING, 146

TRAVEL BUDDY PROJECTS, 114

U

UNITED STREAMING, 24

UNIVERSITY OF ILLINOIS, 158–159

UNIVERSITY OF MASSACHUSETTS, 38

U.S. DEPARTMENT OF STATE, 131

U.S. LIBRARY OF CONGRESS: American Memory, 8; website, 152

V

VENN DIAGRAMS, 111, 111f

VIDEO MICROSCOPES, 157

VIDEO TECHNOLOGY, 8, 202

VIRGINIA TECH: Evaluating Web Information, 209

VIRTUAL LEARNING, 204

VISUAL LITERACY, 150

VOCABULARY, 37

VOLCANO WORLD (WEBSITE), 36

W

WADE HOUSE, 148, 149f

WARWICK SCHOOL (FREMONT, CALIFORNIA, USA), 109

WASHINGTON STATE UNIVERSITY VANCOUVER, 160

WEB ASSIGNMENTS (TASK CARDS), 36–37

WEB LESSONS, 39

WEB66, 145

WEBCAMS, 36, 39–41

WEBFOLIOS, 45f, 59–60, 215; Mrs. Silverman's Webfolio, 90, 116, 215, 222; Online Portfolios (website), 53

WEBLOGS, 153–154, 160–164; comments, 162; Ms. Kreul's Class Blog, 154, 154f, 222

WEBMUSEUM, 36

WEBPAGE DEVELOPMENT, 49–50

WEBQUESTS, 7, 99, 188–192; essential components of, 189–192; Miss Rumphius Site: Teachers Helping Teachers Integrate Technology into the Classroom, 189, 189f, 190–192, 193–195, 195–196, 222; process, 191–192; resources,

X–Z